FROM THE
ENDS OF THE EARTH

THE JEWS IN THE 20TH CENTURY

FROM
THE ENDS
OF THE EARTH

THE JEWS IN THE 20TH CENTURY

MARTIN GILBERT

Picture research by Sarah Jackson

and Franziska Payer Crockett

CASSELLPAPERBACKS

First published in the United Kingdom in 2001 by Cassell & Co
Wellington House, 125 Strand, London WC2R 0BB
This paperback edition first published in 2002 by Cassell paperbacks

Copyright © Endeavour Group UK, 2001
This book was created, designed and produced by Endeavour Group UK
813 Fulham Road, London SW6 5HG Fax 44 (020) 7348 7260
Text copyright © Sir Martin Gilbert, 2001

A CIP catalogue record for this book is available from the British Library

ISBN 1841 881864
Project Manager Franziska Payer Crockett
Picture Research Sarah Jackson with
Franziska Payer Crockett and Mia Stewart-Wilson
Editor Roger Hudson
Design Paul Welti
Production Mary Osborne
Typesetting Peter Howard
Typeset in Garamond
Origination by @atColor Srl, Milan, Italy
Printed by Nuovo Istituto Italiano d'Arti Grafiche SpA, Bergamo, Italy

CONTENTS

AUTHOR'S NOTE

THE idea of combining history and contemporary photographs as presented in this book came from Charles Merullo of the Endeavour Group UK, and was made possible by the collective efforts of Sarah Jackson and Franziska Payer Crockett in the photographic realm, Paul Welti on the design front, Roger Hudson on the editorial side and Mary Osborne in production. It has been a very special team with which to work. I am also grateful to Tim Aspden for transforming my rough drafts into two maps showing every European and Middle East location mentioned in the text and captions. On specific points I have been helped by Max Arthur, Professor John Klier and Enid Wurtman. Kay Thomson assisted at every stage. Susan Ralston of Schocken Books has been a pillar of support. The following reference books provided valuable information:

Ralph Carlson (Editorial Director), *American Jewish Desk Reference*, Random House, New York, 1999.

Joan Comay, *Who's Who in Jewish History*, Weidenfeld & Nicolson, London, 1974.

Susan Hattis Rolef (Editor), *Political Dictionary of the State of Israel*, The Jerusalem Publishing House, Jerusalem, 1993.

Elinor Slater and Robert Slater, *Great Jewish Women*, Jonathan David Publishers, New York 1998

Robert Slater, *Great Jews in Sports*, Jonathan David Publishers, New York, 1992.

Alan Symons, *The Jewish Contribution to the 20th Century*, Polo Publishing, London 1997.

Geoffrey Wigoder, *Dictionary of Jewish Biography*, Simon and Schuster, New York, 1991.

Half-title page: *Two Israeli girls from the Bukharan community in Jerusalem, celebrating Shevuot – the harvest festival – in the 1960s.* [PHOTO: MARLI SHAMIR]

Title page: *At a celebration in a Tel Aviv private apartment in 1948, a couple dance to an accordion.*
[PHOTO: ROBERT CAPA]

EDITOR'S NOTE

ALTHOUGH produced in a different format, this book follows in the tradition of *The Russian Century, The Chinese Century, The British Century, The Irish Century* and *The German Century*. Its pictoral elements are the result of extensive research in archives, museums and private collections in Germany, Israel, the United States and Britain, where we have benefited once again from the extraordinary holdings of the Hulton Getty Archive. The YIVO Institute for Jewish Research collections in New York City and those of Vivienne Silver-Brody, Rona Sela and Ilan Roth in Israel have been invaluable. We also gained a great deal by access to private albums such as those of the Dangoor, Jakobovits and Rothschild families in Britain. We owe special thanks for additional research undertaken by Andrea Stern in Israel, by Amy Heller and Amy Pastan in Washington, and by Mia Stewart-Wilson, Leon Meyer and Tom Worsley in London.

Once again we have enjoyed help and support from all our publishing partners. In particular, Susan Ralston at Schocken Books in New York has been involved in the book from its earliest stages and has provided invaluable assistance at every point.

As always it has been our policy to treat the images as historical documents and to avoid altering them in any way. The photographers' names, when known, are credited in the captions. The sources of the photographs are listed on page 366.

Copyright page: *A Jewish couple take a ride in a 'fiaker' through the streets of Budapest at the turn of the century.*

Contents page: *Orthodox schoolboys in the USA peer from their school bus, 1954.* [PHOTO: LEONARD FREED]

Left: *American Jews – children and adults – at a march and rally in New Jersey, 16 May 1948, one of hundreds held that day throughout the United States to celebrate the establishment of the State of Israel.*

of Finland

St. Petersburg/Petrograd/Leningrad

STONIA

Lake
Peipus

Lake
Ilmen

Lake
Pskov

LATVIA

Riga

Dvinsk

HUANIA

Moscow

EUROPE

Atlantic Ocean

FRANCE

Odessa

ITALY

Adriatic

Constantinople
(Istanbul)

Black
Sea

Brunete   Madrid

SPAIN

Salonika

GREECE

CORFU

Izmir

Tangier   Gibraltar

M e d i t e r r a n e a n   S e a

SICILY

ZANTE

Athens

RHODES

Marrakech

ALGERIA

Tunis

MALTA

CRETE

0   kilometres   750

MOROCCO

TUNISIA

0   miles   400

Tripoli

Tobruk

NORTH AFRICA

LIBYA

vno   Vilna   WHITE RUSSIA
(BYELORUSSIA)

Katyn

Ponar

R U S S I A

Lida

Minsk

Maly Trostenets

Mir

Grodno   Dubrovna

Tatarsk

ialystok

Starodub

dlce

Kursk

kow

Brest-Litovsk

czew

Pinsk

bibor

VOLHYNIA

zec

Tuczyn

Babi Yar

Dubno

Kiev

Kharkov

Stalingrad

Krzemieniec

Astrakhan

Lvov

Kamenets-Podolsk

emysl

U K R A I N E

EASTERN

ALICIA   Buczacz

Vinnitsa

unkacs

Rostov

Beregszasz

Caspian
Sea

ORTHERN
NSYLVANIA

Jassy

Kishinev

Nikolayev

Sea of
Azov

Odessa

CRIMEA

C a u c a s u s

R O M A N I A

Bucharest

B l a c k   S e a

Batum

0   kilometres   500

0   miles   300

Constantinople
(Istanbul)

© Martin Gilbert 2001

9

*Jews from the Yemen, recently
arrived in Israel, look at a map of their
new homeland.*

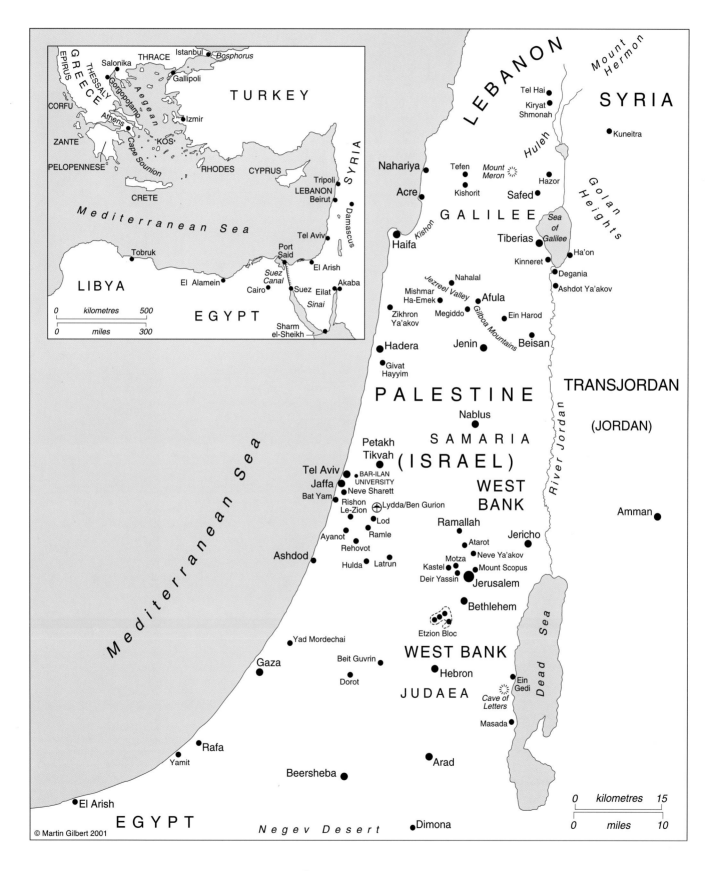

CHAPTER ONE

MIGRATION, ASSIMILATION, THE PROMISED LAND

1900-1914

JEWS HAVE BEEN VARIOUSLY PORTRAYED, AND HAVE portrayed themselves, as a religion, a race and a nationality. According to Jewish rabbinic law, anyone with a Jewish mother is Jewish. People born Jewish, or having Jewish ancestry, might convert to Christianity, or to any other religion, yet still be considered Jewish under rabbinic law. Under Hitler's definition (which sent millions of people to their deaths) anyone with one Jewish grandparent was Jewish. Anyone who considers himself or herself of recent Jewish antecedents might be defined as a Jew. Since 1951, any Jew who wishes to do so may enter the State of Israel and become a citizen on request. This 'Law of Return' has enabled more than two and a half million Jews to go to Israel and live there as citizens, and as 'Israelis'. Other Jews, while openly defining themselves as Jews, whether religiously observant or not, are content to be 'British' or 'American' or 'French', depending on their nationality and citizenship.

No Jew has to go to synagogue, or be a member of any formal Jewish community, or even appear on the statistics of the number of Jews in any country, to be Jewish. Throughout the twentieth century, individual Jews who did not in any way proclaim their Jewishness made their mark on the life and society around them, as much as those for whom being Jewish was a vital part of their identity and even self-esteem. It is the struggles, hopes and achievements of all Jews, in every land, that are portrayed and celebrated here.

With the French Revolution, a period of enlightenment began which saw the disabilities from which Jews had suffered since the Middle Ages reduced and swept away in most Western industrial nations. But, throughout the nineteenth century, Jews still had to struggle against laws which discriminated against them, restricting the places in which they could live, and the jobs they could do. Even when granted equal rights of citizenship, they were seen by many as a people apart, a difficult people, a clannish and un-neighbourly, even an alien, community.

People of the Book. *Jews from Yemen, a community dating from the 1st century BC, study the Torah, the code of Jewish law based on the Five Books of Moses (the Pentateuch). Torah study is the principal intellectual and spiritual activity of observant Jews. By 1914 several thousand Yemenite Jews were living in Palestine, mostly in Jerusalem.*

To protect themselves against the suspicions and hostilities of the outside world, and against the intensification or re-emergence of anti-Semitic prejudice, the Jews were held together and strengthened by their religion, their tradition of education and by language. At one end of the religious spectrum were the ultra-Orthodox and Hassidic Jews, for whom the outside world mattered little: their world was centred exclusively on prayer and faith. Jews of more mainstream Orthodoxy mingled with the non-Jews among whom they lived, but adhered to the basic tenets of their religion, keeping the Sabbath, the fasts and the festivals. Reform Jews, and Jews of various even looser forms of worship, conducted their religious life in synagogue – often using the local language as well as Biblical Hebrew in their services – and carried out the domestic rituals of Friday night supper in the family home, but were not noticeably Jewish at work or in the street.

Education was a Jewish imperative in every century. Throughout the Jewish world, its base since antiquity was the study of the Bible. The age-old interpretations of the Bible by generations of rabbis and scholars, always learned in the original Hebrew, served to stimulate both scholarly discussion and religious practice. Literacy in Biblical Hebrew was a hallmark of even the poorest and most remote of Jewish communities. From their earliest age, young Jewish boys sat at the benches in the Beit Midrash – the House of Study – mastering the ancient texts and ethical code. Two features predominated throughout the years of study, which for Orthodox Jews lasted a lifetime. One was dialectical argument, the skill of reasoning and debate, using

Sephardi youngsters in Palestine, *studying in a Cheder – literally, in the Hebrew language, a room, in fact a class where Hebrew language and Jewish practice are taught in every Jewish community. Sephardi Jews are the descendants of the Jews expelled from Spain in 1492 (Sepharad is Hebrew for Spain). By 1914 they were the majority of the Jewish population in Palestine and Jerusalem. Sephardi communities also flourished in the Balkans, Greece, North Africa, Egypt and Iraq.* [PHOTO: E.M. LILIEN]

the Biblical texts and commentaries as starting point. The other was social justice, the call for equity and fair dealing, not only between Jew and Jew, but between Jew and Gentile.

By the start of the twentieth century, Jews had come to speak the languages of all the people among whom they lived – to speak and write and conduct their daily personal and professional life in the language of the 'host' country: in Russian, Polish, Lithuanian, German, French, Italian, Hungarian, English, Turkish, Persian, Arabic, and a dozen other languages. They also had their own languages, each of which served as a bond of inner solidarity, in speech, writing and song.

When the twentieth century began the most widely spoken and written language of daily Jewish life was Yiddish. Written in Hebrew characters, it had evolved from early medieval German. In 1900 it was spoken in a wide geographic arc from St. Petersburg to San Francisco: its heartland was Russian Poland and the Galician provinces of Austria-Hungary. Another Jewish language, Ladino, had its origins in late medieval Spain. With the expulsion of the Jews from Spain in 1492, Ladino had spread throughout the Mediterranean and the Balkans, from Gibraltar to Constantinople, and as far north as Britain and Holland. A third Jewish language, Judaeo-Tat – the origins of which dated back to the settlements in Persia two thousand years earlier – was still spoken in the remote mountain valleys of the Caucasus, and on the western shore of the Caspian Sea; those who spoke it were known as 'mountain Jews'.

A family Bar Mitzvah, 1906. *At the age of thirteen a Jewish boy assumes the religious responsibilities of an adult, and is called up for the first time to read the blessings over the weekly portion of the Law in synagogue, as well as reading – usually chanting – the portion itself, and is welcomed in festive manner by his family and friends into the adult community. The women are grouped on the one side, the men on the other. Bar Mitzvah means Son of the Commandment.*

During the nineteenth century, the willingness of nations to accept the Jews as an integral part of society varied considerably. In the Russian Empire most Jews were confined to the western provinces, and outbursts of popular violence against them were frequent, coming to a climax in the 1880s with a series of pogroms – violent attacks on Jewish communities, the widespread destruction of Jewish property, and murder. In several countries, among them Turkey, Russia, Bulgaria, Austria-Hungary and Germany, the nineteenth century saw ritual murder accusations made against Jews: an utterly fictitious 'blood libel' dating from early medieval times, that the unleavened bread used by Jews on Passover – to celebrate the Biblical exodus from Egypt – had to be baked using the blood of a Christian child. Whenever this charge was made, a

SEPHARDI JEWS. *The Dangoor family (above) in Baghdad before the First World War – emigrating to Britain after the Second World War they were among the leaders of the Iraqi Jewish community in London. The man is wearing traditional headdress, while the boy wears the more modern fez. Allegre Amar (near right) wearing the traditional dress of married Jewish women in Salonika, one of the most flourishing Sephardi communities, until destroyed by the Nazis. A Jew from Tangier (far right) wearing typical Moroccan costume, a hooded cloak and cummerbund. The first Tangier newspaper was edited by a Jew: Jewish authors and poets, writing in Spanish, flourished there. In 1914 the Jews of Tangier numbered 10,000.*

16

SEPHARDI, ASHKENAZI, SAMARITAN. *Two beautiful Sephardi girls from Bukhara (above) in 1906, when there were 5,000 Jews in the city, and a further 35,000 in the rest of Central Asia. Bukharan Jews also had a vigorous community in Jerusalem. An Ashkenazi Jew from Romania (far left). The Ashkenazis were originally from Germany (Ashkenaz is Germany in Hebrew). A Samaritan from Palestine (near left). The Samaritans believe they are descended from the Israelite tribes of Ephraim and Manasseh. Living mostly in Nablus (Shechem in Hebrew), they numbered less than 200 in 1914. In 1949 they were recognized as citizens of Israel, where their first synagogue was dedicated in 1963.*

[PHOTOS THIS PAGE: E.M. LILIEN]

Jewish New York. *Hester Street, at the heart of the Jewish district in Manhattan, at the time of the great migration of Russian and Eastern European Jews. By 1910 there were nearly five million Jews in New York, by far the largest Jewish population of any city in the world.*

Amsterdam, the Jewish Quarter *in 1906, when there were 60,000 Jews in the city. Many of them worked in the diamond industry where they established the first Trade Union in Holland.*

local mob would hurl itself on the Jews with ferocity and hatred. In Austria-Hungary the poverty of the Jewish communities in the eastern provinces was a barrier to advancement. In Germany dislike of Jews could be found at all levels of society, often startlingly obvious in royal and aristocratic circles, while the much admired composer Richard Wagner was known to be especially hostile to Jews, whom he wanted removed from German cultural life. There was reluctance in both Britain and the United States to admit Jews into the upper reaches of society, to include them in gentlemen's clubs, or to accept them as equals in public life and society; this applied even to rich and successful Jews. In every country some form of quota was imposed on the number of Jews who could enter universities or medical schools.

Even as the laws and social disabilities were being challenged and overcome, the burdens which they had created were leading to a variety of Jewish reactions. When the twentieth century opened there were three main ways of life which Jews followed, or aspired to. The first was the settled life of those who sought to survive and flourish on every continent, in the countries of which they were citizens, and to acquire the full rights of citizens. Many went so far as to have assimilation as their goal: total participation not only in the life but in the morality, patriotism and even religion of the countries in which they lived. The second avenue was that of migration away from the places where persecution or economic hardship or social barriers often made life almost unbearable, to lands – primarily the United States – where Jews

Baron Edmond de Rothschild *in 1914, on his fourth visit to Palestine. He had given crucial support to the first Jewish settlements when they fell into serious financial difficulties in the 1880s. In all, he helped more than thirty settlements. On the right of the picture is Abraham Shapira, a pioneer of Jewish self-defence, who organised the protection of Petakh Tikvah, one of the early settlements financed by 'the Baron'.*
[PHOTO: SHLOMO NARINSKY]

believed they could live a life of political freedom and economic opportunity. The third was to pin one's hopes on the future bringing about a revolutionary change in the Jewish situation: on the one hand the revolution envisaged by Socialists and Marxists in the whole order of society, and on the other hand the re-birth of a specifically Jewish nationalism – the intensification of the age-old emotional call for a Jewish homeland in Palestine.

Only three years had passed since the call for a Jewish State had been put forward at the first Zionist Congress held in the Swiss town of Basle, with delegates from all over the world, the majority from the Russian Empire, but some from Western Europe, Britain, the United States and Palestine. The leader of this political Zionism was Theodor Herzl, a journalist and novelist born in the Austro-Hungarian city of Budapest. At the end of their deliberations the delegates committed themselves to seek 'the establishment of a home for the Jewish people in Palestine secured under public law'. Palestine – known to the Jews by its Biblical Hebrew name *Eretz Yisrael*, the Land of

Israel, had been the historic homeland of the Jews until the destruction of the Second Temple by the Romans nearly two thousand years earlier. In fact, long before 1897 there had been a reviving Jewish community there, thousands of whose members were poor immigrants. Russian Jews in particular had, since the early 1880s, been emigrating and working as farmers in the inhospitable soil of the 'Promised Land': the land which, in the Bible, God promised to the descendants of Abraham. In 1889 the Chovevei Zion ('Lovers of Zion') societies in Russia – which were at the centre of the establishment of Jewish settlement in Palestine in the decade before Herzl began his political and diplomatic efforts – sent the first of six annual cash donations to their needy members. Answering appeals from the Jewish settlers, wealthy Jewish philanthropists, chief among them Baron Edmund de Rothschild, financed factories and vineyards and towns. There had been a Jewish majority in Jerusalem since 1870. Jews, Muslim Arabs, Christian Arabs and Armenian Christians lived in their respective quarters in the crowded Old City. But, beginning in 1870, the Jews of Jerusalem had also built a growing number of suburbs outside the city walls. The first was financed by the American Jew, Judah Touro, and carried out by the British Jewish philanthropist, Sir Moses Montefiore.

Writing in his diary when the 1897 congress ended, Herzl declared triumphantly: 'Were I to sum up the Basle Congress in a word – which I shall guard against pronouncing publicly – it would be this: At Basle I founded the Jewish State.' As to when that State would come into being, Herzl forecast: 'Maybe in another five years, at the utmost fifty years.' Fifty-two years after Herzl wrote these apparently boastful words, the State of Israel was declared. Herzl and his fellow Zionist leaders were convinced that they could persuade the Turkish Sultan, whose empire included Palestine, to grant them rights

Wine in Palestine: *the workers at Zikhron Yaakov making barrels in the cask workshop. The settlement was founded in 1882 by Jews from Romania. The wine industry in Palestine owed much to the patronage of Baron Edmond de Rothschild: Zikhron Yaakov – the Memory of Jacob – was named after his father James.*

[PHOTO: BERNARD A. EDELSTEIN]

Theodor Herzl *in front of the synagogue in Basle(above), during the 1903 Zionist Congress, and posing in his neat office in Vienna (right). He was insistent that delegates wore formal dress, to distance themselves from the image of the ghetto Jew in trailing coat and wide-brimmed hat. After the establishment of the State of Israel in 1948, Herzl's remains were re-buried on a hillside outside Jerusalem. His desk became a central feature of his reconstructed room in the nearby museum.*

there. Herzl also believed that he could influence the German Kaiser, William II, to support their quest. But when Herzl and the Kaiser met in Jerusalem in 1898, the Kaiser was non-committal.

Herzl published his book, *The Jewish State*, in 1896, writing it at great speed, his only relaxation coming, ironically, from listening to the music of the notorious anti-semite Wagner. The book, issued in many languages and many editions over the next few years, explained why Palestine, and Palestine alone, was the place in which he sought a Jewish homeland. 'The very name Palestine would attract our people with a force of marvellous potency,' he wrote. 'Supposing His Majesty the Sultan were to give us Palestine, we could in return undertake to regulate the whole finances of Turkey. We should there form a portion of the rampart of Europe against Asia, an outpost of civilisation as opposed to barbarism. We should as a neutral State remain in contact with all Europe, which would have to guarantee our existence.' Herzl explained that he wanted the Jews to guard the Christian holy sites in Palestine, and 'form a guard of honour about these sanctuaries, answering for the fulfilment of this duty with our existence'. This guard of honour would, he believed, 'be the great symbol of the solution of the Jewish question after eighteen centuries of Jewish suffering'.

In 1901 Herzl travelled to the Turkish capital, Istanbul. The Sultan agreed to receive him, and expressed an interest in Herzl's proposal to use Jewish money to improve Turkey's financial situation. When Herzl returned to western Europe, however, he found no wealthy Jews willing to support such a project. Travelling once more to Turkey nine months later, Herzl was offered a permit for Jewish settlement in Mesopotamia (now Iraq), but Palestine was specifically excluded from any such settlement plan. Herzl turned the offer down. He returned a third time to Turkey five months later, in July 1902, but the Sultan remained unwilling to grant Palestine to the Jews, either as an independent State, or as an autonomous homeland within his wide-spread dominions. The most he would allow was that individual Jewish settlers, and groups of settlers, could go on entering Palestine as immigrants. Even then, from time to time, restrictions were imposed, limiting the number of Jews who were allowed in: one of the very humiliations that a Jewish homeland was intended to prevent.

Herzl continued to travel throughout Europe, to argue the case for a Jewish homeland, and to urge that it should be in the Biblical land with which the Jews had been so intimately associated for so many years, the land of their patriarchs, Abraham, Isaac and Jacob, and of their biblical kings, including King David.

Travelling to Britain in 1902, Herzl appeared before a Royal Commission, where he put the case for Zionism. In a powerful exposition of the Jewish situation in the Tsarist and Austro-Hungarian Empires, he told the Commissioners that the reason why Jews flocked to Britain and America was 'a desire for the freedom of life and soul which the Jew cannot under present

conditions know in eastern Europe'. The Commissioners must remember, Herzl told them, that this 'self-imposed sentence of exile is not with Jews as with those of other nationalists for a term of years – with the Jews it is a life sentence'.

Herzl was also entertained by Samuel Montagu, the first Baron Swaythling, the most successful operator on the foreign exchanges of his day, who suggested buying Palestine for £2 million. His son, Edwin Montagu, though a member of Lloyd George's War Cabinet, was to be a fierce opponent of Zionism in 1917. In 1903, when Herzl visited Vilna – the city known to the Jews as the 'Jerusalem of Lithuania' – he was acclaimed 'Herzl the King' by thousands who thrilled as he spoke to them of his vision for a Jewish homeland; a homeland that would be free from internal hostility and repression. 'In the numerous addresses I was enormously over-praised,' he wrote in his diary, 'but the unhappiness of these sorely oppressed people was genuine. Afterwards all kinds of delegations, laden with gifts, called on me at the hotel, in front of which crowds kept re-gathering as fast as the police dispersed them.'

Max Nordau, *Herzl's closest colleague, and like him, born in Hungary. When a critic of Zionism told Herzl he was insane to want to settle the Jews in Palestine, Nordau consoled him with the words: 'If you are insane, we are insane together. Count me in!' He later distanced himself from the Zionist movement when he felt it was failing to focus sharply enough on the target of Jewish statehood.*

The Jews of Eastern Europe knew what Herzl was seeking on their behalf. In 1902 he published a novel, *Altneuland* ('Old-New Land') which rapidly became a best seller. In it he stressed the need, once the Jews were established in Palestine, for good relations with the Arabs. Tolerance was a theme of the book, as was the importance of using science and technology in building up Jewish life in Palestine. A Peace Palace was to be created, to co-ordinate Jewish and non-Jewish efforts to alleviate the effect of natural disasters. 'Wherever in the world a catastrophe occurs – earthquake, flood, famine, drought, epidemic – the stricken country telegraphs to this centre for help. Here there is always a stock of the necessary supplies, because both the gifts of such supplies and the requests for them are centralized here. A permanent committee chosen from among all the nations sees to it that the distributions are justly made.' Herzl wanted the world to see the Jewish nation as a model. The motto of the book became the Zionist motto: 'If you will, it is no fairytale.'

Such hopes were powerful and seductive, but reality was against them: the Sultan did not wish to grant the Jews their own autonomous status in Palestine. Many Zionists, frustrated by the Sultan's repeated refusal, began to look – as Jews had done in previous centuries – at the possibility of 'other Zions'. In the wake of renewed pogroms in Russia, the establishment of some place of refuge seemed urgent, wherever it might be. In October 1902, three months after his third unsuccessful visit to Turkey, Herzl was received in

London by Joseph Chamberlain, the British Colonial Secretary, who offered an area in East Africa – then it was part of Uganda, today it is inside Kenya – for Jewish settlement.

Many Zionists wanted to accept the 'Uganda Scheme', as it was known, and build some form of Jewish territory on British goodwill. Herzl himself gave 'Uganda' his approval when he spoke at the Sixth Zionist Congress, held in Basle in August 1903. During the debate, however, Herzl's deputy, Max Nordau, spoke passionately against the idea of any *Nachtasyl* ('nightshelter') for the Jews, even at times of persecution in Russia, insisting that Palestine alone was the true aim of all Jewish territorial and national aspirations. Although Herzl replied that Uganda could not replace Palestine as the ulti-mate Zionist goal, there was so much opposition among the delegates to accepting it even in the short term that when a vote was taken in support of sending a survey team to East Africa, critics of the scheme walked out of the congress hall. At the last session of the congress Herzl sought to re-assure the delegates of his commitment to the true Zion by declaring, in the words of the Old Testament: 'If I forsake thee, O Jerusalem, let my right hand forget her cunning.'

Returning to his diplomatic efforts for a Jewish homeland in Palestine, Herzl asked the Russian government to take up the Zionist request direct with the Turks. Then, in January 1904, he met the Pope, seeking Roman Catholic support for a Jewish homeland in Palestine, and offering Jewish protection over the Christian holy places. Exhausted by his efforts, Herzl was taken ill. He died in Vienna, just forty-four years old, on 3 July 1904.

Herzl's funeral procession *in Vienna, More than a thousand people followed his hearse from his home in the suburbs to the cemetery. Jews all over the world, especially those in Eastern Europe, mourned his pass-ing. The figure bottom left appears to be conducting some singers, out of the picture.*

25

The Austrian-Jewish writer Stefan Zweig was an eye witness in Vienna in the days before Herzl's funeral. 'Suddenly, to all the railroad stations of the city, by day and by night, from all realms and lands, every train brought new arrivals,' he wrote. 'Western, Eastern, Russian, Turkish Jews; from all the provinces and all the little towns they hurried excitedly, the shock of the news still written on their faces; never was it more clearly manifest what strife and talk had hitherto concealed – it was a great movement whose leader had now fallen.' Zweig marvelled at the scenes of grief during the funeral procession through the streets of Vienna, and at the cemetery: 'It was this gigantic outpouring of grief from the depths of millions of souls that made me realize for the first time how much passion and hope this lone and lonesome man had borne into the world through the power of a single thought.'

In his last will and testament, Herzl asked to be buried next to his father in Vienna, until such time as his remains could be taken to the Jewish homeland in Palestine in which he so believed. His faith was rewarded forty-five years after his death, soon after the establishment of the State of Israel in 1948.

Herzl had given political direction to the longings of generations who had already seen many thousands of Jews move to Palestine in the thirty years before his death. His search for diplomatic recognition, for international agreements, turned Zionism from a vision held by multitudes of individual Jews into a modern national movement whose aims had begun to make themselves felt, at the highest level of government, in many European capitals. Could this new Zionism survive its founder's death? The anniversary of his death became an annual day of remembrance among Zionist societies around

A clothes shop *in the Jewish quarter of Vilna (Vilnius) in about 1910. When Napoleon looked into its Great Synagogue on his way to Moscow in 1812 he said, 'Surely this is the Jerusalem of Lithuania', and such the Jews called it thereafter. More than 60,000 Jews lived in Vilna in 1910, almost half the city's total population.*

the world, and especially in eastern Europe where his influence had been so strong – until eastern European Jewry was itself virtually wiped out. One of the most remarkable 'Herzl Days' was that held in the Kovno ghetto in 1943, shortly before the ghetto itself was destroyed and most of its surviving inhabitants murdered.

However tenaciously pursued by those who believed in it, Zionism was a dream: a dream held by a minority of Jews. All twenty million Jews in the world when the twentieth century began were subject to the laws of non-Jewish nations

Jewish watercarriers *in Lida, Russian Poland, 1910. A Jewish community existed in the town from the early seventeeth century. By the time this picture was taken, the 5,000 Jews in Lida made up almost 70 per cent of the population. The thirteen synagogues and houses of prayer, one for each main trade, were grouped around the square.*

and empires. They lived everywhere as minorities, often flourishing, but also at times persecuted and discriminated against. There was also widespread poverty among Jews in certain areas, especially parts of Russian Poland and Ukraine, and the Eastern Galician province of the Austro-Hungarian empire. Poverty and discrimination helped to fuel Zionism: but they also made the appeal of revolutionary socialism a strong one among Jews, especially in Russia and Russian Poland, where a quarter of all the Jews in the world lived in 1900.

Just as the first Zionist Congress had been held in 1897, so too, that same year, the Bund – the General Jewish Workers Union in Lithuania, Poland and Russia – was established. Its aim was that Jews should remain in eastern Europe, but act as a spearhead of social justice and equality within the Russian Empire and beyond. Its most visible weapons were mass demonstrations and strikes.

The advent of organized Jewish socialism within the Diaspora had an even greater appeal than Zionism when the Bund was launched publicly, in the Russian city of Minsk, in 1898. Jewish revolutionary socialism was to continue to win over the Jewish masses in Russia until the crushing of the Bund after the Communist Revolution in 1917, towards which it had made its own powerful contribution in the previous twenty years. Even then, outside Russia, the Bund survived as a socialist force: particularly in Poland. Many Bundists also made their way to the United States.

One of the founders of the Bund, Rosa Luxemburg, was among the first Bundists to be arrested. Born in Russian Poland, she had been forced to flee Tsarist Russia before the turn of the century to avoid arrest. In Germany she became active in the left-wing of the German socialist movement. She was imprisoned there in 1900, aged twenty-nine, for speaking publicly against militarism and war, released, and then imprisoned again four years later. Returning to Russian Poland, and to its capital city, Warsaw, she took part in the 1905 Russian Revolution, after which she was imprisoned for a third time, this time by the Russian authorities. After her release she returned to Germany, where she continued to work to promote revolution. It was while leading a Communist attempt to seize power in Berlin in 1919 that she was murdered.

The climax of Bund activity came during the Russian revolution of 1905, when it was a leading and highly organised

Rosa Luxemburg, *who took part in the 1905 revolution in Warsaw: a prison photograph taken in 1906 in Germany where she had been arrested for advocating a general strike. Murdered while leading the failed revolution in Berlin, 1919.*

A mass demonstration *organised by the Bund – the General Jewish Workers Union in Lithuania, Poland and Russia – in support of the 1905 Russian revolution. This demonstra-tion was held in Dvinsk, in Russian Latvia, on 17 October 1905. By the end of the year the uprising had been crushed, and many Bundists were among those exiled to Siberia.*

component of the wider Russian revolutionary activity. On the eve of that revolution – the first Russian revolution – there were more than 4,000 Bundists in Tsarist political prisons, alongside the Mensheviks (whom the Bundists supported) and the Bolsheviks, in both of whose ranks many individual Jews were also active. With the failure of the 1905 revolution, the Bund, while in no way losing its revolutionary fervour, turned its practical attention more and more to Jewish cultural issues, calling for greater autonomy in Jewish life within Russia, and an end to discrimination against Jews by the government of the day. It never lost its Jewish as well as its Socialist impetus.

Between them, Zionism and Socialism held hundreds of thousands of Jews in thrall. But millions more Jews sought relief from poverty and discrimination by leaving Eastern Europe altogether, looking for opportunities for a less harsh life in other lands, and greater opportunities of advancement, particularly in the United States – the *Goldene Medina*, or Golden Realm, of Yiddish lore and Eastern European Jewish aspirations. The crossing of the Atlantic was seen as a prelude to a life of hard work, rewards for that hard work, and an end to continual discrimination. The ability to live in the United States and remain Jewish – to preserve Jewish worship and culture – was the great hope, and it was fulfilled.

Between 1881 and 1914 the astonishingly large number of 2,600,000 Jews emigrated from Russia and eastern Austria-Hungary to the United States. New York was the transatlantic magnet for the largest single number of these immigrants. When the century began there were 350,000 Jews in New York, only a few thousands fewer than in Warsaw. By 1914 the number of New York Jews – many of them penniless immigrants from Russian Poland – was one million. This was more than twice the Jewish population of Warsaw. A vast swathe of eastern European Jewry was being transposed, by its own efforts, from the Old World to the New. They came through the quarantine and immigration procedures of Ellis Island, in New York harbour, to a city where Jewish life pulsated in the busy streets of the Lower East Side, and where the Yiddish language, with its wealth of wisdom and humour, was on all lips.

Alongside the Zionists, the Socialists and the emigrants, there existed in many lands contented, openly practising Jews, as well as those who increasingly assimilated into national life and cultures. 'Seek ye the peace of the city where I have caused you to be taken captive, for in that peace you will find peace' had been the Biblical command. It was heeded even when it was no longer a question of captivity, but of emancipation and participation. The twentieth century began, as it ended, with tens of thousands of people who had been born Jewish – the children of two Jewish parents – assimilating or even converting to Christianity. But many of these retained their Jewishness in one form or another: in external and facial characteristics (so cruelly and cynically derided by Hitler) and in internal feelings, too, of affinity to some aspect of Jewishness.

FIGHTING FOR THE BUND.
Leivick Halpern (above), arrested in 1906 for taking part in a demonstration against the Tsar. He later escaped from Siberia and made his way to the United States. Two women Bundists (above right), photographed in the Black Sea port of Nikolayev, and later exiled to Siberia. Four Bundists (far right), originally from Pinsk, in Minsk prison in 1903, having been sentenced to four years hard labour for killing a police agent. Moshe Citrin, second from left, later escaped from Siberia. Bundists in Siberia (right), a postcard issued in the United States by the Association for the Political Prisoners in Siberia.

TO THE NEW WORLD.

Jewish immigrants from England (left) await inspection at Ellis Island, New York, before entering the United States. Perhaps the father arrived some time before, as many did, to establish a home for his wife and children. Immigrants from Russia, (right) sitting on a hatch cover on board a ship sailing from Antwerp to New York. A Jewish immigrant from Russia (below), Ellis Island, 1905. The metal rails in the background helped to keep queues orderly. Jews constituted 23 per cent of New York's population by 1910.

[PHOTO BELOW: LEWIS W. HINE]

In the early years of the twentieth century, as in every century preceding it, anti-Jewish hatreds, prejudice and violence were never far below the surface. For the Jews of France, these years were dominated by the repercussions of the Dreyfus Affair: the charge levelled in 1894 against Colonel Alfred Dreyfus – a Jewish officer in the French army – that he had sold secrets to the Germans. Although Dreyfus was eventually re-instated in 1906 after the treason charges were proved false, the bitterness generated during and after the trial left French Jews uneasy about the extent of anti-Semitism in their midst. It seemed a warning sign that the steady evolution of greater Jewish rights in the nineteenth century – both in France and elsewhere – could be rapidly eroded by upsurges in popular prejudice.

The *Protocols of the Elders of Zion*, an anti-Semitic forgery, first published in St. Petersburg in 1903, and widely circulated in the coming years, claimed to be evidence of a world Jewish conspiracy, the sinister aim of which was to dominate and undermine all the great European empires. The pogroms in Russia were a visible sign of hatred – even of mass hatred – against the Jews. These pogroms, which had been widespread in the 1880s, were renewed again in the new century, culminating in the Kishinev pogrom in 1903. In a few

'I am innocent'. *Captain Alfred Dreyfus standing before his judges in a courtroom in Paris in 1894, hearing the sentence of life imprisonment for treason. Dreyfus, who had entered the army as an engineer, was the only Jew on the French General Staff. He was brought back from the penal colony on Devil's Island off French Guiana in 1899, retried, found guilty with extenuating circumstances and pardoned. Exonerated and reinstated in1906, he reached the rank of Lieutenant-Colonel in the First World War.*

hours of mob violence, forty-nine Jews were killed, and thousands injured, by Russian anti-Semites who also ransacked Jewish shops and houses.

When Herzl had visited Russia shortly after this pogrom, he had seen Witte, who was to become the Russian Prime Minister two years later. Witte had reminisced about conversations with Alexander III, who had been Tsar during the 1880s. Witte told Herzl that he had said to the Tsar, 'If it were possible, Your Majesty, to drown six or seven million Jews in the Black Sea, I should be perfectly satisfied. But if it isn't possible, we must let them live.' In Kiev, in 1911, Mendel Beilis was accused of the medieval blood libel accusation of using Christian blood for the Passover meal. Jews world-wide, and especially in Britain and the United States, protested at the absurdity of the charge. In Russia, 20,000 Bundists – Jewish revolutionary socialists – carried out a protest strike in Kiev, where the trial was to be held. But the trial went ahead, creating great anguish among Jews. So absurd was the charge, and so strong the world-wide public outcry, that Beilis was acquitted. He made his way first to Palestine, and then to the United States. In Jerusalem, he was seen by the city's Muslim Arabs as a Jewish hero against Russian Tsarist oppression, and welcomed by the Muslim clergy to the Dome of the Rock.

Wounded victims. *Survivors of the Kishinev pogrom, who had been injured during attacks by an anti-Semitic mob. The 5,000 Russian soldiers in the city, who could have held back the attackers, did nothing. A letter of protest written in the United States was handed to the President, Theodore Roosevelt, who forwarded it to the Tsar. The Tsar refused to receive it.*

SYNAGOGUE AND MARKET PLACE.
A massive synagogue proudly dominates the market square at Przemysl (left), in Austria-Hungary. In 1910 the city's Jewish population of 16,000 made up 30 per cent of the total. Jews celebrate a new Torah scroll (right) with music and dance in the synagogue of Dubrovna, a small town in Tsarist Russia. Two boys and a man hold up the new scroll at the back. Dubrovna's main industry was textiles, and almost all the Jewish prayer shawls for the Russian Empire were made there.

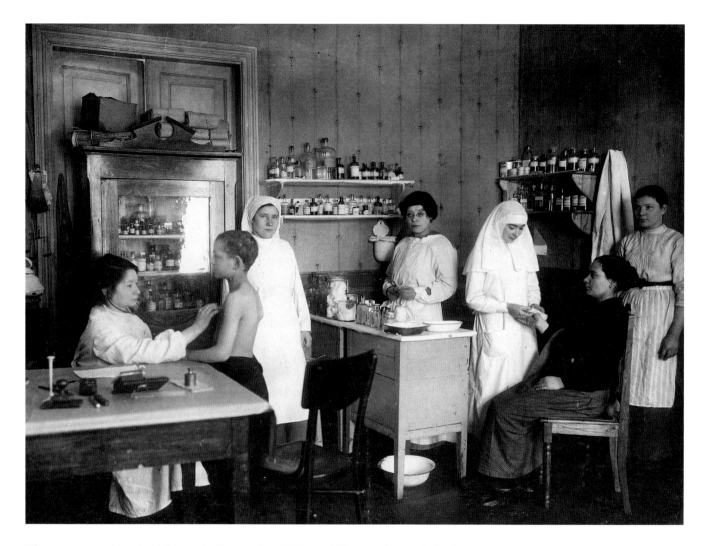

The most populous Jewish city in Europe in 1900 was Warsaw, the capital of Russian Poland. Jewish newspapers, books, theatres, schools and hospitals proliferated. The Tlomackie Street synagogue was at the centre of a vigorous religious life. In every Jewish community, even the smallest, the synagogue provided a focus of creative spiritual worship that reached far beyond the portals of the house of prayer. When, in 1900, the cantor Joseph Rosenblatt (known as Yossele) took up a position in the Austro-Hungarian town of Munkacs – he was then only eighteen years old – his powerful, melodic voice quickly entranced the congregation at the daily services, Sabbath and festivals. It was his first step on a road that would make him one of the great masters of the cantorial art so beloved of Jews in their synagogues throughout the world: and a voice heard and enjoyed on early gramophone records by thousands of non-Jews.

In parts of Russian Poland, and throughout the Ukraine, more than a fifth of all Jews were in receipt of poor relief from their local Jewish community. Among the charitable organizations set up to help them were those which

Health for all. *Nurses of OSE, the Society for the Protection of the Health of the Jewish Population, and their patients. The society had clinics throughout the Jewish-populated regions of Russia, and also ran a number of children's convalescent homes in resort towns in the Crimea and in the Baltic. It was based in the capital, St Petersburg.*

supplied poor students with clothes, gave kosher food to Jewish soldiers serving in the Russian army, and gave technical education to orphans, provided free medical treatment for the poor, free meals for those who had no money at all, and dowries for poor brides. ORT – 'The Society to Promote Trades and Agriculture' – was active in Russia from 1889, setting up trade schools and agricultural colonies for 120,000 Jews before the outbreak of the First World War. OSE, founded in St. Petersburg in 1912, established hospitals, kindergartens and children's homes for those Russian Jewish families who did not have sufficient resources to care for their children.

In 1905 a Polish Jew, Ludwig Zamenhof – an advocate of humanistic Judaism, freed from dogma – presided over a congress in Paris to promote a single universal language, Esperanto, which he had invented eighteen years earlier. In 1910 a second congress was held in Washington, at which Zamenhof delivered his lectures in the new language.

In Warsaw, in 1912, Janusz Korczak (born Henryk Goldszmit) was appointed director of a new Jewish orphanage, at which his revolutionary – and also humanistic – approach was to encourage the children to self-government, as well as to draw them into active participation in the running of the orphanage. He urged all those who taught children or looked after them to regard the emotional life of each child with respect. Once, while lecturing in a Warsaw hospital to medical students on 'The Heart of the Child', Korczak brought a small boy on to the rostrum, took off the child's shirt, and, placing a fluoroscope lamp behind him, turned off the overhead light. The audience could see the child's heart beating rapidly on the screen. Korczak then told the students: 'Don't ever forget this sight. Always remember what a child's frightened heart looks like.' In 1942, when in his mid-sixties, he was deported with his orphans to their deaths at the Nazi concentration camp of Treblinka, to the east of Warsaw. He had given life-long service to the Polish nation, as well as to the Jews.

Jews made their contributions to every field of professional, scientific, commercial and social endeavour. This was so, and remarkably so, even in Russia, despite the restrictions imposed on where Jews could live, and what jobs they could pursue – they were excluded altogether from government. Samuel Poliakov was among the main financiers of railway building that had begun to link the vast empire. Baron Horace de Gunzburg, millionaire owner of gold mines in Siberia, was a philanthropist who virtually sustained through his own personal munificence the poor Jews of St. Petersburg, as well as being the main contributor to the building of the magnificent Choral Synagogue in the city. Serge Koussevitsky, soloist and later conductor, who had been baptized at the age of fourteen because Jews were not then allowed to live in Moscow, gave his first public concert in Moscow in 1900. The painter Marc Chagall moved from Russia to Paris in 1910.

Two wealthy Russian Jews, Izrail Brodsky and Klonimus-Wolf Wissotsky, were the main manufacturers of sugar and tea. Russian Jews, among them

Leon Trotsky (born Lev Bronstein), were prominent in the most extreme revolutionary movements. After the 1917 Bolshevik revolution in Russia there was a popular jingle: 'The sugar belongs to Brodsky, the tea to Wissotsky, the country to Trotsky'.

A majority of French Jews lived in Paris: 40,000 out of a total of 60,000 at the start of the First World War. As many as 10,000 were part of the mass westward emigration of Jews from Russia and Russian Poland that had begun in 1881. A further 15,000 had come from the main Jewish population centres in the Ottoman Empire: Istanbul, Salonika and Izmir, making France their home.

Some French Jews reached positions of high respect and authority. In 1904 Sylvain Levy, a distinguished orientalist, was made head of the Institute of Indian Studies at the Sorbonne. He was an early and forceful advocate of Jewish nationhood in Palestine. In 1908 another French Jew, Gabriel Lippman – a physicist and pioneer of colour photography – won the Nobel Prize. In Paris, Sarah Bernhardt's theatre was in its second year when the twentieth century began. As a child she had been baptized and placed in a convent – because she interfered with her Dutch-Jewish mother's life as a courtesan. She was always aware of her Jewish origins and proud of them, though when asked what she thought of the Ten Commandments by a reporter, she replied, 'Zey are too many'. When she was eighteen she was extracted from the convent and went on the stage. From the 1880s she toured all Europe, America, Australia and South Africa. At her new theatre in Paris, which was named for her, one of her most acclaimed roles was that of Hamlet, Prince of Denmark.

In Britain, as much as in any other western industrial country, the Jews found themselves from the first years of the century in a land of extraordinary opportunities. Jews had lived in Britain in early medieval times, until the expulsion of 1290. A Jewish community was re-established in 1656, invited to do so by Oliver Cromwell. It was initially a Sephardi community, descendants of the Jews who, having been expelled from Spain and Portugal, had first settled round the Mediterranean and in northern Europe. When the Dutchman, William of Orange, became King of England in 1688, several Jewish families

Yiddish writers. *Mendel Elkin (left) and his lifelong friend, the playwright Peretz Hirschbein, in elegant attire. Both wrote extensively for the Yiddish theatre, first in Russia, where this photograph was taken in 1910, then in Poland, and later in the United States.*

Pondering her lines. *Sarah Bernhardt, one of the leading actresses of her day, famous for playing Hamlet, and also Napoleon's son. In 1905 she injured her knee while jumping off a 'cliff' in a stage scene. The wound was neglected and in 1915 her leg had to be amputated. After that, roles were specially written for her so that she never had to stand up. In the First World War she was carried around the war zone on a sofa to give performances to the troops. She died in 1923, at the age of seventy-nine.*

came from Amsterdam, followed in the succeeding decades by many more. In the next two centuries, British Jews migrated throughout Britain's far-flung maritime empire, reaching Bombay, Tangier and New York.

The first Ashkenazi community, of northern European Jews, was set up in London in 1690. While the Sephardi Jews were mainly in commerce and the professions – one of them became clerk and librarian of the Royal Society early in the eighteenth century – the Ashkenazi Jews were mostly poor. In 1881 Britain had a Jewish population of 65,000. Michael Marks was part of the mass influx of 235,000 Jews who emigrated to Britain from Russia and Russian Poland between 1881 and 1914. He set himself up as an itinerant peddler, carrying his goods in a pack on his back across the Pennines from Leeds to Manchester, seeking to sell something, for the smallest of profit margins, in a dozen northern towns. It was a hard struggle, but twenty years later,

LEADING FAMILIES.

(far left) The British Rothschilds and Sassoons amuse themselves at a country house in Scotland, in a break, no doubt, from pursuing deer, salmon and grouse like other rich Edwardians. The Rothschilds were originally from Frankfurt, the Sassoons from Baghdad. Marie Louise Beer (left), on the day of her wedding to Lionel de Rothschild. Louise Perugia, (below) who married Arthur Sassoon, on holiday in Scotland, posing with her King Charles spaniel and the salmon she has just caught.

in 1907, Marks and Spencer (Spencer was a non-Jew who helped with the accounting side of the business) opened its sixtieth high street store. Today there are more than 250.

So many and so poor were the immigrants, or most of them, that Yiddish-speaking communities sprung up in vastly overcrowded areas – usually slums – of many British towns, including London's East End, Manchester, Liverpool, Leeds and Glasgow. At the beginning of the twentieth century, forty per cent of the Russian-Polish immigrants who had work were tailors. More than twelve per cent were in the boot and shoe trade, including my paternal grandfather, who arrived from Russian Poland just before the turn of the century, and ten per cent were in the furniture trade, most of them cabinet makers. Dressmaking absorbed tens of thousands of Jewish women,

A peddler's progress. *Michael Marks sold his wares with the slogan: 'Don't ask the price, it's a penny'. After one of his assistants died of pneumonia, caught while working in an open market, he moved into the covered market, then opened his own high street stores. This one, in Sheffield, opened in 1897. One notice says, 'Every item 4d this section', thus following the original principle of simplicity and uniformity. Marks provided his shopgirls with wooden platforms, so that their feet would not get cold.*

44

usually in terribly over-crowded conditions in 'sweat-shops' where hours of work were long and wages low. Two of my great-aunts were dressmakers, while my maternal grandfather made buttons. An immigrant from Lithuania, he lived in the East End of London: a Bangladeshi family lives in his house today (it escaped destruction in the Blitz, unlike many of the houses near it).

The early years of the twentieth century saw a vast outpouring of Jewish energy in the crowded areas of Anglo-Jewish immigrant settlement. Yiddish and Hebrew newspapers were published, the Yiddish theatre flourished, Jewish trade unions were created. By 1914 many immigrant Jews were beginning to find their way out of the ghetto, to earn enough money, often only just enough, to provide for their children the education they themselves could never have afforded. Immigrant children were encouraged to speak English, sent to schools where English was the language of instruction, and made welcome at clubs and youth groups where competition with non-Jewish youngsters in sports and other club activities was encouraged. As Jewish families moved out of the ghetto areas into the more affluent, greener and less crowded suburbs, many new synagogues were opened.

Jews were to be found in many varied aspects of public life. In 1898 Lilian Baylis became manager of the Old Vic theatre, and her remarkable pronouncements started to be recorded by her company there: 'I'm all for everybody having their proper mate in life, but I don't like it going on in the wings.' In 1913 the boxer Ted 'Kid' Lewis (Gershon Mendeloff), became British featherweight champion. Wealthy Jews became patrons of the arts, were active in both Jewish and non-Jewish charitable causes, and set a pattern for communal responsibility. Montague Burton, born in Russia, made his fortune out of ready-made men's clothes. His philanthropy was widespread. So too was that of the British branch of the Rothschilds. In the Liberal government which came to power in 1905 there were two Jewish Cabinet Ministers: Rufus Isaacs, later Viceroy of India, and Herbert Samuel, later leader of the Liberal Party.

Pressures on the Jews could be considerable. There was hostility to Jewish immigration among those who felt threatened by what seemed to be a fierce Jewish work ethic, and they pressed for restrictions on 'alien' immigration. An act imposing restrictions became law in 1905, in the final months of the outgoing Conservative administration. In the event, under the Liberal government, its clause allowing in victims of political persecution was interpreted in such a way as virtually to restore the immigration numbers to what they had been before the act came into force. There was, however, an outbreak of anti-Jewish rioting in South Wales in 1911, when coal miners vented their rage against poor pay and conditions in the mines on the Jewish shopkeepers in their towns: shopkeepers who were hardly better off than the miners themselves. No one was killed, but many Jews were injured and much Jewish property damaged. It was Britain's only pogrom.

There were more than 600,000 Jews in Germany in 1910, and they were

Lilian Baylis. *Her famous series of Shakespeare productions at the Old Vic in London, beginning in 1914, laid the foundations for what became the National Theatre. In 1931 she re-opened Sadler's Wells Theatre.*

able to participate in every aspect of German life. Both the Liberal and Social-Democrat parties had many Jewish members of Parliament, but Jews were excluded by law from becoming government ministers, a barrier that was not swept away until after the First World War. They did participate, however, in building up Germany's military strength: a Jewish industrialist, Albert Ballin built warships for the Kaiser.

Many German Jews had assimilated completely into German ways, through intermarriage, renunciation of Judaism, and conversion to Christianity. The relationship between Jewishness and national patriotism was, however, much discussed among Jews. The German painter Max Liebermann remarked: 'And if throughout my life I have felt a German, my

Shipbuilder and patriot. *(left) Albert Ballin, a German shipping magnate, on board one of his Hamburg-Amerika liners. During the First World War he organised the shipping of foodstuffs to Germany, circumventing the Allied shipping blockade. Because he refused to convert to Christianity he never received a patent of nobility. He and his British friend and fellow-Jew, Sir Ernest Cassel – the most important figure in the City of London at the time – had both tried to dissuade their respective monarchs from getting into a dangerous race for naval supremacy.*

The Jewish Quarter *in Frankfurt am Main, with one of the three main synagogues, each of which was burned down by the Nazis in 1938 (right). The first Rothschild bank was in a house similar to the ones shown here, a few doors to the right of the synagogue. In 1910 there were 22,000 Jews in the city, 8% of the total population. One of Germany's most influential liberal daily newspapers, the* Frankfurter Zeitung, *was founded by a Jew, Leopold Sonnemann.*

vivid sense of belonging to the Jewish people has been no less strong.' Jewish communal life was sustained by an impressive network of schools, youth organizations and charities. In Berlin the Hilfsverein organisation, founded in 1901, helped Jewish emigrants bound for the United States. Also, in the thirty years before the outbreak of the First World War, large numbers of Jewish immigrants came to settle in Germany from eastern Europe. These were Yiddish speakers, with their more traditional appearance, the women in headscarves, the boys with their ringlets, the men with their thick beards and – each Sabbath – wearing their flowing prayer shawls. They too had opportunities to do well. In 1906 Yossele Rosenblatt had moved on to become chief cantor at the main Hamburg synagogue, and began recording some of his

47

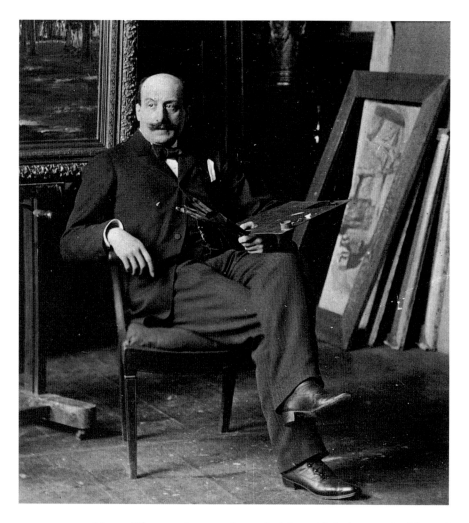

Max Liebermann *a painter of international renown who introduced Impressionism to Germany. When Hitler came to power he announced, 'As it is my conviction that art has nothing to do with either politics or descent, I can no longer remain a member of the Prussian Academy of Art, of which I have been a full member for over thirty years and whose president I was for twelve years, as my standpoint is no longer considered valid.' Later his house was looted while the police stood by laughing.*
[PHOTO: MAX VON RÜDIGER]

own compositions. These early records made him widely known inside and beyond Germany.

Among the German Jews who succeeded, even to the point of arousing jealousy among their less successful non-Jewish competitors, were prominent bankers, department store owners, leading merchants in the grain and metal industries, in the textile and clothing trades, in building construction and in heavy industry. In Berlin, Isidor Loewe was the head of the largest rifle factory in the world. He also manufactured cars, and some of the first aircraft. A Jewish engineer, Emil Rathenau, founded the General Electric Company (AEG): by the time of his death in 1915 it employed more than 70,000 people. His son Walther was also an industrialist, but a man of radical insights too. In a book published in 1912 he condemned the current faith in technology, rationalism and materialism, and urged a return to deeper moral and social values. Among German Jews who made a contribution to the health of mankind was Paul Ehrlich, the founder of modern chemotherapy, winner of the Nobel Prize in 1908.

It was above all in the United States that Jewish life flourished, despite initial poverty and hard struggles. The range of Jewish personalities in public life, the arts, science and commerce there was remarkable. Carl Laemmle, German-born, became the leading partner in the Motion Picture Patents Company, making some of the very earliest successful one-reel and two-reel films. Laemmle also initiated the 'star' system when he signed up the 'Biograph Girl', Florence Lawrence, taking her away from her home studio. Irving Berlin (born Israel Baline, in Russian Siberia) wrote the song 'Alexander's Ragtime Band' in 1911, becoming a household name overnight. Later he was to write 'God Bless America' and, his most recorded song, 'White Christmas'. In 1912 cantor Yossele Rosenblatt emigrated to the United States from Germany, to conduct services at the First Hungarian Congregation in New York's Harlem. 'Vast crowds – including non-Jewish music lovers – flocked to the services he conducted as well as to his concerts,' writes the historian Geoffrey Wigoder. The violinist and child prodigy Mischa Elman reached the United States from the Russian capital, St. Petersburg, at the age of sixteen. Aged twenty-seven, Max Factor, soon to become a leading cosmetician, reached the United States from Russian Poland. Helena Rubinstein, born in Russian Poland in 1871, and living in London from the age of twenty-three, emigrated to the United States in 1914. Among the cosmetics she pioneered were waterproof mascara and medicated face

Yossele Rosenblatt, *cantor and composer whose musical genius emerged when he was a boy in Austria-Hungary. He recorded some of the earliest gramophone records. In 1912 he moved to New York, where his own compositions of liturgical music won him a vast following.*

cream. She also developed the selling technique of home demonstrations.

The role of Jews in the United States spanned every profession and walk of life. Florenz Ziegfeld, the showman, launched the Ziegfeld Follies in 1906. Albert Michelson, a pioneer in modern optics, became, in 1907, the first American Nobel laureate in the sciences. Judge Louis Brandeis, a leading jurist, was on the United States Supreme Court for twenty-three years. Many American Jews also represented the United States overseas. Henry Morgenthau, an immigrant from Germany, was American Ambassador to Turkey in the years just before the outbreak of the First World War, active in trying to persuade the Turks to grant greater protection to their Christian, Armenian and Jewish minorities (his son Henry Morgenthau Jr was to be one of President Franklin Roosevelt's principal advisers in the Second World War). Hannah Solomon, who was at the forefront of the struggle for women's rights in the two decades before the First World War, was chosen by the National Council of Women in the United States – made up of women of all religions, races and national origins – to go to Berlin in 1904 as their representative on the International Council of Women. Her ability to speak fluent English, French and German (her father had emigrated from Germany to the United States in 1845) made a strong impact on the delegates.

Abraham Goldfaden, a Russian-born pioneer of the Yiddish theatre,

New York extremes. *Helena Rubinstein (above) in a ball gown. Her name became synonymous with beauty aids for women and she made a fortune in the process. A twelve-year-old boy on piecework (left) pulling threads in a garment trade sweat-shop. He had sworn that he was sixteen, but according to inspectors who examined his teeth, he was only twelve.*

[PHOTO LEFT: JACOB A. RIIS]

reached the United States in 1903, his comedies having been banned by the Tsarist government for fear of their revolutionary impact on the Jewish masses. Goldfaden wrote sixty plays for the Yiddish theatre. The title-hero of one of his early comedies, *Shmendrik*, quickly became the proverbial, gullible, good-natured fool. Goldfaden became a strong critic of Jewish assimilation and participation in the life of other nationalities. In his play, *Ben Ami*, ('Son of My People') he called for Jewish national redemption in Palestine as an answer to the Russian pogroms. The play's aristocratic hero, on discovering his Jewish origins and witnessing a pogrom in Odessa, leaves the bloodstained soil of Russia for a new life, not in America, but in Palestine. Once there, the hero sets as his task the training of Jewish youth to till the soil and to work for the national regeneration of the Jewish people. As assimilation gained ground in the United States, and Zionism saw emigration to Palestine as the countermeasure to it, Goldfaden's play – it was the last that he wrote – held a particular resonance.

Jews in the United States developed their own Yiddish-American humour, delivered in thickly-accented English. One of the first 'dialect' comedians, David Warfield (born Wohlfelt) enacted the part of Sigmund Cohenski, a Jewish millionaire on holiday in Paris whose daughter Uneeda was in love with an American naval officer: 'The captain is my idea of hero', Uneeda told

Leaving synagogue *after the Jewish New Year service, Rivington Street, New York.*

her father. 'A hero! Is dot a business? A tailor is a business, a shoemaker is a business, but a hero? Better you should marry a bookkeeper.' 'A bookkeeper? I suppose you think the pen is mightier than the sword?' the girl sneered. 'You bet my life', said papa Cohenski. 'Could you sign checks with a sword?'

Irving Berlin wrote a song 'Goodbye Becky Cohen', in which she tells her boyfriend not to go off and fight:

> *'Where's the percentage in that?*
> *No, you'd better mind your store.*
> *Let McCarthy go to war.'*

The Triangle Building. *Garment workers, mostly Jewish and all women, jumped to their deaths from the top windows, later cooled by the fire hoses from below. Protests and action by trade unions later led to fire escapes being installed all over New York.*

Among the American Jews who heeded the call to leave the New World for the Old were two nurses who, travelling to Jerusalem just before the outbreak of the First World War, established a small clinic which was to be the basis of the Hadassah Hospital, since 1939 a prominent Jerusalem landmark. With them on board ship was the American philanthropist who financed their efforts, Nathan Straus – the grandson of an immigrant from Germany who had arrived in the United States in 1852. For four years New York's parks commissioner, and then health commissioner, Straus had already, before his Jerusalem venture, established a series of milk distribution centres in New York, as well as boarding houses which provided cheap bed and breakfast for the poor in the city.

One nineteenth-century Jewish tradition that continued in the twentieth century was intervention on behalf of Jews in distress elsewhere. Throughout the reign of Queen Victoria a British Jew, Sir Moses Montefiore, had travelled widely, including to Russia, to protest to government ministers about anti-Jewish actions and legislation, and in 1903 a distinguished American Jew and jurist, Louis Marshall sought a means of protesting against the plight of Russian Jews. Using his political influence, and the power of his moral advocacy, he was able to obtain the abrogation of the 1832 Russian-American Friendship Treaty, as a protest against the Kishinev pogrom of 1903.

Closer to home, American Jewry had to face a tragedy in 1911, when a fire broke out at the Triangle Building in New York: 147 women working in the building, most of them Jewish, were killed. At one of the many anguished public meetings that followed, Jewish trade union leaders warned against the perpetuation of bitterness against the women's employers for the appalling conditions of work. But Russian-born Rose Schneiderman, a champion of women's rights in factory and workplace, told the audience: 'To speak of peace and harmony now would be treason to the dead!'

By 1914, there were 45,000 Jews living in Jerusalem – out of

Home from school. *Two Jewish children at Petakh Tikvah ('Gateway of Hope') in Palestine, before the First World War. Behind them is an Arab on horseback. To protect themselves from repeated attacks by Bedouin marauders, the villagers organised the first Jewish self-defence group, headed by Abraham Shapira (see page 20), but their relations with the neighbouring Arab villages were good. 800 Jews lived in Petakh Tikvah in 1900, more than 8,000 in 1930, and 80,000 in 1970.*

[PHOTO: SHLOMO NARINSKY]

a total city population of 60,000. They constituted almost half the total number of Jews in the whole of Palestine. A turning point in Jewish enterprise in Jerusalem, and indeed in Palestine, was the founding, in 1906, of the Bezalel Art School. It sought to encourage modern Jewish arts and crafts, in a predominantly secular Jewish setting. The Zionists also had an ambitious plan, strongly advocated by Chaim Weizmann – a Russian-born Jew who had become professor of chemistry at Manchester University, in England – to establish a Hebrew University in Jerusalem. Its supporters wanted it to provide higher education in both the arts and sciences for Jews throughout the Ottoman Empire including Palestine, and from all over the world. Two years before his death, Herzl had explained, in a letter to the Turkish Sultan, that with the creation of such a university, Jewish students living in Palestine 'would no longer need to go abroad. They would stay in the country and obtain the most advanced scientific training without ceasing to be under the laws of their country.' Herzl stated confidently and proudly: 'The Jewish University should bring together all the scholarly qualities of the best universities, technical schools and schools of agriculture.' A house and fifty acres of land for the project was bought to the north-east of the city, on Mount Scopus, early in 1914, from a British non-Jew who owned the site. Only the coming of war prevented the scheme from being carried out during the Turkish times: the university was eventually opened under British rule in 1925.

The largest influx of Jews into Palestine at the start of the twentieth century was from Russia. Many were Labour Zionists, determined to till the soil and make the land fertile again, after hundreds of years of Turkish neglect. A.D. Gordon, a Russian agricultural pioneer, settled in Palestine in 1904. David Ben Gurion, born in a small town – Plonsk – in Russian Poland, was working as a labourer in the vineyards at Rishon le-Zion in 1907. It was Russian Jewish immigrants who, that same year, set up the first Jewish self-defence units in Palestine. To meet the needs of growing numbers of immigrants, the town of Tel Aviv was founded in the sand dunes in 1909. Immigrants also helped build up the town of Zikhron Ya'akov, where a

A city in the sand. *On 11 April 1909 a group of Jews assembled on the sand dunes north of Jaffa, to take part in a lottery for plots of land for the future town of Tel Aviv ('Hill of Spring'), the first all-Jewish city. A man who was present later recalled how the secretary of the neighbourhood committee 'stopped and pointed with a cane. Here will be a public park, here a theatre and here a town hall'. He had earlier gathered sixty*

white and sixty grey shells on the shore, writing the name of each family involved on a white shell and lot numbers on the grey shells. A boy and a girl then drew one of each at the same time. The first sixty houses were built using a loan from the Jewish National Fund head office in Cologne. The fund was a philanthropic organisation, active throughout the Diaspora, for encouraging Jewish settlement in Palestine. [PHOTO: AVRAHAM SOSKIN]

Teachers' Federation was founded in 1903, for Jews throughout Palestine. Among the Jews who lived and worked in Zikhron Ya'akov was the Ukrainian-born, Swiss-educated physician, Dr Hillel Joffe, a pioneer in the fight against malaria. It was he who advised the planting of eucalyptus groves to help soak up the marshy waters.

Collective farming was a Labour-Zionist ideal. The first kibbutz was established at Degania, the second at Kinneret, with American Zionists among the earliest settlers; both were on the southern shore of the Sea of Galilee. Fear of attacks by marauding Bedouin was widespread, and on each kibbutz a watchtower was the first building to be erected, as at the foundation of Kinneret in 1909. Three years later, as the kibbutz grew, a girls' agricultural training farm was set up there, and then the first date palm grove was planted nearby, serving as the model for date cultivation throughout the area.

Turkish rule over Palestine meant that the growing number of Jewish settlements there before 1914 were dependent on Turkish political goodwill,

The first kibbutz. *An armed Jewish horseman in Arab dress guards the settlers of Degania, just south of the Sea of Galilee, photographed in 1912. The kibbutz had been founded three years earlier, inspired by Arthur Ruppin, a German-born Jew who saw the potential of agricultural work and self-reliance. The money for buying the land and building the kibbutz was given by the Jewish National Fund.*

[PHOTO: YA'ACOV BEN DOV]

and in the main this was extended to them. Shortly before the coming of war, however, Muslim Arab politicians from Jerusalem were able to convince the authorities in Istanbul to put restrictions on Jewish immigration. By 1914 that immigration, mostly from Russia, had brought the Jewish population to 90,000.

Almost no corner of the globe failed to attract some Jewish immigration, some hopes of a better life than that in Eastern Europe. In South Africa, Jews had come from Europe early in the nineteenth century, when first the Dutch rulers and then the British who succeeded them at the Cape offered full religious toleration. Individual European Jews were among the early pioneers trading and settling deep in the interior. Jews from Britain and Germany, and even from the United States and Australia, were drawn after 1869 by the opportunities of diamond mining, and after 1886 by the development of the gold mines. The gold rush coincided with the flight of Jews from the Russian pogroms; many of those who made their way to South Africa were from the Lithuanian province of the Russian Empire, increasing the South African Jewish community from 4,000 in 1880 to more than 40,000 in 1914. There were those who described South African Jewry as 'a colony of Lithuania'. Johannesburg was known as 'Jewburg.'

From the beginning of the century, individual Jews took part in the struggle against anti-coloured discrimination in South Africa. The young Indian lawyer, M.K. Gandhi, then championing the rights of Indians in South Africa, was helped by two Jewish friends, Henry Polak and Hermann Kallenbach. Fifty years later Jews were to take part in the struggle for Black rights in both South Africa and the United States.

At the beginning of the century, a Hamburg-born Jew, Alfred Beit, head of several leading gold and diamond companies in South Africa, devoted himself to the opening up of Rhodesia (which had been named after the British imperial pioneer, Cecil Rhodes). Alfred Beit's aim was to achieve Rhodes's vision of a railway linking the Cape of Good Hope with Cairo. No such railway was ever completed, but after Beit's death in 1906, at the early age of fifty-three, the Railway Trust Fund which he set up constructed five major railway bridges, the first being across the Limpopo river, linking South Africa and Rhodesia. The first town on the Rhodesian side of the river was named Beit Bridge in his honour. Beit also left money to enable poor but promising students to have a university education.

Like South Africa, Rhodesia proved an attractive area of settlement for Jews, many of whom also came from Lithuania. The new towns of Rhodesia offered many opportunities for tradesmen and shopkeepers. The first Jewish community, of some twenty Jews, had been established in 1894. With the coming of the railway, many more Jews came up from Cape Town, though a future mayor of Salisbury, Joe van Praag, a Jewish immigrant from Europe, walked all the way from the Portuguese port of Beira, a distance of almost three hundred miles.

Jewish patriotism to the countries of which they were citizens was a strong feature of every decade of the twentieth century. In the Boer War, which was being fought in South Africa at the start of the century, Jews fought in both the Boer and British armies, supporting, often with their lives, the respective claims of the nationalists and the imperialists in whose countries they lived.

The Jews in the Ottoman Empire traced their origins to Greek and Roman times, although most had come to Turkey following the expulsion of the Jews from Spain in 1492. They lived in every city of the Empire, more than 50,000 of them in Salonika by 1914, where they were to be found in every profession: doctors, teachers, shopkeepers, workers in the tobacco factories, and stevedores in the docks. So high a percentage of the dockworkers

Place your bets. *Jack Cohen's betting shop, Johannesburg, South Africa. By 1900, when this photograph was taken, there were 25,000 Jews in South Africa, many of them immigrants from Lithuania escaping Tsarist persecution and pogroms. In the next four years the numbers had grown by a further 8,000. During the Boer War, Jews fought in both the British and Boer armies.*

of Salonika were Jews that each Saturday – the Jewish Sabbath and day of rest – the large, usually bustling port came to a standstill.

Following the Young Turk revolution of 1908, when the powers of the Sultan were curbed, the new government lifted the restrictions on non-Muslims serving in the Turkish army. Because of the Jewish fear of being conscripted in an army known for its harshness and the isolation of its postings, this led to a considerable emigration, mostly to the United States. At the same time, the tendency of the regime towards greater political freedom led to a growth of Jewish socialist activity in Turkey. Zionist activity was also allowed, and proliferated. In Salonika, by 1914, thirty Zionist organizations were active.

The Ottoman Empire stretched from the Aegean Sea to the Persian Gulf. One of its largest cities was Baghdad, where Jews had lived since Biblical times, maintaining a great centre of learning, prosperity and self-help, 50,000 strong in the decade before the First World War. Families like the Sassoons and Dangoors held high positions in public and commercial life, spreading the trade and influence of Baghdad Jewry to India and the Far East.

Under the auspices of the Paris-based Alliance Israélite Universelle school system, Jewish schools were opened in many Turkish towns, among them one of the remotest places in the empire, Basra, at the head of the Persian Gulf, home to a small community of 1,500 Jews. A boys' and a girls' school were both set up before the First World War. Another 'Alliance' school was set up in Izmir, for four hundred years a centre of Jewish religious scholarship, philosophy, medicine, printing and commerce. In 1901, however, the Jews of Izmir were victims of a charge of blood libel, the sixth brought against them within forty years. From a Jewish population of 40,000 when the accusations began, emigration reduced the numbers to 25,000 by the time of the Young Turk revolution, with its emphasis on toleration of minorities.

The Young Turks had a Jewish dimension: among their leaders was Djavid Bey, the descendant of Jews who had earlier been forcibly converted to Islam, but who retained their sense of Jewishness. Following the revolution he was three times Minister of Finance, including during the final years of the First World War. He was executed in 1926, after the imposition of Ataturk's stern rule, on charges of trying to revive the Young Turk movement.

In central Europe, with the establishment of Austria-Hungary in 1867, Jewish intellectual, scientific and artistic life flourished, especially in the two capitals, Vienna and Budapest. By the beginning of the twentieth century, both cities were power houses of Jewish activity. In Budapest, in 1910, eighteen-year-old Alexander Korda – later a leading British filmmaker – turned a small building in the city into a simple film studio, and began to experiment with making motion pictures. Another Austrian Jew, Alfred Fried, was the founder of the German League for Peace, a pacifist movement. He received the Nobel Peace Prize in 1911. Because of his views he was accused of high treason after the outbreak of the First World War, and had to take refuge in Switzerland. Returning to Vienna after the war, he was an early and vigorous

Sigmund Freud, *(top) the father of psychoanalysis, who regarded all religions, including Judaism, as a collective delusion, and effectively founded his own, rooted in psychoanalysis, stating with the fervour of any religious convert, 'We possess the truth'.*

Gustav Mahler. *His nine completed symphonies, like all his compositions, were banned by the Nazis as 'degenerate Jewish music'.*

advocate of European union, as a means of preserving peace in the future.

Sigmund Freud and Alfred Adler, pioneers of psychiatry, worked in Vienna. Freud published his *Interpretation of Dreams* in 1900. Among Jewish musicians in Vienna was Gustav Mahler, the music director of the Imperial Opera. In order to take up this appointment he had been required to accept baptism as a Catholic. Austrian Jews were also at the forefront of medical science. In 1902, Karl Landsteiner – later a Nobel prizewinner – established blood groups. In 1914 Robert Barany won the Nobel Prize for his work on the structure and functions of the inner ear. He was denied a professorship in Austria-Hungary, however, because he was Jewish.

The laws against Jews in employment and education had mostly been swept away, but the examples of Mahler and Barany, both of whom had to face anti-Jewish prejudice in their careers, highlighted the curse of anti-Semitism that could affect even the most cultured and scientific nations. For several years the mayor of Vienna, Karl Lueger – appointed in 1897, the year of the first Zionist congress in Basle – was an outspoken anti-Semite, refusing to employ Jews in the municipality and restricting the number of Jews who could attend high school and university. The young Adolf Hitler was among those who absorbed Lueger's anti-Semitism. The influx of eastern Jews from the poorest parts of the empire into Vienna, Jews in Orthodox garb, with beards, black hats and ringlets, led to an intensification of ridicule, as well as contempt and disdain, a crude sniggering and finger-pointing.

Three rabbis *at a conference in the Austro-Hungarian resort of Karlsbad that had been developed by Jewish entrepreneurs, and was a popular holiday and meeting place for Czech Jews. (Now called Karlovy Vary.)*

LITERATURE AND ART *Arthur Schnitzler (left), Viennese doctor and dramatist, like his Russian contemporary, Anton Chekhov. He said, 'I had as little relationship to the so-called beliefs of my fathers – to that which was truly belief and not merely memory, tradition, atmosphere – as to any other religion,' but nevertheless often wrote about Jewish themes. His play* Professor Bernhardi *and his novel* The Road to the Open *described the anti-Semitism prevalent in the early years of the century. Franz Werfel (below), Viennese playwright, novelist and poet. His best known novel,* The Forty Days of Musa Dagh, *portrayed the plight of the Armenians massacred by the Turks in the First World War. His play* The Eternal Road *told the story of medieval Jews who accepted exile because of their adherence to their faith. He said that alienation was 'the arch-feeling of my life'. Maria Likarz (right), a Jewish artist in Vienna between the wars, who worked for Wiener Werkstätte, the leading Austrian arts and crafts firm, dedicated to good design. The photograph was taken by Trude Fleischmann, a leading portrait photographer.*

CHAPTER TWO

THE FIRST
WORLD WAR

1914-1918

THE CONFLICT BETWEEN THE EUROPEAN EMPIRES, which began in 1914, continued with great slaughter for just over four years. By the time Italy and the United States had both been drawn in, Jews from every warring nation were fighting in the armed forces on both sides of the European divide. The scale of Jewish participation in the First World War was considerable. Of more than 1,500,000 Jews who fought in it, 140,000 were killed. Their graves, often marked with the Star of David carved into the headstones, are to be found in the war cemeteries in every war zone, particularly on the Western Front.

For the Jews, as for so many peoples, the First World War proved a turning point, leading to the creation in its early months of a specifically Jewish fighting force which was to make a major contribution to the prospect, even before the war ended, of a Jewish National Home in Palestine. As well as their role as soldiers, individual Jews were also prominent in the call for an end to war, and in the struggle to create a new world order, either to bring the conflict to an end by workers' strikes and world revolution, or to see new democratic nations emerge on the ruins of the fighting empires, or to make future conflicts impossible.

From the first week of the war, Jews living on the Eastern Front were among those civilians and bystanders who were forced out of their homes. As the German army drove across the Russian border, villages with large numbers of Jewish inhabitants found themselves at the centre of the fighting, their wooden houses set ablaze in the fierce artillery duels being fought between the Germans and Russians. Tens of thousands of Jews fled from the battle zone. To help them with food, clothing and shelter, the American Jewish Relief Committee – later called the American Jewish Joint Distribution Committee, or 'Joint' – was set up in the first month of the war by American philanthropists. America was neutral at that stage, so the money which they collected could be sent to both sides of the front line without danger of accusations of helping the enemy.

Berlin, the Unter den Linden. *Ludwig Börnstein, seen off to the front in 1914 by his friends Fritz and Emma Schlesinger. This photograph was among the most widely published German patriotic pictures at the outbreak of war, but all three had to emigrate to Palestine after Hitler came to power.*

Mlawa.

A RUSSIAN-POLISH TOWN CONQUERED. *German officers ride through the main Jewish street of Mlawa (above). When the Germans entered such towns they were often met by Jewish crowds welcoming them as liberators. The town's 5,000 Jews, their community dating from the sixteenth century, formed almost half the population.*

JEWISH BOYS *enthusiastically hold up sheet music for a German military band (above right); a photograph from a German wartime newspaper.*

A FORMAL DINNER *for German-Jewish soldiers in the Palais Baudoin, Brussels to celebrate Rosh Hashanah, the Jewish New Year, in 1917.*

Eight hundred villages in which Jews lived were overrun during the first six months of fighting. Many thousands of Jewish villagers were evacuated by the Russians as the German army drove eastward. These evacuees were sent deep into the Russian interior, to towns that had neither the facilities nor the desire to help them. A thousand Jews reached the town of Ekaterinoslav, hundreds of miles from the battle zone; they had just begun to find work when the local authorities deported them elsewhere. When 7,000 Jewish evacuees reached Kursk by freight train, the local town council refused to let them leave the wagons. For a month they were forced to live in the trains – including some who were extremely ill – in conditions of great hardship.

Considerable help for the refugees who were sent into the Russian interior was provided by one of the leading Jewish self-help organisations in Russia, the

Refugees. *Jews look warily at Austro-Hungarian soldiers, on the left, as they flee from the war zone in Galicia, a province of Austria-Hungary that was overrun by the Russians in 1914 and then reconquered by the Austrians a year later.*

St Petersburg-based Society to Promote Trades and Agriculture among the Jews of Russia (ORT). It provided money to Jewish workers' cooperatives to enable them to fulfil Russian government orders for military goods. In Vilna a number of large shoemaking shops were set up, and in Dvinsk a home-based tailoring project began making uniforms for the army. So chaotic was the Russian army's commissioning system, however, that the cooperative projects had to be discontinued after only four months. More successful were the Labour Bureaus which ORT set up in over seventy cities to which Jews had been evacuated. Jobs were thus found for the evacuated Jews in cities throughout the interior

Waiting for a train. *Jews in flight (left) from central Europe at the end of the war, sitting on their bundles at a railway station on the German-Polish border.*

Lower depths. *A destitute Jewish mother and her child (above), straw sticking out of their mattress, the sleeping father's boots visible on the other bed, in a Polish town.*

of Russia, including tailoring, office work, leather work, metal work and manual labour. To enable the Jews to survive, ORT also set up cooperative restaurants and lodging houses. In these endeavours the Jewish principle of charity through self-help found an urgent practical application. By the end of 1915, more than 170,000 refugees had been aided.

A mass flight of Jewish refugees also took place in the area where the Austro-Hungarian and Russian armies were in conflict in some of the poorest regions of Eastern Galicia. Then, after the Russian troops had advanced, and the Galician Jews had fled westward in search of shelter behind the Austrian lines, the direction of the fighting was reversed, which meant that the houses, shops and farms of hundreds of thousands of Jews were once again in the battle zone. When the Russians were finally driven back across the border, and the Galician Jews were able to return, for many there was nothing left of their homes.

Jewish soldiers fought and died on every battlefront of the First World War. Even in Serbia, the first country to be attacked in 1914 – by Austria-Hungary – there was a small Jewish community. There were 1,200 Jews in the Serbian army; 250 of them were killed in battle. Jews also served in the Austro-Hungarian and German forces that attacked Serbia and, despite an initial and prolonged military setback, eventually defeated her. Among the German Jews who fought on the Serbian front was the novelist and playwright Arnold Zweig; as a result of his experiences he became an outspoken pacifist, using his novels to attack Prussian militarism and wartime miscarriages of justice, most powerfully in *The Case of Sergeant Grischa*, which became an international best seller in 1927. In 1933, as the Nazis burned his books, he emigrated to Palestine.

A Jewish doctor in the Austro-Hungarian army, Dr Jan Levit, was working in a garrison town in Bohemia where the Serb student Gavrilo Princip, whose assassination of the archduke Franz Ferdinand precipitated the war, was being held in a prison cell. Dr Levit tended him as best he could, but in 1918 his patient died of tuberculosis. Twenty-four years later Levit was brought back to that same garrison town of Theresienstadt, as a prisoner himself, before being deported to Auschwitz and his death. Although he was a second-generation practising Christian, Nazi racist laws determined that he was a Jew – because at least one of his grandparents had been Jewish.

Levit was one amongst the 320,000 Jews who served in the Austro-Hungarian army, many on the Russian front, of whom 40,000 were killed. Of the 650,000 Jews who served in the Russian army, 100,000 were killed in action. Inevitably many Russian Jewish soldiers shot at and killed Austro-Hungarian and German Jewish soldiers in the opposing trenches. A month after the outbreak of war it was reported from St Petersburg that the Tsar had awarded the very highest military decoration, the Cross of St George (the equivalent of the British Victoria Cross) to Leo Osnas 'for exceptional bravery on the field of battle'. Osnas was not only the first Russian soldier to receive this high award during the First World War, he was also a Jew, and it was widely believed both in Russia and among Jews elsewhere that as a result of this act of bravery the Tsar had decided to end all anti-Jewish restrictions. A British newspaper, the *Yorkshire Herald*, reported that Osnas 'has won freedom for the Jews in Russia; he has gained for his race the right to become officers in the Russian army and navy, hitherto denied them, and he has so delighted the Russian government that it has since proclaimed that henceforth Jews in the Empire shall enjoy the full rights of citizenship.' In fact the Jews of Russia did not receive full citizenship during the war, nor did they escape repeated violent attacks on them by Russian townsmen and villagers looking for scapegoats for Russia's military setbacks.

As the German army began to advance from East Prussia deep into the Russian borderlands, Jewish shops, homes and synagogues were looted, the local population accusing the Jews of secretly wanting the Germans to win the war. For many Jews in the Polish and Baltic provinces of Russia the possibility of German rule did indeed seem an opportunity for an end to discrimination: the Jews of Kovno were among those who welcomed the German army and were well-treated by the German military administration. Russians elsewhere were infuriated; in a report from St Petersburg the French ambassador informed the Foreign Ministry in Paris that Jews were 'being hanged every day' because of their alleged sympathy for Germany. As German military successes continued, Russian soldiers were assured by their officers 'that were it not for the Yids – traitors – the Prussian army would have been utterly routed'.

FIGHTING FOR HIS COUNTRY – GREAT BRITAIN. *Lithuanian-born Morris Chaim Blake, who emigrated before 1914 to the United States, where he joined the Jewish Legion, a British Royal Fusiliers battalion that fought against the Turks and Germans in Palestine. He is wearing a Royal Fusiliers cap badge. Wounded in a gas attack, he was in hospital in Britain, before returning to the United States. He died in 1997, aged 98.*

FIGHTING FOR HIS COUNTRY – GERMANY. *Albert Lilienfeld, a German Jew who volunteered to fight in the German army, serving on the Russian front. He is photographed here at Passover 1917, after the Bolshevik revolution in Russia brought the war to an end. After Hitler came to power in Germany, he emigrated to Palestine with his family.*

FIGHTING FOR HIS COUNTRY – POLAND. *Jacob Shatzky, Jewish historian, the author of a three-volume history of the Jews of Warsaw, published in 1914, just before the outbreak of war. He was wounded in action while fighting in the Polish Legion against the Germans for the independence of Poland. Polish Jews also served in the Russian, Austrian and German armies. In 1922 he emigrated to the United States.*

FIGHTING FOR HIS COUNTRY – TURKEY. *A Jewish officer in the Turkish army. On each of the Turkish war fronts, at Gallipoli, in the Caucasus, in Mesopotamia and in Palestine, other Jews were in the opposing armies. In 1914 many Zionist settlers in Palestine, including David Ben Gurion, were keen to fight for their Turkish overlords, but their offer was turned down.* [PHOTO: AVRAHAM SOSKIN]

Of the 100,000 German Jews who fought in the German army, on all fronts, 12,000 were killed in action. More than 31,000 won the Iron Cross for bravery. The first German parliamentarian to be killed in action was a Jew. On the Western Front, a Jewish captain in a German infantry battalion, Hugo Gutmann, was so impressed by the bravery of a (non-Jewish) corporal under his command – Adolf Hitler, the company runner – that he nominated him, successfully, for the Iron Cross, First Class for what he described as 'personal bravery and general merit'. This was an unusual decoration for a corporal, and

FOOD QUEUES. *Jews in the market place of Vilna (Vilnius) then a Russian town under German occupation, later in Lithuania. The city's 70,000 Jews, including many refugees from the war zones, had welcomed the German authorities to the city, hoping they would be less harsh than the Russians had been, but the Germans quickly imposed discriminatory levies on them. When the Germans left and Polish rule came to the city, eighty Jews were massacred by Polish troops during an anti-Semitic rampage.*

JEWISH PORTERS *wait for work, in front of the State Theatre in Vilna, 1916. The poster, in German, says 'Beware of spies'.*

Hitler wore the medal with pride for the rest of his life. After he came to power in 1933, he was embarrassed when Gutmann said publicly, 'I pinned the Iron Cross on Hitler'. The Nazis protested that 'no Jew could have done it' and Gutmann was arrested. He was taken into Gestapo custody three times before he was allowed to leave for the United States in 1934.

Of the 6,000 Italian Jews who fought in the war, 500 were killed in action. Among the Jews who fought in the Italian army was Ernesto Nathan, who in 1907 had become Mayor of Rome, the first Jew to hold that position. He was seventy years old when Italy entered the war in 1915; yet to demonstrate his patriotism, he volunteered to serve as a junior officer on the Austrian front. He was accepted, and survived the conflict. A leading Italian mathematician, and one of the Senators for Rome, Vito Volterra, whose family had lived in Italy for many hundreds of years, was among those who supported Italy's entry into the war in 1915, and in 1917 publicly opposed an Italian Socialist initiative to take Italy out of the war by making a separate peace. To back his patriotic views with action, at the age of fifty-five he joined the air branch of the army engineering corps, and later established the Italian Office of War Inventions.

There were 50,000 Jewish soldiers in the British army, of whom 8,600 were killed in action, among them Isaac Rosenberg. His death in 1918 came just as he was beginning to be recognized as an important English poet. He had insisted on enlisting, despite a lung disorder. When the Germans launched their offensive in the spring of 1918, Rosenberg's dawn patrol was in the direct line of German fire. His body was never found.

The pain and horror of trench warfare were the dominant theme of the poetry of Siegfried Sassoon, one of the British members of the Sassoon family which had came to prominence in Iraq half a century earlier. His courage

on the battlefield led to the award of the Military Cross 'for conspicuous gallantry and devotion to duty' during a raid on the German trenches where he 'remained for one and a half hours under rifle and bomb fire collecting and bringing in our wounded'. Later, having been shot through the neck, he was sent back to Britain, where, in protest against the war, he issued a statement that he would no longer serve in the army. He was sent to a hospital for those with shell-shock. Recovering, he returned to the battlefield, serving in both France and Palestine, and was again wounded. His cousin

Soldier-poet. *Siegfried Sassoon, in British military uniform. He fought with distinction and his poetry exposed the cruelties and grotesqueness of war from the perspective of the soldiers in the trenches, a universal cry of pain.* [PHOTO: GEORGE C. BERESFORD]

Philip Sassoon was also a soldier in the British army, first serving at the Front, and later becoming Military Secretary to the British Commander-in-Chief in France, Sir Douglas Haig, at whose headquarters the poems of Siegfried Sassoon were regarded almost as treason.

Leslie Hore-Belisha, a member of a Sephardi family that had lived in Britain for 150 years, served in France and Greece, and was mentioned in despatches; in the two years leading up to the Second World War, as Secretary of State for War, he was responsible for the expansion of armoured and mechanized forces. Two members of the British Rothschilds served in the trenches: Captain Anthony de Rothschild, who was wounded at Gallipoli (and who thirty-five years later financed the building of the Knesset, the Israeli parliament) and Major Evelyn de Rothschild, who was killed leading his men in an attack on a Turkish stronghold in Palestine.

Call to arms. *A wall poster in the City of London urges British Jews to join the army. It was put up by Messrs Rothschild and declared: 'The country's call for men has been nobly responded to by Jews of all classes. Are you holding back?'*

The first of five Jews to win the Victoria Cross in the First World War was a Londoner, Lieutenant Frank Alexander De Pass. A British officer serving with the Indian Corps on the Western Front, on 24 November 1914 he led two of his Indian soldiers into the sap of a German trench that had been pushed out to within ten yards of the Indian line. The sap was destroyed. De Pass made an even more dangerous foray the next day, when he and an Indian soldier faced German machine-gun fire across a two hundred-yard stretch of No-Man's Land in order to bring back a badly wounded Indian soldier. On his third day in the trenches De Pass went forward again, this time to repair a front line parapet. Seeing a German sniper at work, he tried to shoot him, but was himself shot through the head and killed. The official history of the Indian Corps in France wrote of him: 'He was the very perfect type of British officer. He united to singular personal beauty a charm of manner and a degree of valour which made him the idol of his men. He was honoured in death by the Victoria Cross. No one in war earned it better.'

The armies of the British Empire also had many Jewish soldiers in their midst, from Australia, New Zealand, Canada, South Africa, Gibraltar and Jamaica. The St John's Ambulance Brigade units raised in India had a Jewish section. Indian Jews fought against the Germans in East Africa and against the Turks in Mesopotamia. Surgeon B. Reuben of the Indian Medical Service was among those killed in action. In the Australian army, John Monash, in peacetime a civil engineer whose expertise was railway and bridge building, led an Australian infantry brigade on the Gallipoli peninsula. When the order came to withdraw he managed to take off all his men without a single casualty. Raised to the rank of Major-General, he commanded the Australian Army Corps in France, taking a leading part in the breakthrough of the German lines in the summer of 1918. It was the first time infantry and tanks had been used in a coordinated – and effective – manner. After the battle the German army was unable to mount any further offensives. For his skill in battle he was knighted at his military headquarters by King George V, the first time in almost two hundred years that a British monarch had knighted a commander in the field. Later, Monash was the first Australian, and also the first Jew, to be promoted to the rank of full General. Born in Melbourne in 1865, in the first half of the nineteenth century his family had been printers of Hebrew books in Vienna.

In the French army there were 55,000 Jews, of whom 9,500 were killed in action. Alfred Dreyfus, against whom the false charge of treason had been brought by anti–Semitic army officers twenty years earlier, returning to active service in 1914, was promoted to Lieutenant-Colonel and awarded the Légion

Major-General Sir John Monash *decorates an Australian sergeant with the Victoria Cross in 1918, four months before the end of the war. Monash, the most senior Jewish general in any of the warring armies in the First World War, was then commanding the Australian Army Corps on the Western Front.*

Tanks on the Western Front. *Lieutenant-Colonel Alfred Stern, a Jewish officer in the British army, and Director of Tank Supply at the Ministry of Munitions in 1916, was one of the pioneers in developing this new weapon and ensuring it would play a decisive part in the final battles of the First World War. For this achievement he was knighted by King George V. Among the British troops in the foreground are several German prisoners of war (in flat caps). The devices on three of the tanks are for dropping into trenches, to assist the tanks' passage over them.* [PHOTO: ALFRED STERN]

d'Honneur in 1916. René Cassin, severely wounded and awarded the Croix de Guerre and the Médaille Militaire for his bravery, was later Professor of Law in Paris and, after 1946, President of the United Nations Commission on Human Rights: he was the main author of the Universal Declaration of Human Rights, issued in 1948. Another young soldier, Marc Bloch, was later a distinguished historian, who also served in the French army in the Second World War. Reflecting on his position as a Jew and a Frenchman, Bloch wrote: 'By birth I am a Jew, though not by religion, for I have never professed any creed, whether Hebrew or Christian. I feel neither pride nor shame in my origins… I am at pains never to stress my heredity save when I find myself in the presence of an anti-Semite… France will remain the one country with which my deepest emotions are inextricably bound up. I was born in France. I have drunk the waters of her culture. I have made her past my own… I breathe freely only in her climate, and I have done my best with others, to defend her best interests.' Working as a codebreaker and messenger in the French resistance, in 1944 Bloch was arrested by the Gestapo, tortured and shot. His last words, as he faced the firing squad, were said to have been 'Vive La France!'

A French officer who served as interpreter with British troops on the Western Front was Emile Herzog, from a Jewish cloth-manufacturing family. Among the British officers for whom he acted as a liaison with the local population was Winston Churchill. After the war, Herzog, under his writing name of André Maurois, wrote a satire contrasting British and French attitudes to the war, *The Silence of Colonel Bramble*.

Neutral for the first two years of the war, the United States declared war on Germany in April 1917, after German submarines had begun the systematic sinking of American merchant ships in the Atlantic. In June 1917, under the Selective Draft Act, registration for military service began throughout the United States for all men between twenty-one and thirty. The *New York Times* wrote that the act gave 'a long and sorely needed means of disciplining a certain insolent foreign element in this nation', a harsh reference to America's Jews, whose pacifist elements were no greater, by proportion, than those of other Americans. Indeed, one American rabbi insisted that universal military service was an institution deriving from the time of Moses. He also cited in support of American Jewish participation in the war the same verse in the Psalms which British Jews had cited two years earlier as their religious justification for going to war: 'Blessed be the Lord, my Rock, Who teacheth my hands to war and my fingers to fight.'

Within two months of the passage of the Selective Draft Act, Jews made up six per cent of the American armed forces, although they were only two per cent of the population. As many as a quarter of a million Jews served in the American armed forces, 3,400 of whom were killed on the battlefield. Among those who served was Herbert Lehman, responsible for procurement and transportation on the American General Staff; he was awarded the Distinguished Service Medal. He was later Governor of New York State for five terms – longer than anyone in the State's history – and then a Senator. He had been a founding member of the Joint in 1914 and after the war headed its reconstruction committee, finding the funds to restore Jewish life in those areas of Eastern Europe devastated by the war. Another New York Jew, Walter Lippman, who served as a captain in Military Intelligence, and also as an assistant to the Secretary of War, wrote a series of articles that influenced President Wilson in his support for a postwar set of principles of international conduct; principles which, through the League of Nations, were intended to bring an end to war.

In addition to Jewish soldiers who served in the armies of every nation during the four years of war, individual Jews made considerable contributions to the national war efforts. The newspaper despatches of the Hungarian playwright Ferenc Molnar (born Neumann) from the Austro-Hungarian front were so vivid that they were reprinted in the *New York Times*, even after Austria-Hungary had become an enemy power. In Germany, one of the world's leading chemists, Fritz Haber, the director of the Kaiser Wilhelm Institute for Physical Chemistry in Berlin, worked from the outbreak of war

SERVING HIS COUNTRY–
WALTER LIPPMAN *(1889-1974),
American political journalist and analyst. A graduate of Harvard, he helped to found the liberal weekly magazine* New Republic. *He was twice awarded the Pulitzer Prize, in 1958 and 1962, for his regular newspaper column in the* New York Herald Tribune, *which was syndicated in 250 newspapers. He was a most perceptive commentator on all topics – except those involving the Jews. Despite never gaining entrance to the innermost sanctums of the American establishment, he clung to his ultra-assimilationist stance and hostility to Zionism. Perhaps his greatest failure was to underestimate Nazi anti-Semitism in the 1930s. He never mentioned the death camps at all.*

[PHOTO: PIRIE MCDONALD]

SERVING HIS COUNTRY –
FRITZ HABER *(1868-1934), the son
of a successful German chemical and dye
merchant. In 1911 he became Professor of
Physical Chemistry at Berlin University,
and in 1918 was awarded the Nobel Prize.
Without the Haber-Bosch process for
extracting nitrogen from air, the German
army would have run out of shells by the
end of 1914. When Germany was presented
by the Allies after its defeat with a massive
demand for reparations, he tried to extract
gold from seawater.*

SERVING HIS COUNTRY –
WALTHER RATHENAU *(1867-
1922), the son of an industrialist who
founded the AEG company, he held radical
views on State planning, social reform and
international co-operation. A convinced
assimilationist, he believed that his German
identity took precedence over his Judaism,
but his long-term ideal was the merger of
much of Europe under the title
Mitteleuropa, a precursor of the European
Union. In 1922, while Foreign Minister of
Germany, he was murdered by German
anti-Semites. Later under Hitler a memorial glorifying his assassins was unveiled in
Berlin, but on the thirtieth anniversary of
his murder the West German government
issued a stamp bearing his portrait.*

SERVING HIS COUNTRY –
BERNARD BARUCH *(1870-1965)
started work in New York as an office boy. A
decade of playing the stock market saw him
a millionaire. In 1912 he was a major contributor to Woodrow Wilson's presidential
campaign. At the Paris Peace Conference in
1919 he helped frame the economic clauses
of the Versailles Treaty, which imposed heavy
reparations payments on Germany. He
brought up his children in his wife's
Episcopalian faith, though this did not prevent his daughter being turned away from a
smart Manhattan school. He remained hostile to Zionism, and instead proposed that
Jewish refugees from the Second World War
should be settled in Uganda.*

SERVING HIS COUNTRY – ANDRÉ CITROËN *(1878-1935). He began producing motor cars in 1908. In 1922 he sponsored a crossing of the Sahara Desert by car, pioneering motor exploration throughout the world. In 1934 he made motoring history by introducing cars with front-wheel drive.*

on the development of chlorine and mustard gases, which were then used by the German army when attacking the British and French forces on the Western Front. Another chemical process which he developed before the war was used for the production of the nitrates needed in explosives: after the war it was used for the production of fertilizers. Having rejected Judaism and converted to Christianity, Haber was initially exempted from the Nazi persecution, but when the authorities demanded that he dismiss the Jewish members of his institute he refused, and resigned. He died in exile in Switzerland in 1934. A fellow-chemist, Richard Willstaetter, who was awarded the Nobel Prize in 1915 for his work on the structure of chlorophyll and blood cell pigments, worked in Berlin on the development of gas masks, for the better protection of soldiers caught in gas attacks. For this he was awarded the civilian Iron Cross. Neither his Iron Cross nor his Nobel Prize could prevent him from being ordered out of Germany by the Gestapo in 1939: he too went to Switzerland.

Albert Ballin, a multi-millionaire shipping magnate who had built up Germany's merchant marine – including transatlantic liners and luxury cruise ships – organized the shipping of food to Germany in such a way as to avoid the British naval blockade in the North Sea. As Germany's war effort, fighting in the West and the East at the same time, came under severe strain, the industrialist Walther Rathenau was given charge by the German War Ministry of the supply and distribution of raw materials throughout Germany. It was he who approved the deportation of 700,000 Belgian workers, from German-occupied Belgium, to work in the munitions factories and coal mines of Germany, but his opposition to unrestricted submarine warfare against neutral as well as allied merchant shipping, on which Germany embarked in 1916, then led him to resign.

In the United States, Bernard Baruch, a multi-millionaire financier, worked at President Wilson's request to build up America's industrial readiness for war before 1916. Once the United States entered the conflict, he co-ordinated the purchase of raw materials and the production of munitions. A leading American labour leader, and opponent of revolutionary trade unionism, Samuel Gompers, who had been born in London in 1850 and reached the United States as a teenager, was a main force in persuading organized labour in the United States to support the war effort.

In France, André Citroën, a successful motor car manufacturer, was made responsible for most of France's munitions production. The arms factory which he built in Paris produced millions of artillery shells for insatiable guns. After the war he used his munitions assembly line to mass-produce a small car, ten years before the Germans embarked upon the Volkswagen. A fellow-Jew, Marcel Dassault, whose brother later became a general, was asked by the French government to design aeroplanes. His special expertise was with propellors, one of which survives to this day as a monument in Paris.

From the first days of the war, the charge of being a 'German-Jewish trai-

Rufus Isaacs *(1860-1935), with his wife in a London park, 1916. The only Jew to be Viceroy of India, his liberal sympathies won the respect of Indian nationalists. His career had been a steady progression from Attorney General via the offices of Lord Chief Justice and Lord Chancellor until he was given the title of Marquess of Reading. The only hiccup had come in 1912 with his involvement in the Marconi Scandal, a case of insider share trading in which Lloyd George and Herbert Samuel were also implicated. Isaacs was cautious about Zionism, but felt that: 'The Jews ought to have a place of their own and a government of their own.'*

tor' was bandied about in the popular newspapers against the British industrialist Alfred Mond, whose parents had reached Britain from Germany fifty years earlier. He brought a successful libel action, but the charge was again levelled against him. He turned his country house into a military hospital, opened his London house to refugees from German-occupied Belgium, and focused the resources of his factories on the manufacture of explosives and the production of the first British gas masks. The government also turned to him for advice on how to maintain industrial production, and prevent economic bottlenecks. The founder of the Shell Oil Company, Marcus Samuel, a former Lord Mayor of London – the third Jew to hold that position – was the main supplier of oil fuel for ships and aviation fuel: he refused to avail himself of the wartime inflation of prices and profits, charging only pre-war prices. He also built a factory to manufacture toluol, the basic explosive ingredient of TNT, and by 1917 was providing eighty per cent of all the explosives used by the army and navy. Another British Jew, the painter Solomon J. Solomon, turned his artistic skills to developing camouflage techniques; using his design, the hulls of ships were painted to make them virtually invisible. The development of the tank as a weapon of war was itself under the supervision of a Jewish officer, Lieutenant-Colonel Sir Albert Stern, a banker who had turned to invention and tactics.

At the highest level of political life, British Jews played their part in the conduct and prosecution of the war. The Lord Chief Justice, Rufus Isaacs – the first Jew to hold this high office – was sent on an urgent mission to the United States where he negotiated a $500 million war loan. Edwin Montagu, from a Sephardi family that had lived in Britain for more than a hundred years, served in 1916 as Minister of Munitions, and toured India to investigate how greater Indian self-government could be instituted. The Zionist leader, Dr Chaim Weizmann, by profession a chemist, while working under the auspices of the Admiralty, discovered a method of manufacturing acetone, a potato-based raw material that could be used to make explosives.

The part played by Weizmann in the evolution of the Balfour Declaration of 1917 – promising the Jews a homeland in Palestine – was decisive. Russian-born, educated in Germany, and coming to Britain in 1903 to teach chemistry at Manchester University, he was an attractive and persuasive personality.

It is said that when he first met Arthur Balfour, a former Prime Minister, in Manchester, Balfour asked him why the Zionists had rejected Uganda as a national home. Weizmann answered: 'Mr Balfour, supposing I were to offer you Paris instead of London, would you take it?' 'But Mr Weizmann, we have London,' was Balfour's reply, to which Weizmann retorted, 'That is true. But we had Jerusalem when London was a marsh.' According to another Zionist legend, when Balfour, then First Lord of the Admiralty, asked Weizmann what reward he would like for his discovery of acetone, which had enabled Britain to renew and accelerate its war effort, Weizmann replied that he wanted nothing for himself, but a homeland for his people. Two years later, Balfour, then Foreign Secretary, signed the official British government letter promising to support a Jewish National Home in Palestine after the war.

Individual Jews were active in the pacifist and anti-war movements that flourished – despite almost universal popular hostility – in every warring nation. In Berlin, Albert Einstein was among those who led the call for an end to the fighting. 'Nationalism,' he said, 'is an infantile sickness. It is the measles of the human race.' Refusing to join the mass of German scientists and academics who issued patriotic calls stressing the rightness of Germany's cause, he called for an immediate end to the war. Reflecting on his Jewishness, and on its impact upon his own thought, Einstein said: 'The value of Judaism lies exclusively in its ethical and spiritual content, and in the corresponding qualities of individual Jews.' He saw pacifism – and also Zionism – as reflecting those values and enhancing those qualities. For him Zionism was not so much a potentially aggressive national movement as an opportunity for application of Jewish ethical values to the modern world. In September 1917 the French Christian philosopher Romain Rolland commented in his diary: 'It is noteworthy that Einstein is Jewish, which explains the internationalism of his position and the caustic character of his criticism.' Replying to a German academic who rebuked him in February 1918 for his continued hostility to the war, Einstein wrote: 'Your ostentatious Teutonic muscle-flexing runs rather against my grain. I prefer to string along with my compatriot Jesus Christ, whose doctrines you and your kind consider to be obsolete. Suffering is indeed more acceptable to me than resort to violence.'

In Italy, a leading socialist parliamentarian, Vittorio Emanuele Modigliani – the elder brother of the painter – spoke in Parliament against Italy joining the war. But eight months after the war began, Italy did join, after Britain and France had promised her substantial gains of land from both Austria-Hungary and Turkey. Shocked by this cynical bargain, Modigliani was among the Italian socialists who believed that, when the war ended, neither Italy, nor any other nation, should make territorial gains. The two leaders of the anarchist movement in America, Alexander Berkman and Emma Goldman, both Russian-born, urged Americans to refuse to be conscripted. They were sent to prison for the duration of the war – it lasted two more years – and were then

Anarchist Emma Goldman *(1869-1940), born in Lithuania, emigrated to the United States when she was seventeen. A brilliant orator, she could inspire audiences in Yiddish, Russian, German or English. This photograph was taken in 1919, after she had spent two years in prison in the United States, and shortly before she was deported to the Soviet Union. She soon became disillusioned with Soviet Communism.*

Abel Gance *(1889-1981) seen here (left) with the film director D.W. Griffith. Gance, an actor and dramatist who turned to film making during the First World War, pioneered the triple-screen, and the use of distorting mirrors to present images from the point of view of a madman. His six-hour long masterpiece* Napoleon, *one of the greatest works of the silent screen, was revived in 1979.*

expelled from the United States to the land of their birth. After the assassination of President McKinley in 1901 by an anarchist, Emma Goldman had been accused in the American newspapers of incitement to murder the President, charges which she denied, but which gave the Jewish role in anarchism a high profile and a bad name. She was also a fervent advocate of many causes that gained in respectability in the years before her death in 1940 – including birth control, the right to form trade unions, and women's rights. Another American Jew who opposed America's entry into the war was Lillian Ward, a pioneer of public health nursing. She was fifty when the United States entered the war, and president of the American Union Against Militarism. As a result of her anti-war stance many of her former patrons withheld funding for her Visiting Nurse Service for the poor, and for her community projects for poor women and children. At her suggestion, however, one of her nurses became director of the United States Army School for Nursing.

In Berlin, Gershom Scholem, a seventeen-year-old schoolboy, who was later to be the leading scholar of Jewish mysticism, spoke out against the war on the grounds that it was against Jewish interests. As a Zionist, he believed emphatically that Jews should be working together to create a specifically Jewish national home irrespective of their present nationalities; and should not be shooting each other in the trenches. For distributing anti-war literature he was expelled from school. In the last year of the war, in France, the film director Abel Gance directed one of the most powerful anti-war films ever made. He called it *J'accuse* ('I accuse'), and made use of real soldiers for a remarkable sequence in which the dead soldiers rise up from the battlefield to question the value of their sacrifice. Most of these extras were killed in battle a few days after they had taken part in the film.

One of the most forceful voices speaking out against the war in Germany was that of the Polish social democrat Rosa Luxemburg. Arrested because of her pacifist writings and speeches in the early months of the war, she was imprisoned in February 1915. Two months later she smuggled out of prison an anonymous appeal, signed with the name Junius: widely circulated, it was known as the Junius Pamphlet. 'The spectacle is over', she wrote. 'The trains carrying the reservists now leave in silence without the enthusiastic farewells of fair maidens.... The crisp atmosphere of the pale rising day is filled with the voices of a different chorus – the hoarse clamour of the vultures and hyenas of the battlefields. Ten thousand tents, regulation size, guaranteed! One hundred thousand kilograms of bacon, cocoa powder, ersatz coffee, immediate delivery, cash only! Grenades, drills, ammunition bags, matchmakers for war widows… serious offers only! The patriotically glorified cannon fodder … is already rotting on the battlefields… Disgraced, shameful, bloodstained, filthy – that is the true face of bourgeois society… The well-groomed, cosmetic mask of virtue – culture, philosophy, and ethics, order, peace, and constitution – slips and its real, naked self is exposed. During this witches' Sabbath a disaster of world-wide magnitude occurred - the capitulation of the International Social Democracy.'

David Ben Gurion *as a soldier in the British army, with the Star of David insignia of the Jewish Brigade. When the First World War broke out his offer to fight for the Turks had been spurned. His overriding loyalty was to the Jewish people, and to Zionism.*

The position of the 90,000 Jews in Palestine when war broke out was precarious. After Britain and France declared war on Turkey in October 1914, the Turkish authorities feared that they might act as a fifth column, secretly working for a British or French victory in the hope of gaining support for Jewish autonomy in Palestine. Within a week of the outbreak of war the local Turkish ruler, Jemal Pasha, rounded up five hundred recent Russian Jewish immigrants and deported them by sea from Jaffa. This was a mistake, as these potentially loyal would-be Turkish subjects found themselves under British rule in Egypt, hoping for a British victory over the Turks which would enable them to return to their new homes. Jemal Pasha made another mistake in the first weeks of the war, when it was discovered that a number of Zionists had obtained permission from the governor of Jerusalem to form a Jewish militia to help defend Palestine against the British. Instead of welcoming this gesture, Jemal disbanded the militia and announced that anyone found with a 'Zionist' document on him would be put to death. He also expelled from Palestine two of the leading Zionist supporters of Jewish participation in the Turkish army, David Ben Gurion and Yitzhak Ben-Zvi. Both were manacled and put on board ship at Jaffa with a note from the governor of the port: 'To be banished forever from the Turkish Empire.' Later they were to help raise troops for a specifically Jewish force to

Joseph Trumpeldor *as a prisoner-of-war of the Japanese, 1905, when he organised a Zionist group for emigration to Palestine. Inside the Star of David is the word 'Zion'. The sign says: 'Son's of Zion in Japan: Barracks'. Having fought as a soldier in the Russian army against Japan, he then fought the Turks at Gallipoli as a British officer in the Zion Mule Corps. In 1920 he was killed defending the settlement of Tel Hai in the Galilee against Arab attack. His last words as he lay dying were said to have been: 'Never mind, it is good to die for our country.'*

fight against the Turks. Three decades later Ben Gurion was be the first Prime Minister of Israel and Ben-Zvi the second President.

Thousands of Jews were sent by the Turks to do forced labour in Syria, where harsh conditions lead to many deaths. By the end of 1914 twelve thousand had been put on board ships in Jaffa and expelled to Alexandria. There, the British authorities were approached by Joseph Trumpeldor, a veteran of the Russo-Japanese war of 1904–5 when he had lost an arm, and Vladimir Jabotinsky, who had organised Jewish self-defence in Russia against the pogroms and was then in Egypt as war correspondent of a Moscow newspaper. They urged the British to make use of these men. At first the British were reluctant to allow a specifically Jewish force, being doubtful of Jewish fighting competence, and said that they could serve only as mule-skinners. This disillusioned Jabotinsky but Trumpeldor persevered. On 15 March 1915, under his enthusiastic leadership, a Palestine Refugees' Committee, set up in Egypt, passed a resolution 'to form a Jewish Legion and propose to England its utilisation in Palestine'. Within a few days, five hundred Palestinian Jewish refugees had enlisted. The British relented, and agreed to the formation of the Zion Mule Corps, to serve on the Gallipoli peninsula in the struggle against the Turks. The men and their mules were made responsible for carrying essential food and military supplies from the narrow beaches up the precipitous cliffs and ravines to the front line, often under heavy Turkish fire.

Most of the 737 men who volunteered to serve in the Zion Mule Corps were Russian-born Jews. Their commander was Lieutenant-Colonel Henry Patterson, who had fought in the Boer War fifteen years earlier; of Irish-Protestant origin, he persuaded the British military authorities to provide his men with kosher food and matzo (unleavened bread) for their Passover celebration while they were still in training in Egypt. The deputy commander was Trumpeldor.

On 25 April 1915, together with the first British, Australian, New Zealand and French troops, the Zion Mule Corps landed on the Gallipoli peninsula, their badge a Star of David. The point chosen for their landing was Cape Helles, the southernmost tip of the peninsula, where they were met by heavy Turkish shelling and machine gun fire. Their first award for bravery, a Distinguished Conduct Medal, was made to Private M. Groushkowsky, who, in order to prevent his mules from stampeding under the heavy bombardment, exposed himself to Turkish fire. Despite being wounded in both arms by shrapnel bullets, he 'kept hold of the animals and delivered the ammunition'. Trumpeldor himself was shot through the shoulder but refused to leave the battlefield for treatment until that day's fighting was over. Patterson later wrote: 'Many of the Zionists whom I had thought somewhat lacking in courage showed themselves fearless to a degree when under heavy fire, while Captain Trumpeldor actually revelled in it, and the hotter it became the more he liked it…'

Patterson and Trumpeldor returned to Egypt in July, where they spoke to a large gathering of Jews in the Cairo synagogue, recruiting 150 as volunteers. Once they returned to the peninsula, Patterson was taken ill and sent back to Egypt; Trumpeldor took over as the Commanding Officer. For the first time in the war, a Jew was in command of an all-Jewish military force. It remained on the peninsula until January 1916, when all the allied forces were evacuated. After three months in Egypt, the Corps was told that it was to be sent to Ireland, to help put down the Easter Rising, the Irish rebellion against the British. Its men refused to go; they had joined the army, they said, in order to fight the Turks, not the Irish; to fight for a Jewish homeland, not to be sent against Irishmen who wanted independence. No further fighting against the Turks being in prospect, they were disbanded. It had been a small but impressive episode in Jewish history.

Inside Palestine a small group of Jews decided to work for the defeat of Turkey by helping the British with intelligence information about the Turkish forces. One of those at the centre of this espionage activity was Sarah Aaronsohn, the daughter of a Jewish farming family from Zikhron Ya'akov, an early Jewish settlement in Palestine. In 1915 she and her brothers formed a secret organisation to make contact with the British military authorities in Cairo. While travelling back to Palestine from Constantinople, she had seen thousands of Armenians being driven southward by the Turks under the harshest conditions, and feared that in due course a similar fate might await the 50,000 Jews still living in Palestine.

The Zion Mule Corps *in Egypt, before embarking for Gallipoli. Members of the Corps won the highest awards for courage under enemy fire.*

The Aaronsohns called their group 'Nili', an acronym of the Hebrew Biblical quotation Netzah Yisrael lo yishaker – 'the Strength of Israel will not fail'. In January 1917 a member of the group, Avshalom Feinberg, was killed by Bedouin while crossing the Sinai desert to try to reach British lines on the Suez Canal. Shortly after the Six-Day War of 1967, when Israeli troops occupied Sinai, they found his remains underneath a date palm which had sprung from dates that he had with him on his journey.

The British also made direct contact with Sarah Aaronsohn, sending a naval supply ship, the *Monegan*, along the coast of Palestine, to land a British emissary, to whom she then delivered her Intelligence information. Later rumour said that the emissary was Lawrence of Arabia, then working in Intelligence gathering in Cairo, and that the mysterious 'SA' to whom he dedicated his book *Seven Pillars of Wisdom* was in fact her. She was also given money, sent by Jews from the United States, to help the starving Jews inside Palestine, who were suffering continued Turkish oppression, many Jewish men having been sent by the Turks to do forced labour in Syria.

In October 1917 the Turks uncovered the Nili spy ring. Sarah Aaronson was arrested and tortured. As further tortures were being prepared, she killed herself with a pistol which she had managed to hide in her clothing when she was captured. She was twenty-seven years old.

Britain and Germany had both tried to win the allegiance of the Jews, and both offered support for some form of Jewish homeland in Palestine. But the Germans, despite their military help to Turkey, and the presence of German generals on all the Turkish war fronts, could offer little hope of an eventual Turkish victory. In contrast, since October 1917 the British had a large army, including Australian and New Zealand troops, inside the border of southern Palestine, commanded by General Allenby, a veteran of the battles on the Western Front, who was determined to capture Jerusalem, and to drive the Turks from Palestine altogether. Once Turkey was defeated it would be in Britain's power to give the Jews the right to live in Palestine, to emigrate there in large numbers, and to build up Jewish national and self-governing institutions.

Three factors made the British government keen to support the Zionist aim. First there was a natural sympathy with Jewish national aspirations, which had been patiently and enthusiastically explained to leading members of the government by Dr Weizmann and his Zionist colleagues, and which had been stimulated by the British determination to drive the Turks from Jerusalem. Second, there was a strong British desire to persuade Russian-born

Food for the soul. *At a United States army supply depot in France in the First World War, soldiers prepare packets of matzos (unleavened bread) to be sent to Jewish soldiers at the front, for Passover. Earlier, Michael Adler, the first Jewish chaplain on the Western Front, had bought matzos for the first Passover of the war, only for them to get lost in a depot in Le Havre.*

A moment of respite. *Two Jewish volunteer soldiers in the Zion Mule Corps at Gallipoli. Their task was to take munitions and other supplies up to the Allied front line trenches, where Turkish shelling and sniper fire were intense.*

Jews then living in the United States to volunteer to fight in Palestine, and thereby augment the British forces which had still to drive the Turks from the centre and north of the country. The third incentive was to persuade the Jews in Russia that they should speak out openly in favour of keeping Russia in the war, at a time when Bolshevik anti-war propaganda was gaining enormous support among the Russian troops. If Russian Jews felt that a British victory would accelerate the Zionist dream, then – so the British argument went – they would be keen to press their government to continue with the war. If Russia withdrew from the fighting, the German High Command would be able to transfer enormous numbers of troops from the Eastern to the Western Front, defeat Britain and France (as they nearly did in March 1918), and thus make any British promise with regard to Palestine impossible to fulfil. The situation for the Allies had become desperate. On the Western Front, the French army was beset with mutiny. In the Ypres salient, the British army was fighting yard by yard through the mud towards Passchendaele, which was to become a symbol of military stalemate and waste.

There was one Jew, however, in the British government, Edwin Montagu, who was reluctant to support Zionism. He feared a backlash of anti-Semitic prejudice that might result in all Jews being urged to go to Palestine, and thus put a brake on the pace of Jewish participation in national life. But his fellow Jewish Cabinet Minister, Herbert Samuel, saw great virtue in a Jewish national home, and urged his colleagues to support it. Even Samuel, however, warned: 'The dream of a Jewish State, prosperous, progressive, and the home of a brilliant civilisation, might vanish in a series of squalid conflicts with the Arab population.' To attempt to realise 'the aspiration of a Jewish State a century too soon,' Samuel feared, 'might throw back its actual realisation for many centuries more.'

Samuel's fears were overshadowed among the urgent needs of war. Most importantly, Balfour, who had once told Weizmann that he was an anti-Semite, was won round to the sense of Jewish destiny as seen by the Zionists. A considerable impact was made on the British policymakers by Sarah Aaronsohn's brother Aaron, who had managed to reach London, and

impressed those to whom he put the Zionist case by the record of farming and agricultural work already achieved in Palestine. It was he who convinced Mark Sykes, the War Cabinet secretariat's expert on Palestine, of the reality and potential of Jewish constructive enterprise there. On 2 November 1917, a day which marked a dramatic turning point in Jewish history, the British government announced its support for the Zionist call for a Jewish homeland in Palestine. A letter from Balfour himself, sent to a leading British Jew, Lord

Zionism rejoicing. *Dr Chaim Weizmann, head of the Zionist Commission to Palestine, tells the villagers at Rishon le-Zion about the Balfour Declaration, on 16 April 1918. Although the war was still being fought in*

northern Palestine, all the Jewish settlements in the south, including Rishon le-Zion, had been liberated by British, Australian and Indian troops five months earlier.

Rothschild, promised that Britain would 'view with favour the establishment in Palestine of a National Home for the Jewish people, and will use their best endeavours to facilitate the achievement of this object'. There was a double caveat: 'it being clearly understood that nothing shall be done which may prejudice the civil and religious rights of non-Jewish communities in Palestine, or the rights and political status enjoyed by Jews in any other country'. In the first of these two caveats were the seeds of much future conflict.

When Mark Sykes brought the text of the Balfour Declaration out of the Cabinet room, he said to Weizmann, who was sitting outside, 'It's a boy!' But when he heard the wording of the declaration, Weizmann said it was not the boy that he had expected, and he did not like it. He had been hoping for the promise of a Jewish State, not a 'National Home'. The Foreign Office, on the other hand, had wanted no more than the word 'Sanctuary'.

A persuasive farmer. *Aaron Aaronsohn, an agricultural pioneer in Palestine, later leader of the Nili group spying on the Turks for the British. His sister Sarah took her life when captured. He died in a plane crash in 1919.*

As part of its determination to use the Balfour Declaration to win both American- and Russian-Jewish support for the war, the British government made immediate plans to despatch a number of prominent Zionists to the United States and Russia to try to activate pro-war sentiment there; Weizmann was to go to both, while Jabotinsky would go to Russia and Aaron Aaronsohn to the United States. 'Information from every quarter shows the very important role the Jews are now playing in the Russian political situation,' a senior official wrote to Balfour on October 24. 'With skilful management of the Jews of Russia,' another official wrote to him, 'the situation may still be restored by the spring.' Unfortunately for British plans the calendar was against them. The Balfour Declaration was issued on 2 November 1917 and the Bolshevik revolution took place five days later. The Bolsheviks' first official act was to withdraw Russia from the war, enabling the German army to begin at once, with new confidence, to prepare a spring offensive on the Western Front.

In Britain, two thousand mostly Russian-born Jews were recruited for a specially created military force, the 38th Battalion of the Royal Fusiliers. The idea for this came from Jabotinsky, who was made a lieutenant in the battalion. Known as 'Judaeans', they would fight in Palestine, where the Turks remained in control of the whole country north of Jerusalem, including Galilee. As Jews were being recruited in Britain, parallel recruitment of Russian-born Jews took place in the United States for a 39th Battalion of the Royal Fusiliers. David Ben Gurion was one of those in charge of this recruiting; another future Prime

91

CELEBRATING LIBERATION.

The joyous return of Torah scrolls (left) to Tel Aviv after the town was liberated from the Turks. The scrolls had been taken for safety to Rishon le-Zion, and hidden there. The Sephardi Chief Rabbi of Palestine (above) adds his signature to the list of dignitaries – including his colleague the Ashkenazi Chief Rabbi – who had laid the twelve foundation stones of the Hebrew University of Jerusalem, on Mount Scopus, overlooking the city. The twelve stones represented the twelve tribes of Israel.

[PHOTO LEFT: AVRAHAM SOSKIN]

Minister of Israel, Golda Meir, heard him speak in Milwaukee of his hopes for the Jewish liberation of Palestine. Having undergone military training in Nova Scotia, the two thousand men of the 39th Battalion were sent by ship to Palestine, which they reached in June 1918. Among them was Russian-born Nehemia Rubitzov, who remained in Palestine after the war and whose son Yitzhak, born in 1922, later took the surname Rabin.

A third group of volunteer soldiers were Jews living in those parts of Palestine, including Tel Aviv and Jerusalem, that had been liberated by the British in October 1917. They became the 40th Battalion, Royal Fusiliers. Before they left Tel Aviv for training camps in Egypt, Chaim Weizmann addressed them in the main synagogue and presented them with a large Star of David flag, which had been sewn for them by the women of Tel Aviv.

The men of the three Royal Fusilier battalions saw action in the final struggle to drive the Turks out of Palestine in September 1918 and were among the first troops across the Jordan river, their 'good fighting qualities' being praised by General Allenby. Lieutenant Theodore Fligelstone, of the 38th Battalion, won the Military Cross when, with his machine gun, he drove the Turks 'off two miles of our front' at the crossing of the river.

One Russian-born Jew who served the British cause did so, not like the Royal Fusiliers in British uniform, but disguised as a serving German officer. Sidney Reilly had been born Sigmund Rosenblum, in Odessa. Making his way to Germany through neutral countries, and then using different 'German' identities, he enlisted in the German army. On one of his missions, dressed as a German army colonel, he attended a meeting with the Kaiser and his senior generals, passing back the details to his British spymasters.

The Jewish Legion. *At the railway station in Jaffa (left), relatives say good-bye to recruits for the 40th Battalion of the Royal Fusiliers, made up entirely of Palestinian Jews, on their way to the final battles against the Turks, in Samaria and Galilee, summer 1918. American volunteers for the 39th Battalion (above), with their Star of David arm bands, about to leave the United States for the Turkish front in Palestine.*

Major James de Rothschild, *son of 'the Baron', with some of the recruits for the 40th Battalion of the Royal Fusiliers. He was later a British Member of Parliament, and a leading philanthropist during Israel's first decades. His wife Dollie, from a leading Sephardi family, the Pintos, was a patron of myriad Jewish causes, including support for Soviet Jews in the 1980s.*

Star quality. *Irving Berlin (left), one of America's greatest songwriters. Born Israel Baline in Russia, his family, took him to the United States aged six, when they fled the pogroms. Seen here in a still from the 1918 film* Over There, *in which he played an American soldier. When on his way to England after the Second World War he received a mysterious summons to lunch on board ship with Winston Churchill only to discover that he had been mistaken for the Oxford philosopher Isaiah Berlin, whose wartime reports from Washington Churchill admired. Theda Bara (below), the Hollywood film star who appeared in more than forty films between 1914 and 1919. Fanny Brice (right) in the* Ziegfeld Follies, *1916.*

In the world beyond the trenches and the fury of battle, life went on between 1914 and 1918 for millions of people, continuing on the surface at least as if no daily slaughter was taking place. Theatres played to full houses in all the capitals of the warring powers. Old stars continued to make their mark, and new stars were born. In 1915 a twenty-five-year old American Jewish actress, Theodosia Goodman – born in Cincinnati, Ohio – starred in the film *A Fool was There*, playing, under the name Theda Bara, the role of a 'vamp' – a vampire. She was the first film star to be promoted by the American film studios as an object of sexual desire. Fanny Brice was another Jewish 'star'. Her parents had immigrated to New York from Hungary at the turn of the century. In 1916 she made her first appearance in the Ziegfeld Follies. For her act, she put on an American Indian costume

and spoke with a Yiddish accent. Of her subsequent 'Jewish' routines, many of which centred around 'Mrs Cohen at the Beach' gossiping with her friends and telling her husband what to do, she said: 'In anything Jewish I ever did, I wasn't standing apart, making fun of the race. What happened to me on stage is what could happen to them. They identified with me, and then it was all right to get a laugh, because they were laughing at themselves as well as at me.'

In 1917 the German conductor Otto Klemperer obtained his first major post, as music director of the Cologne Opera: following Hitler's rise to power he was among the hundred thousand German Jews who found refuge and continued their careers in the United States. As Jewish Orthodoxy continued to be a powerful factor for Jewish cohesion, even while secular Judaism and assimilation gained more and more adherents, Cantor Yossele Rosenblatt made headlines throughout the Jewish world in 1918 by declining $1,000 a night to sing the part of Eleazar in Halévy's *La Juive* at the Chicago Opera. A deeply observant Jew, he could never agree to appear in love scenes on the opera stage.

NEW HOMELANDS. *The ceremony laying out a new neighbourhood in Tel Aviv in 1913 (above), today bisected by Allenby Street in one of the busiest parts of the city. Jews in New York on the day, in 1916, when* *they became American citizens (right). Most of them had been born subjects of the Tsar in the Russian Empire. Now they proudly wave the Stars and Stripes, the flag of their new homeland.* [PHOTO ABOVE: AVRAHAM SOSKIN]

CHAPTER THREE

THE CRUCIBLE YEARS

1919-1929

THE AIM OF THE COMMUNIST REVOLUTION IN RUSSIA was to destroy the capitalist system first there and then throughout the world. Within two years, similar revolutions had broken out in Germany (both in Berlin and also in Bavaria), Austria, and Hungary, but had been crushed. In each of these revolutions – the one that succeeded and the four that failed – individual Jews were prominent, creating a backlash of anti-Jewish feeling among millions who saw these Jewish revolutionary leaders as part of a sinister and destructive conspiracy. For these Jews and their followers the revolutionary ferment of Communism appeared to offer great opportunities, equalities hitherto denied them, and social justice, for which they had been active campaigners in their own movements, or in national Social Democrat movements inspired by Marxism and a belief in the replacement of the capitalist system by a workers' and peasants' utopia. Other Jews, far more numerous than those who led or supported these revolutions, were to be victims of Communist policy and ideology. Jewish political organisations and Jewish mass movements were as much the enemies of Communism, and persecuted by it, as capitalism, bourgeois society, the class system, economic free trade and democratic values. For them, revolution posed even greater dangers than defeat in war, challenging both their desire to assimilate into the existing democratic and capitalist societies, and to live as practising Jews, or threatening to eclipse the project of a Jewish nation in Palestine. Communism was fierce in its opposition both to religion and to nationalism, including Zionism; it offered instead an internationalist, universal and uncompromising 'dictatorship of the proletariat', based on the one-party state.

On 20 March 1917, five days after the abdication of Tsar Nicholas II, the new Provisional Government issued a decree abolishing all the restrictions which had for centuries prevented Jews from leading lives as ordinary Russians. On November 6 that government was overthrown and the Bolsheviks came to power. One of their leading figures – second only to Lenin in charisma and power – was a Jew, Leon Trotsky. Although he had long

Soldier of revolution. *Leon Trotsky, born Lev Bronstein to a wealthy Jewish farming family in the Ukraine, at a parade of Red Army troops in Moscow's Red Square. As Commissar for War, he masterminded the defeat of the enemies of the Bolshevik Revolution.*

before turned his back on any links with Judaism, his looks and his real name (Lev Bronstein) marked him as a Jew and stimulated anti-Semitism among millions of Russians – especially among the peasants still steeped in Orthodox Christianity, with its anti-Jewish theology and superstitions. It was widely rumoured in 1918 that the Tsar and his family, whose murder had been organised by Yakov Yurovsky, a Jewish convert to Catholicism – and then to Communism – had been killed in a Jewish ritual manner, although no such ritual existed: even so, that charge re-surfaced in the year 2000 when the Tsar and his family were formally made Saints in a ceremony in a Moscow cathedral.

Lenin, the leader of the Bolshevik revolution, was not a Jew, but he kept secret – as did subsequent Soviet historians – the fact that his mother's father, Asher Blank, was Jewish. It was only in order to be able to practice as a doctor in an area of Russia barred to Jews that his grandfather had converted to Christianity, changing his first name to the quintessentially Russian Alexander. Under Hitler's definition of who was a Jew – a person with at least one Jewish grandparent – Lenin was Jewish. There were many Jews among his closest colleagues in the revolution, at the heart of the establishment of Communism in Russia. Yakov Sverdlov, whose original name was Solomon, as First Secretary of the Central Committee of the Communist Party, was the first Head of State of the Soviet Union. It was he who barred the more moderate Mensheviks from crucial policy meetings; Stalin said of him that he was 'an organiser to the bones of his brains'. His sudden death in 1919 at the age of forty-four deprived the revolution of a forceful leader, although he had been so troubled by the order to execute the whole Russian royal family that, in reporting to the Central Committee that the deed was done, he only mentioned the execution of the Tsar.

It was Leon Trotsky who, as President of the Petrograd Soviet, directed the

Old Bolsheviks: *Karl Radek (left) and Grigori Zinoviev. Radek was instructed to bring revolution to the West and was imprisoned in Germany during the Spartacist rising in 1919. When the historian John Wheeler-Bennett interviewed him in 1935 he said, 'I am a Bolshevik and I'd like to cut your throat, so let's start here.' Zinoviev was thrown out of the Politburo in 1926 for opposing one-party government. Both were executed in Stalin's purge in the late 1930s.*

armed uprising in November 1917 which brought the Bolsheviks to power. Then, as People's Commissar for Military Affairs, he established the Red Army as an effective fighting force, capable of pushing back the anti-Bolshevik White Russian armies. Far from seeing anti-Semitism as a reason for Jewish solidarity, Trotsky regarded it as a sickness of bourgeois society that would disappear with the revolution. For that reason he urged Jews to support the Bolshevik efforts, while at the same time arguing that the best solution for the perils which beset Jews as a result of their separateness was total assimilation. He rejected entirely, and opposed, both the Jewish revolutionary socialists of the Bund, and the Zionists.

When Lenin died, Trotsky was regarded by many as his natural successor but Stalin outmanoevred him and became ruler of the Soviet Union. Trotsky, at first in opposition and then in exile, was finally murdered on Stalin's orders in Mexico in 1940. By then, Stalin had murdered or sent to their deaths in Siberian labour camps almost all the Jewish members of Lenin's first government, not because they were Jews but because, like all the revolutionary leaders of 1917, they were a threat, in his own mind at least, to his absolutism.

Among the Jews whom Stalin murdered was Karl Radek (born Sobelsohn) whom Lenin had put in charge of plans to spread the revolution to Germany. Radek had worked hard to persuade the Russian Jewish masses that the revolution would be to their advantage. He also appealed to the Labour Zionists to join the Communist International and to recognise that revolution would be the best solution to Jewish isolation, as it would bring equality and fair-dealing to all members of society, of whatever race or background. The Zionists were not convinced, though a strong pro-Bolshevik element among them emigrated to Palestine and set up left-wing settlements where even Stalin's name was admired. Radek, an opponent of Stalin, was later appointed by him to be editor of the two Party newspapers, *Izvestia* and *Pravda*, where his articles on literature and theatre were much admired, but he was arrested in the 'Great Purges' of 1936 and 1937, sentenced to ten years hard labour, and never seen again. Grigori Zinoviev was also arrested in 1936, and then executed. Born Radomysylski, to a middle-class Jewish family, in 1919 he had been appointed Chairman of the Communist International, instructed by Lenin to promote revolution worldwide.

For more than three years, from November 1917 until the middle of 1920 a vicious civil war was fought in southern Russia, and particularly in the Ukraine, as Russian anti-Bolsheviks tried to overthrow the Bolshevik regime. The forces of anti-Bolshevism, including Ukrainian nationalist *haidamaks*, a White Army and a Green Army, largely motivated by loot, carried out as many as two thousand violent pogroms as they advanced through towns and villages with large Jewish populations who had sometimes shown sympathy with the Bolsheviks, or at least not opposed them. During these pogroms as

many as 85,000 Jews were murdered. This was the worst mass slaughter of Jews since the Chmielnicki massacres in the seventeenth century, when 100,000 Jews had been murdered in this same region. In response to the attacks, which reached a climax in the summer of 1919, Jewish self-defence units were formed in many towns, and had some success in beating back the attackers. Tens of thousands of Ukrainian Jews fled westward to Poland, Romania and Yugoslavia. Some made their way to the United States, Western Europe, Britain and Palestine, while 13,000 fled eastward, forming new communities in the Manchurian city of Harbin and the Chinese port of Shanghai. With the recapture of southern Russia by the Red Army the anti-Jewish excesses ended, and Jewish members of the Soviet secret police were active in finding, and often executing, those who had led the anti-Bolshevik campaign, and the pogroms.

The part played by Jews within the Soviet secret police in imposing the Red Terror in the early days of the Bolshevik regime created deep animosities among many non-Jews inside Russia and beyond. In Petrograd, the first head

The aftermath. *Following one of the many pogroms in southern Russia, probably by anti-Bolshevik forces, Jews examine desecrated Torah scrolls and prayer books in a synagogue vandalised in May 1920.*

of the secret police (then known as the Cheka) was a Jew, V. Volodarsky. After he was assassinated by an anti-Bolshevik Social Revolutionary he was succeeded by another Jew, M.S. Uritsky. He too was shot dead – by a young Jew seeking to avenge the death of a friend at the hands of secret police. On the day of Uritsky's murder, 30 August 1918, Fannie Kaplan, a Jewish woman who had earlier been exiled by the Tsarist authorities in Siberia for her part in a plot to kill the governor of Kiev, attempted to assassinate Lenin. One of the three shots which she fired hit Lenin at the juncture of his jaw and his neck, permanently affecting his health and leading to his early death six years later. She had objected to his suppression of the Constituent Assembly, an act which effectively ended democracy in Russia for more than seventy years. She was executed four days after her attempt on Lenin's life. It is said that Lenin did not want her executed, and that she was killed before he could intervene from his sickbed. A non-Jew, Feliks Dzerzhinsky, was then appointed to lead an intensification of the counter-revolutionary terror. Several Jews were his assistants; many more were his victims.

Solidarity. *British Jews march through the East End of London on 26 June 1919, to protest against the pogroms in Poland, where several hundred Polish Jews were murdered, and to call for action against the killings.*

In Germany, the final surrender of the once victorious Imperial army on 11 November 1918 and the fall of the monarchy encouraged the extreme German socialists and revolutionaries, led by a Jew, Rosa Luxemburg, and by Karl Liebknecht, who was not Jewish. He wanted an immediate seizure of power in Berlin. Luxemburg opposed this as impractical, but Liebknecht's will prevailed. They attempted to seize power from the new Republican government, but during the fighting with the government forces, and with right-wing militias, both of them were captured and killed. Rosa Luxemburg's body was thrown into the Landwehr canal at the point where it flows past the Berlin Zoo. On the following day the uprising was crushed.

In Vienna, an uprising by the Communist 'Red Guard' was led by Egon Kisch, a Prague-born author and journalist active before 1914 in Czech-Jewish literary circles. With the failure of the uprising he was imprisoned and then expelled from Austria. In later years he fought with the Spanish Republicans against Franco, and having emigrated first to New York and then to Mexico, returned after the Second World War to became president of the Prague Jewish community. By then his revolutionary fervour had been replaced by a democratic passion for the 'good European' which he had always aspired to be.

Red revolution also broke out in Bavaria, where a number of Jews were at the forefront of the attempt to impose Communist rule. The successful seizure of power in Munich was carried out on 7 November 1918 – four days before Germany's final surrender – by the Social Democrat leader Kurt Eisner, the son of a wealthy Berlin businessman. Having opposed Germany's entry into the war in 1914, once war broke out he set up an anti-war discussion group in Munich. In 1917 he was made leader of the Independent Social Democratic party, committed to the overthrow of the monarchist and capitalist systems. In 1918 he organised a series of anti-war strikes in Munich factories, for which he was imprisoned without trial or charge; only the imminent ending of the war led to his release. Marching at the head of an estimated 50,000 Bavarian workers and soldiers he presided over a bloodless revolution.

In February 1919 Eisner was murdered by Count Anton von Arco-Valley, a right-wing aristocrat and army officer, who wrote

Kurt Eisner, *German journalist and politician (centre, with dark coat), in Switzerland at a socialist conference, 1917. A year later, Eisner, the son of a wealthy Berlin merchant, led a Communist revolution in Bavaria. Three months after that, while walking to the Parliament building in Munich, he was assassinated.*

Ernst Toller, *the German writer who participated in the Communist revolution in Bavaria in 1919, seen here in prison after the failure of the revolution. When Hitler came to power, his books were banned and burned. Emigrating to the United States, he raised funds for the republicans fleeing from Franco's forces in the Spanish Civil War. When Madrid fell to Franco in 1939, he was overtaken by despair and committed suicide.*

in his diary shortly before he killed Eisner: 'He is a Jew. He is not German. He betrays the fatherland.' By an irony the Count was discovered to be of Jewish descent and therefore refused membership of the anti-Semitic, racist Thule Society which for several weeks had been circulating pamphlets calling for Eisner's death. Eisner was succeeded as Prime Minister of Bavaria by another, more extreme Jewish revolutionary, Gustav Landauer, who established the Bavarian Soviet Republic. The new republic was short-lived, and in the anti-Communist reaction which followed its overthrow, strong anti-Semitic feelings were stimulated. Landauer himself was captured by reactionary army officers who shot him, having trampled on him with their iron-studded army boots. His last words to his killers were said to have been: 'To think that you are human!' Landauer was a cultured man; his lectures on Shakespeare, published after his death in two volumes, were highly regarded. Despite his belief in world revolution and a strong early attachment to anarchism he supported the idea of workers' communes in Palestine within the framework of a wider Zionist political spectrum.

With Eisner and Landauer dead, a third German Jew, Ernst Toller, a twenty-six-year-old dramatist and poet, emerged as a leader of the Bavarian revolution. In the First World War he had fought in the trenches on the Western Front until wounded in 1916. Within the Bavarian Soviet he opposed the excesses of revolutionary terror. On 13 April 1919, as troops loyal to the government in Berlin moved against Toller's forces, yet another revolutionary regime – the Second Bavarian Soviet Republic – was declared in Munich. Its leader was Eugen Leviné, a thirty-eight-year-old Russian-born Jew who announced in triumph that 'the sun of world revolution has risen'. Toller moved quickly against this challenge from within the revolutionary ranks, forcing Leviné to resign, and telling his followers: 'I favour the dictatorship of the proletariat, but it must be a dictatorship of love and not of hate.' As Berlin continued its military offensive, the revolutionaries, in a desperate attempt to avert defeat, took sixteen hostages, most of them civilians. Adolf Hitler, still serving as a corporal in the Second Bavarian Infantry Regiment, was reportedly among those who managed to avoid being taken. Ten of the sixteen hostages were then killed, before Toller arrived and ordered an end to the executions. One of those in Munich at the time was the Papal Nuncio, Cardinal Pacelli, later Pope Pius XII, for whom the 'bestial hostage murder' blackened the name of both Jews and Communists. Hitler, who might so easily have been a victim of the Red Terror, saw in the Jewish leadership of the revolution proof of the destructive, anti-patriotic nature of Jewry.

The government forces quickly crushed the revolutionaries. Leviné was found guilty of treason and shot. Toller was sentenced to five years in prison. Of his Jewishness he had written, in words which many Jewish revolutionaries committed to a new world order in the 1920s could have echoed: 'A Jewish mother bore me, Germany nursed me, Europe educated me, the earth is my homeland, the world my fatherland.'

The Hungarian revolution that broke out in March 1919 was led by a Jew, Bela Kun – his surname a variant on the name Cohen – who had served in the Austro-Hungarian army and been captured by the Russians. While a prisoner of war he joined the Russian Bolshevik Party and met, and was impressed by Lenin. In 1918 he organised an International Unit of the Red Army, fighting alongside Soviet soldiers to beat back the armed forces of counter-revolution. Returning to Hungary in November 1918 he founded the Hungarian Communist Party. Imprisoned in February 1919 and badly beaten by his Hungarian captors, he managed to direct the revolutionary cause from inside prison. On 21 March 1919 he was released; on the following day the Hungarian Soviet Republic was declared. Kun was made Commissar for Foreign and Military Affairs, and the virtual dictator of Hungary. A number of Jews held high office in Bela Kun's administration. With him, they took over control of banks, large businesses and landed estates. Opposition groups were suppressed, including those within the Communist Party, and a Red Terror, modelled on that of the Soviet Union, tyrannised critics of the regime. Seeking to regain territory that had been lost to Romania and Czechoslovakia, Kun found the military task beyond his new nation's capacity, and when hoped-for Soviet help did not arrive, he had to watch powerless as Romanian forces entered Hungary and defeated his forces. His overthrow led to a violent anti-Semitic backlash: three hundred Jews, mostly Communist leaders and functionaries, were killed as Red Terror was replaced by White Terror. Bela Kun escaped, making his way to Moscow, where he became a leading figure in the Communist International, only to be shot during Stalin's purges in the 1930s.

Only in Soviet Russia did the Communist regime survive, and at first there was a flourishing of Jewish culture there. In 1924 the silent film *Jewish Luck* was issued, starring the comic actor Solomon Mikhoels, and with the linking screen texts by Isaac Babel. A year later the filmmaker Sergei Eisenstein, whose father was Jewish, produced *Battleship*

Bela Kun, *far right, with two fellow-Jewish revolutionaries, Joseph Pogany (left) and Sigismund Kahn (centre) at the height of their powers in Communist Hungary. Their moment of triumph was short.*

Creative conclave. *Yiddish writers who called themselves 'Di khalyastre' ('The gang') gather in Warsaw in 1922. Left to right: Mendl Elkin, Peretz Hirschbein, Uri Zvi Greenberg, Peretz Markish, Melekh Ravitch and Israel Joshua Singer (brother of the Nobel Prize winner,. I.B. Singer). Peretz Markish and Joshua Singer edited* Khalyastre Almanakh, *a Yiddish expressionist literary journal.*

Potemkin, a powerful portrayal of suffering and rebellion at the time of the 1905 Russian revolution. Mikhoels went on to make a screen version of Shakespeare's *King Lear* that marked him out as one of the great tragic actors of his generation. Based in Moscow, the Russian Yiddish theatre strove for the avante garde. But as Communism gained confidence, the Jewish political and social structures which had flourished in the first years of the revolution were destroyed. The first to be crushed was the Jewish revolutionary socialist movement, the Bund. Zionist societies were then closed down, and Jewish newspapers suppressed. Opportunities for Jewish religious worship were curtailed, and synagogues were forced to close. A special Jewish Section (*Yevsektsia*) of the Communist Party was set up, to ensure that all manifestations of Jewishness within the Soviet borders were in strict compliance with the growing monolithic ideology of Communism, and all manifestations of Zionism were banned. Tens of thousands of Jews were able to emigrate before the Soviet regime effectively sealed the borders for the next seventy years.

Among those who managed to leave in this last phase were Marc Chagall, who returned to France and joined the School of Paris (which included another Jewish painter, Amedeo Modigliani), and Simon Kuznets, a twenty-

MARC CHAGALL *in his Paris studio, 1927, with his wife Bella and daughter Ida. In 1937 his works were displayed in Munich as part of the 'Degenerate Art' exhibition there. When he was a child, his uncle refused to take his hand on discovering he had broken the Jewish religious prohibition against idolatry by drawing. As a young man in St Petersburg he had been the favourite pupil of Leon Bakst, the Jewish designer of the Ballets Russes.*

two-year-old economist with the statistical division of the Central Soviet of Trade. Making his way from the Ukrainian city of Kharkov to the United States, Kuznets became a leading expert on the national economy, defining the two concepts of national product and national income. In 1971 he was awarded the Nobel Prize for his 'empirically founded interpretation of economic growth which has led to a new and deepened insight into the economic and social structure'. Another émigré in the 1920s was Roman Jakobson, a professor at Moscow's Higher Dramatic School at the early age of twenty-two, who fled to Czechoslovakia. In 1938 he had to flee again, travelling first to Scandinavia and then to the United States, where for nearly twenty years he was professor of Slavic languages at Harvard. The wandering Jew – of which he was typical, through no choice of his own – had also of necessity to be

Queen of the Yiddish Theatre. *Ida Kaminska (left) as Esmeralda in a Yiddish stage adaptation of Victor Hugo's* Hunchback of Notre Dame.

something of a linguist: Jakobson was fluent in six languages and could read twenty-five.

There was one Jew who made his way not out of Russia but into it in the mid-1920s. This was the Odessa-born British spy Sidney Reilly, who reached Helsinki on 25 September 1925, and then crossed clandestinely into the Soviet Union on a secret mission to stimulate internal opposition to Bolshevism. Two weeks after his arrival there was a report in a Soviet newspaper that three Western agents had been caught on the Russo-Finnish border and shot. Reilly was almost certainly one of them.

Opium of the People. *An anti-religious play performed at the Byelorussian State Yiddish Theatre in Minsk. The letters on the backsides of the actors spell 'kosher'.*

THEATRE OF THE ABSURD.
Yiddish humour was intensely self-mocking.
Zuskin, a Yiddish actor, on the stage in
Moscow in 1928 (above left), in a comedy
by Sholom Aleichem. A scene from the play
Travels of Benjamin the Third *by Mendele*

Mokher Seforim ('Little Mendel the Bookseller'), performed at the Moscow State Yiddish Theatre (above) in 1927. It remained in the repertoire for twenty years. Mendele's real name was Sholem Jacob Abromovitch. Known as 'the grandfather of modern Yiddish literature', he was the first to record the Yiddish of common people and to use it in literature. The scenery in both productions, with its simplifications and strong diagonal lines, is redolent of the Expressionism then fashionable.

The prominence of individual Jews in the violent revolutions which curbed or sought to curb individual liberty, did not prevent the mass of Jewry, in Europe and beyond, from leading constructive, creative lives, which benefited the societies in which they lived. Yet the position of the Jews in newly independent Poland was at times precarious. As Poland itself struggled to secure its eastern borders against the Lithuanians and Ukrainians, and to protect them against the advance of the Red Army (to the very outskirts of Warsaw), a series of pogroms led to more than five hundred deaths. This was far fewer than the slaughter that was taking place in Ukraine, but it was frightening for those who witnessed it, or feared that it was a prelude to further killings. In Vilna, the historic 'Jerusalem of Lithuania', which Poland had annexed from Lithuania – eighty Jews were killed. However, in several Polish towns, including Lvov, Cracow and Oswiecim (the former Austro-Hungarian border town of Auschwitz) Jewish self-defence groups beat off the attackers. Despite the ill omens, from the first days of Polish independence Polish Jews were able to enter Parliament as the representatives of the large Jewish community. Every tenth Polish citizen was a Jew; certain large towns had a substantially greater Jewish element: more than seventy per cent of the popula-

tion of the eastern town of Pinsk was Jewish, more than fifty per cent in Bialystok, Brest-Litovsk and Grodno, and more than a third in the cities of Vilna, Lvov and Warsaw. In many small towns in eastern Poland as many as three quarters of the population was Jewish. The Polish treaty which emerged from the Paris Peace Conference guaranteed the Jews their own schools, and the right to observe the Sabbath. The Polish constitution recognised the Jews as a nationality and gave them, in common with all minorities, the right to foster their 'national traditions', a right which enabled Zionist organisations to flourish. However, anti-Jewish pressures and prejudices were seldom far from the surface. At school and university level quotas were imposed on the number of Jewish students. Jewish students were often taunted in the streets – as later they were to be in Germany – with the cry, 'Go to Palestine'.

The spectrum of Polish Jewish life ran from the totally secular, often Polish-speaking, to the ultra-Orthodox, Yiddish speaking. Orthodoxy itself

Youthful learning. *Boys and their teacher at a religious school in Lublin (above), 1920. This photograph was taken by Alter Kacyzne during his travels through Poland after the First World War. Kacyzne, a Yiddish writer and poet, was murdered by Ukrainian collaborators in 1941. Boys entering a school in Vilna in which modern Hebrew and Jewish history were taught (left). The school was called Mefitzah Haskalah ('Disseminators of Enlightenment'). Jewish boys on holiday near Warsaw, sitting at a wayside café (top left), also photographed by Alter Kacyzne.*

117

was changing: in 1918 a thirty-five-year-old Jewish dressmaker in Cracow, Sarah Schenirer, had set up the first school for Orthodox Jewish women who wished to study the Bible. She did so against two thousand years of Jewish religious tradition which strongly discouraged such studies, but she was determined that women should have the same rights as men to become learned in the holy texts and religious arguments of Judaism. She called her school, where the teaching was in Yiddish, the Beth Jacob (House of Jacob). Within seven years, twenty Beth Jacob schools had been opened throughout Poland. When Schenirer died in 1935 there were more than two hundred of her schools there, with a total student population of 35,000. In her will she told her students: 'My dear girls, you are going out into the great world. Your task is to plant the holy seed in the souls of pure children. In a sense, the destiny

Making parchment *for Torah scrolls (left), a photograph taken by Alter Kacyzne in Lukow, a small Polish town, half of whose 12,000 inhabitants were Jews.*

The old market *in the eastern Polish town of Krzemieniec – in Yiddish, Kremenits – photographed by Alter Kaczyne in 1925. Its a Jewish population suffered terribly during the pogroms of 1918-20, and of the 10,000 Jewish inhabitants in 1939 only fourteen survived the Holocaust.*

of Israel of old is in your hands.' With the German conquest of Poland in 1939 her schools were closed down, and during the following five years most of those who had been pupils were killed. After the war, however, her system was recreated in the United States, so that her aim, to keep girls within the religious fold, was not lost.

In May 1918, while the First World War was still being fought, Chaim Weizmann, as head of the Zionist Commission, had welcomed General Allenby back to Jerusalem, which he had conquered six months earlier, and shown him the enthusiasm of the Palestinian Jews, many of whom had returned from their enforced exile in Egypt. Weizmann also held talks at Akaba, at the head of the Red Sea, with the leader of the Arab Revolt against the Turks, Emir Feisal, with whom he later reached agreement – on 3 January 1919 – that 'all necessary measures' should be taken 'to encourage and stimulate immigration of Jews into Palestine on a large scale, and as quickly as possible to settle Jewish immigrants upon the land through closer settlement and intensive cultivation of the soil'. In taking such measures, the agreement went on, 'the Arab peasant and tenant farmers shall be protected in their rights, and shall be assisted in forwarding their economic development' and that the Zionist Organisation would use 'its best efforts' to assist the Arabs of Transjordan 'in providing the means for developing the natural resources and economic possibilities thereof'. Feisal was convinced that the Arabs would benefit from Zionist enterprise. 'I would welcome any good understanding with the Jews,' he wrote to his senior British adviser a month after the Akaba meeting. 'I admit that some ignorant Arabs despise the Jews, but ignorants everywhere are the same, and on the whole such incidents compare favourably with what the Jews suffer in more advanced lands.' At that very moment in towns and villages throughout the Ukraine thousands of Jews were being murdered.

The Paris Peace Conference of 1919, which led to the Versailles Treaty, listened with sympathy to the view of the Jewish delegation that the Jews, although a minority everywhere, did have collective rights and status. This was put forward most effectively by the United States judge, Louis Marshall, who urged the conference to include minority guarantees for Jews in the establishment of the new States of Europe. In an important definition of Zionist aims in Palestine, Weizmann told the conference: 'The Zionist Organisation did not want an autonomous Jewish Government, but merely to establish in Palestine, under a Mandatory Power, an administration, not necessarily Jewish, which would render it possible to send into Palestine 70,000 to 80,000 Jews annually. The Organisation would require to have permission at the same time to build Jewish schools, where Hebrew would be taught, and to develop institutions of every kind. Thus it would build up gradually a nationality, and so make Palestine as Jewish as America is American or England English.'

Leaving for a new world. *Polish Jewish emigrants on the train to the port of Danzig. From there tens of thousands took passage to the United States, thousands more to Britain, Canada, South Africa, South America and Palestine This photograph was taken by Alter Kacyzne.*

121

From the first days of British rule, the British allowed Jews to enter Palestine in large numbers from throughout the Jewish world; tens of thousands of Jews came from every country in which there were Jewish communities, with first Russia and then Poland providing the biggest numbers. Many Jews also came from western European countries, and from the Americas. From Holland, Lazare Bavly brought his knowledge of agricultural development. From Canada, Bernard Joseph brought the basis of a legal system, as did Harry Sacher from Britain. From the United States, Judah Magnes became the first chancellor of the Hebrew University, and a strong supporter of close Arab-Jewish relations. Russian-born Golda Meir, aged twenty-three, was among several thousand Jews who reached Palestine from the United States in 1921; she worked first as a farmer on a kibbutz – where the ideal was collective work without pay, for the general good of the kibbutz community – and then as a trade union leader. Half a century later she became the first woman to join an Israeli Cabinet and the first (and as yet only) woman to become Prime Minister of Israel.

Between 1920 and 1939 more than half a million Jews entered Palestine, less than five per cent of world Jewry. Jewish life continued to find its main areas of activity and intensity in the Diaspora, where, in those parts of the former Russian empire that had escaped Bolshevik rule, Jewish life recovered from the wartime privations and began to flourish. In Lithuania, where the Jewish population was more than seven per cent of the total, Hebrew-language schools and a strong Zionist tradition encouraged emigration to Palestine, and children celebrated the anniversaries of the Balfour Declaration in dance and song. The capital, Kovno, where twenty-seven per cent of the population was Jewish, was a vibrant centre of Jewish life; at the Jewish hospital, Dr Moses Brauns ran a contagious diseases department which served Jews and non-Jews alike. It was also a centre of Zionist enthusiasms; in 1925 the left-wing Zionist organisation, *Hashomer Hatzair* ('The Young Watchman'), marched proudly through the city to celebrate the opening of the Hebrew University in Jerusalem. Lithuanian Jews also emigrated to new lands, chiefly to South Africa, where they formed a cohesive community, strongly Zionist, and conscious of its Lithuanian-Jewish origins.

Jews could be among the strongest patriots of the new nations of central Europe. In some of his first published poems, Julian Tuwim, the son of Orthodox parents, expressed his joy at Poland's new-found independence. In the Second World War, on the outbreak of which he was by chance in South America, one of his poems became the anthem of the Polish national resistance movement.

In Britain, a Jew, Lord Reading, formerly Rufus Isaacs, became Viceroy of India in 1921. Another British Jew, Alice Marks, began her ballet career, as Alicia Markova, in 1924. Marie Rambert (born Miriam Rambach), a ballet teacher, set up a ballet school in London in 1920 which became a focus of the revival of ballet in Britain. In France, the Romanian-born Jewish poet Tristan

Arrival. *Jewish immigrants disembark at Haifa. Others arrived by train from Egypt. Arab resentment led to protests and violence; also in 1921 the British briefly suspended immigration. Among those not allowed to*

land until the ban was lifted was Golda Meir, later Prime Minister of Israel, who had come from the United States.

[PHOTO: YOSEF SCHWEIG]

Tzara, having been a co-founder of the Dada movement in Zurich in 1916, celebrated surrealism and delighted in the joys of anarchism in language and design. In most countries of the world the 1920s were a period of opportunity for Jews, breaking out of the stereotypes and able to take part in every aspect of national life. More and more countries allowed Jews to rise to the

highest ranks in the army, the judiciary and the civil service. Sephardi as well as Ashkenazi Jews saw a renaissance in the 1920s. In Baghdad the Jewish community contributed to the government of Iraq, like Palestine a British Mandate, where the opportunity to participate in the emerging national life brought Jews into the highest reaches of the administration. The community maintained its own institutions, including a Jewish hospital, high school and Boy Scout troop.

In Shanghai, which had a flourishing Sephardi community of more than a thousand Jews, mostly from Baghdad, Zionist enthusiasms were seen in the Young Judaea youth group, whose Student Study Circle discussed the pros and cons of emigration to Palestine. There was also an Ashkenazi Jewish community in Shanghai, more than 4,500 strong, who had come from Russia between 1917 and 1925. Each had its own communal committee, synagogues and rabbis, but shared the Jewish hospital. One of the members of the Sephardi community, Renée Dangoor, later recalled how her fellow-Jews 'all spoke Baghdadi Arabic and conducted their accounts and correspondence in Arabic… They were without exception devout Jews who led a strictly Orthodox life.'

There was another prosperous Sephardi community in Salonika, with its Maccabi sports club and, among its communal organisations, a Philanthropic

Eastern Diaspora. *The Dangoors (above), one of the leading Sephardi Jewish families, in Shanghai (see p.16). The central seated figure is wearing Chinese dress. Sephardi women (below) in Arab dress, in Baghdad.*

Society for the Distribution of Food to Orphans. Girls and boys had their own youth movements. In Egypt, the Jews of Cairo and Alexandria were prominent in the economic and cultural effervescence which accompanied the stirrings of Egyptian nationhood.

Defeated in war, the once all-powerful Germany struggled to rebuild its economic and national life. The Jews, who had suffered the same sense of defeat and humiliation as non-Jews, were an integral part of that search for recovery. When massive inflation struck, Jewish businesses suffered with the rest, but there were never lacking those who tried to make the Jews the scapegoat, both

Aegean Diaspora. *Jewish girls sorting tobacco in Salonika. When this picture was taken, in the 1930s, there were 35,000 Jews in the city. During anti-Semitic riots from 1932 on, one entire Jewish quarter was burned to the ground. Most of those living there emigrated to Palestine.*

Albert Einstein *in Berlin in 1921, with his wife Elsa. In 1914 his anti-war position, expressed in outspoken language, had alienated him from many of his fellow German scientists. In 1933, in the aftermath of Hitler coming to power, he moved to the United States, becoming a Professor at Princeton. After Chaim Weizmann's death in 1952 Ben Gurion offered him the presidency of the State of Israel as 'the greatest living Jew', but he declined. He was seventy-six, and died three years later.*

for Germany's defeat in 1918, and for the inflation. In 1920 Adolf Hitler began to preach a particularly virulent form of anti-Semitism, telling his followers – few in number at the time, but growing steadily and then rapidly during the coming decade: 'It is our duty to arouse, to whip up, and to incite our people to instinctive repugnance of the Jews'. Two years later, Walther Rathenau, the German Foreign Minister, was murdered by anti-Semites. In 1933 Hitler dedicated a memorial tablet to them, describing them as the 'champions of the new Germany'. Yet even as anti-Semitism reverberated through the German nation, Jewish creativity flourished. In 1921 – the year that Albert Einstein won the Nobel Prize for Physics, for his work on the photoelectric element of the quantum theory – another Jew, Max Born, was appointed professor of theoretical physics at Göttingen University, where, building on Einstein's work, he pioneered the formulation of quantum mechanics. In 1933 he was personally denounced by Hitler as a proponent of 'Jewish physics' and emigrated to Britain. Returning to Germany after the war, he was awarded the Nobel Prize for Physics.

The crude anti-Semitism of Hitler's small, rabble-rousing National Socialist (Nazi) Party seemed a sideline at the time, irrelevant to the wider world of German Jewish creativity and participation in every facet of German national life. When in 1923 an anti-Semitic newspaper was published in Nuremberg, entitled *Der Stürmer* ('The Stormer') its banner headline, repeated in every issue, 'The Jews are our misfortune', seemed a laughable absurdity, a throwback to medieval prejudices which had no place in a modern democratic and cultured society. Yet between 1922 and 1933 there were two hundred instances in Nuremberg of the desecration of Jewish graves.

In 1923 Hitler tried to seize power in Munich. He failed and was imprisoned. While in prison he wrote his book *Mein Kampf* ('My Struggle') which

A fashionable wedding *in Berlin in 1929. The photographer Arthur Himmelreich gets married in full evening dress with his elegant wife in the latest creation.* [PHOTO: HEIDERICH]

was filled with venomous attacks on the Jews, whom he portrayed as the defilers of a 'pure' Aryan race which he, Hitler, wished to save from destruction. 'The black-haired Jewish youth lies in wait for hours on end,' he wrote, 'satanically glaring at and spying on the unsuspicious girl whom he plans to seduce, adulterating her blood and removing her from the bosom of her own people. The Jew uses every possible means to undermine the racial foundations of a subjugated people.' Was there 'any shady undertaking,' he asked his readers, 'any form of foulness, especially in cultural life, in which one Jew did not participate?' and he went on to give his own answer: 'On putting the probing knife carefully to that kind of abscess, one immediately discovered, like a maggot in a putrescent body, a little Jew who was often blinded by the sudden light'. In a dire warning, apocalyptic in its tone, and with all the marks of madness, Hitler portrayed himself as the saviour of mankind: 'Should the Jew, with the aid of his Marxist creed, triumph over the people of this world, his Crown will be the funeral wreath of mankind, and this planet will once again follow its orbit through ether, without any human life on its surface, as

Object of curiosity. *An Orthodox Jew walking with his children in a Berlin street in 1928: an image at the opposite pole to that on the previous page. That year the new British Ambassador to Germany, Sir Horace Rumbold, wrote to a friend: 'I am appalled by the number of Jews in this place. One cannot get away from them. I am thinking of having a ham-bone amulet made "to keep off the evil nose", but I am afraid that even that would not be a deterrent.' There were in fact only 172,672 Jews in Berlin at that time, out of a total population of 4,000,000, but the appearance of Orthodox Jews made them conspicuous, easy targets for ignorance and prejudice.* [PHOTO: WALTER GIRCKE]

it did millions of years ago. And so I believe today that my conduct is in accordance with the will of the Almighty creator. In standing guard against the Jew I am defending the handiwork of the Lord.' On release from prison Hitler rebuilt his Nazi Party – which had briefly been banned – and at two successive 'Party Days', the first at Weimar in 1926 and the second at Nuremberg in 1927, he listened with approval as speaker after speaker advocated driving the Jews out of Germany. During 1927 several Jewish cemeteries were desecrated and synagogues wrecked by Nazi gangs.

Acts of anti-Semitic vandalism, and manifestations of anti-Jewish prejudice, wherever they occurred, threw into greater contrast than would otherwise have been the case the mounting Jewish national aspirations. These had been stimulated throughout the Jewish world by the Balfour Declaration.

In 1921, Winston Churchill was put in charge of the Middle East Department of the Colonial Office. His support for Jewish enterprise in Palestine was crucial. Shortly before this he had published a newspaper article stating that the creation 'in our own lifetime' of a Jewish State in Palestine of three to four million Jews would be an event 'in the history of the world which would from every point of view be beneficial'. From the earliest days of British rule, however, Jewish settlements in Palestine had been vulnerable to Arab attack. In 1920, Trumpeldor was killed defending the small settlement at Tel Hai in northern Galilee. To give such defence a more organised shape, Jabotinsky set up the Hagannah, a Jewish defence force armed and trained to go into action whenever attacks took place.

In 1921 one of the leaders of the Arab riots of the previous year, Haj Amin al-Husseini, was appointed Mufti of Jerusalem by the first British High Commissioner in Palestine, Herbert Samuel, a Jew. The year before, the departing Chief Administrator had given him a small piece of paper to sign:

Master of the Mandate. *Sir Herbert Samuel, the first British High Commissioner to Palestine, ruled impartially between his fellow-Jews and the Arabs, though many Palestinian Jews called him, with pride, 'Our Samuel'. The son of a wealthy Jewish banker, as a university student he had lost his faith in Judaism, but out of deference to his family maintained outward observance. So when he joined the Cabinet in 1909, he was the first Jew to reach that eminence. Early in the First World War he had advocated a British protectorate over Palestine once Turkey was defeated.* [PHOTO: LEO SILVER]

'Received from Major-General Louis Bols, one Palestine, complete'. Samuel had signed but added in jest 'E & O E' – Errors and Omissions Excepted. There undoubtedly were flaws and errors in the country, but Samuel added to them. If he had hoped by this method to curb Haj Amin's extreme views he was gravely mistaken. Slowly but with great skill, Haj Amin eliminated the influence of those moderate Arab leaders who were prepared to accept some element of Jewish immigration. On May Day 1921 Communist and Socialist Jews fell out among themselves during a demonstration march in Jaffa. This gave the opportunity to Arab rioters, inspired by their new Mufti, to attack Jews and Jewish property there and in Jerusalem, demanding an immediate end to Jewish immigration. Among those murdered in Jaffa was the Russian-born writer Joseph Chaim Brenner, who had settled in Palestine in 1909, publishing Hebrew-language novels, short stories and recollections. Brenner doubted if the Jews could escape anti-Semitism in Palestine. Although he did not run when attacked, but fought back, he was the victim of anti-Jewish hatred.

Confrontation and conciliation. *Jews in Petakh Tikvah, one of the late nine-teenth-century Jewish settlements in Palestine, sit down in their orchard with Arab notables from the neighbouring village. This se'uda – meal – had been called after an attack on the settlement by armed Bedouin marauders. The attackers had been driven off by a defence force of local young men, four of whom were killed. Among the dead was Avshalom Gissin, aged 25, who had been born in Petakh Tikvah, and had founded the local Jewish scout movement.*

In response to the Arab riots, Samuel suspended Jewish immigration, but Churchill told him that concessions to the Arabs must be made 'on their merits and not under duress', and lifted the ban. Churchill also prepared the terms of the Mandate for Palestine, which was to be given to Britain by the League of Nations. As a result of the Churchill White Paper of 1922, which the League of Nations accepted, the Jews were to be in Palestine 'of right, and not on sufferance'. Following this bold assertion, on average as many as 8,000 Jews entered Palestine each year for the next seven years.

The British did their best to absorb Palestine into their traditional colonial system, at the same time making themselves at home. Herbert Samuel lectured on Keats; Ronald Storrs, the military governor of Jerusalem, played Shylock in an amateur production of *The Merchant of Venice*. After Sunday morning service in Jerusalem Cathedral, there was cricket, and hunting (jackals not foxes) on other days with the Ramle Hunt. Meanwhile there was an impressive building up of Jewish institutions, including comprehensive education and health systems, trade union and co-operative ventures, and the opening of the Hebrew University. In 1920 the American teacher and social worker, Henrietta Szold, took charge of the organisation she had founded before the First World War, Hadassah – the Women's Zionist Organisation of America, called after the Hebrew name of the Biblical Queen Esther, and set up welfare clinics, dispensaries and medical laboratories throughout Palestine. In Jerusalem, a Nurses' Training School was established and the cornerstone of the Hadassah Hospital was laid on Mount Scopus, overlooking the city. The hospital sought to become – and did become – a centre of medical excellence, available to all the inhabitants of the country, Jew and Arab, Christian or Muslim, religious or secular. Speaking of the conflict between Jews and Arabs, she said: 'I believe there is a solution; and if we cannot find it, then I consider that Zionism has failed utterly.'

The methods pursued by the Zionists, with the support of the British Mandate authorities, were three-fold: first, land purchase, usually from Arab landowners; then settlement on that land by pioneers who had been trained, often in Europe, in agricultural skills; and third, persistent diplomatic negotiations to secure the rights and privileges which the Zionists believed were theirs as a result of the Balfour Declaration and the 1922 Churchill commitment. While most Zionists, including Weizmann and Ben Gurion, welcomed whatever opportunities Britain gave them – and these were many – to press ahead with their self-governing institutions, this acceptance was denounced by a minority of Zionists as too gradualist. In 1923, Jabotinsky resigned from the Zionist Executive. His last task had been raising funds in both Palestine and England for land purchase and the settlement of new immigrants. The previous year he had opposed the creation by Britain of an Arab emirate – Transjordan – east of the river Jordan, believing that as in Biblical times the Jews should be free to settle and to build their national institutions on both sides of the river Jordan. In 1925 he established his own breakaway Zionist movement, the Revisionists, and, speaking throughout Europe to large gatherings of Jews, called for unrestricted mass Jewish immigration to Palestine and the creation of a Jewish fighting force there to meet any emergency that might arise. His appeal was particularly strong among Polish, Lithuanian and Latvian Jews.

With the aim of mobilising the Jewish masses, Jabotinsky also set up paramilitary organisations in Eastern Europe, complete with uniforms and slogans. Contempt was openly expressed for the more moderate counsels of mainstream Zionism – for those leaders who were actually building up the Jewish National

Challenge within the ranks. *Uniformed members of the Revisionist youth movement Betar welcome their leader, Zev Jabotinsky, to the Lithuanian capital, Kovno. Revisionism, which opposed the more moderate Zionism of Weizmann and Ben Gurion, called for the immediate mass immigration of Jews to Palestine, vigorous defence training, a more militant attitude towards the enemies of Zionism, including Arabs, and the rebirth of a Jewish State 'on both sides of the Jordan'. The scene shows that Revisionism was not immune from infection by the revolutionary germ of Fascism, so prevalent in inter-war Europe.*

Art in Jerusalem. *The courtyard of the Bezalel Academy, where Russian-born Boris Schatz (facing the camera, in dark jacket and white trousers) encouraged a modern style of Jewish art, in painting, sculpture and design. With him (bearded, in white shirt and white trousers) is the artist Abel Pan. The climate of Palestine allowed regular outdoor classes.*

Home, institution by institution, settlement by settlement, brick by brick. The most effective and visible of Jabotinsky's creations was the Revisionist youth organization, founded in the Latvian capital, Riga, a centre of Jewish political activism. It was called Betar – an acronym for Brit Yosef Trumpeldor – the Joseph Trumpeldor Pact. Trumpeldor's last words before he was killed in 1920 were said to have been, 'It is good to die for our country' – an echo of the ancient Roman belief, 'It is sweet and noble to die for one's country'. The youth of Betar swore that Trumpeldor's death would not prove to have been in vain, and that Jewish self defence would triumph. Defiantly they called for the immediate establishment of a Jewish State, even if the British had to be fought to obtain it. Unlike the socialist youth movements active among Zionist youth, especially in Poland and central Europe, Betar gave its members courses in military instruction as well as in agriculture. One future head of Betar was Menachem Begin, later Prime Minister of Israel.

From 1921 the Zionist Executive, headed by Dr Weizmann, had been in charge of Jewish creative endeavour in Palestine, and of relations with the British authorities. In 1929 a Jewish Agency was created to accelerate land settlement, immigration and the building up of Jewish national institutions. Its members included Jews living in the Diaspora. Individual Jews who made their mark in the Palestine in the 1920s included the Austro-Hungarian-born novelist Shmuel Agnon, and Boris Schatz, whose Bezalel Academy continued to excel, as it had done before the First World War, in teaching Jewish arts and crafts. The Academy encouraged modern Jewish artistic attitudes far removed from Orthodox Judaism: one of its noted features was its anatomy class.

Farming in Palestine involved hard, even harsh work, with the constant danger of malaria, which killed hundreds, and forced thousands more to return to Europe. Newcomers at Haifa port did not always know what severe conditions awaited them. Swamp draining at Kishon, near Haifa, was one task that newcomers carried out. In the continual modernisation of Tel Aviv, Jewish women laid stones in the main streets to make them passable by motor vehicles. There was also the continual delight in the antiquities and natural wonders of the country. One popular excursion from Tel Aviv was to the ancient Jewish cave dwellings at Beit Guvrin.

At Ben Shemen, Jewish orphans from the First World War, mostly from Russia and Lithuania, were found a home in a special youth agricultural village. One of the basic beliefs of the village's founder, German-born Dr Siegfried Lehmann, was that far-reaching, meaningful concessions had to be made to the Arabs in order to achieve an understanding and live with them in harmony. The German-born founder of the kibbutz movement, Arthur Ruppin was also a leading advocate of Jewish-Arab cooperation. He was convinced that this was essential if the Jews were to be able to live in Palestine without violence. In 1925 he helped establish Brith Shalom ('The

Vote for Mayor. *Youngsters drive through Tel Aviv with election posters during municipal elections in 1928, urging voters to support the anti-Zionist ultra-Orthodox Agudat Yisrael religious Party candidate. Victory went instead to Meir Dizengoff, one of the founders of the city. Born in Russia, and an active Russian revolutionary in his youth, he was mayor from 1921 to 1925 and from 1928 until his death nine years later. One of Tel Aviv's main shopping streets is named after him.* [PHOTO: ZVI ORUSHKES]

WORKING THE LAND. *Jewish workers (above left), most of them new immigrants from Russia, draining the Kishon swamp near Haifa. This area, seen here in 1920, was to become one of the main industrial regions of Israel. Road-building near Nahalal (left), a settlement*

founded in 1921 in the Jezreel Valley. A girls' agricultural training farm was established there eight years later. (above) The Festival of the First Fruits at kibbutz Ein Harod in the Jezreel Valley, 1924. Settlers are gathering from all twenty Jewish settlements in the valley. Behind them are the

Mountains of Gilboa. Fifty years later, thick forests, planted by the early settlers, covered these slopes. [PHOTO OPPOSITE ABOVE AND ABOVE: YOSEF SCHWEIG]

135

FRUITS OF THE LAND. *Packing oranges (left). God had promised the Jews 'a land of milk and honey', to which the pioneers in Palestine added a vigorous arable and plantation economy, of which oranges were a central aspect. Date palms were brought from Iraq and avocados from South Africa: both flourished. Then it was found that bananas could grow in abun-* *dance. An agricultural college was set up, and also an agricultural research branch of the Hebrew University. A child (above) is dressed in orange leaves as the 'spirit of the orange', during the feast of Purim in Tel Aviv, celebrating the ancient rescue of the Jews of Persia from imminent destruction.*

[PHOTO OPPOSITE: YA'ACOV BEN DOV]

[PHOTO ABOVE: YOSEF SCHWEIG]

Covenant of Peace'), an organisation whose aim was to 'prepare the ground for an understanding between Jews and Arabs', living side by side in a single, bi-national State. Ben Gurion, the leader of Mapai (the Party of the Workers of the Land of Israel) opposed him, telling a meeting of Brith Shalom: 'Only one fragment of the Arab people – perhaps seven or eight per cent – lives in Palestine. However, this is not the case with respect to the Jewish people. For the entire Jewish nation, this is the one and only country with which are connected its fate and future as a nation. Only in this land can it renew and maintain its independent life, its national economy and its special future, only here can it establish its national sovereignty and its freedom.'

In 1928 Field Marshal Lord Plumer, who had followed Herbert Samuel as Palestine's second High Commissioner, handed over to his successor, Sir John Chancellor, what appeared to be a comparatively quiescent country. When one of his officials remarked to Plumer that he had said nothing about the political situation, Plumer answered, 'Crosbie, there is no political situation – and don't you create one'. But in 1929 there were renewed Arab riots on a hitherto unprecedented scale against Jewish settlements. These convinced Ruppin that it was necessary to strengthen the Jewish economic base in the country and push ahead with immigration as fast as possible, despite Arab objections. Those Palestinian Arabs – by no means the majority – who followed Haj Amin al-Husseini, the extremist Mufti of Jerusalem, were determined to halt Jewish immigration by violence. Fellow-Arabs who opposed them were denounced as traitors and even killed. The attacks on Jews were widespread. In Hebron, sixty Jews – men, women and children – were killed during a five-hour assault on the Jewish quarter. In a Jerusalem suburb, Agnon's house was set on fire and all his books and manuscripts destroyed. In Motza, a village just outside Jerusalem, six Jews were killed in their homes and their bodies mutilated. Thousands of homes were looted. Arthur Ruppin, seeing the ruins of the Jewish village of Huldah, wrote in his diary: 'I remembered what hopes we had when we built the first house there twenty years ago. But I was not depressed: we shall rebuild what has been destroyed. On the whole, it is strange that I am one of the few optimists. I have a profound mystical belief that our work in Palestine cannot be destroyed.'

Ruppin was convinced that a Jewish community in Palestine would not only continue to exist, but would also 'animate Jewry in the Diaspora'. That Diaspora was alive with creative vigour in the 1920s. In 1926 a Luxembourg-born Jew, Hugo Gernsback, founded the first science fiction magazine in the United States, *Amazing Stories*. Today the annual award for the best science fiction is known as the Hugo Award. In 1921 a Jewish woman became the first woman Senator in the newly independent Irish parliament. Born in London as Ellen Bischoffsheim, it was as Lady Desart, the wife of an Irish Catholic aristocrat, that she devoted herself to Ireland's well-being, and was active in protecting and enhancing Irish culture.

Destruction. (*Oppsite*) *A British Mandate policeman, wearing Turkish-style astrakhan headgear, stands guard by a synagogue desecrated by Arab rioters in Hebron in 1929. There were then 700 Jews in Hebron, living among 16,000 Arabs, but all left after the massacre of sixty from number. When a small Jewish presence was restored in 1967 it caused resentment among the local Arabs, although the town contains the Cave of Machpelah, traditionally bought by Abraham, the father of both the Jews and the Arabs, in which to bury his wife Sarah, and in which he is also buried, as well as his son Isaac and his grandson Jacob. There was a continuous Jewish presence in Hebron for at least five hundred years before 1929, but since the mid-thirteenth century the Muslim rulers of Palestine had refused to allow Jews to visit Abraham's tomb, a rule that was enforced until the mid-nineteenth century.*

In the United States, the world of arts and entertainment saw an upsurge in Jewish participation in the 1920s. When the decade began, Arnold Schoenberg brought atonal music to California. Also in 1920, the Russian-born violinist Jascha Heifetz made his first commercial gramophone record. George Gershwin's 'Rhapsody in Blue' was first heard in 1924, the year in which Samuel Goldwyn – born Shmuel Gelbfisz, in Warsaw, and initially changing his name to Goldfish – founded the Gold-Wyn film studio, later Metro-Goldwyn-Mayer. Among his illogical aphorisms and malapropisms were 'Monogamy is OK in the office but at home I prefer white pine', 'A verbal contract is not worth the paper it's written on', 'Anyone who visits a psychiatrist should have his head examined' and 'Include me out'.

Mixed marriages were increasingly common among wealthy American Jews, as was total denial of one's Jewishness. Jimmie Speyer, inheritor of a large Jewish fortune, was proud of his surname, gave liberally to Jewish charities, and yet insisted that he was not a Jew: he was a member of the prestigious Racquet Club, where Jews were not even welcome as guests. Speyer was married to a Christian woman, Ellin Prince, who could trace her ancestry back to Colonial America. He was so proud of his wife's origins that in his listing in *Who's Who* he included her parents' name, and even her mother's maiden name, but omitted the names of his own parents, Eduard Gompertz and Sophie Rubino Speyer. So hostile could the aristocratic German-born Jews of the United States be towards their fellow Jews from Russia that when Weizmann – himself Russian born – went on his first fund-raising trip to the United States, in the first years of the Mandate, he was advised to take a well-known German-born Jew with him. He took two: Albert Einstein and Arthur Ruppin. This tactic was a success.

The dark side of life could also be found among American Jews, as among all peoples. Jewish gangsters were active in exploiting alcohol prohibition by bootlegging. One of them, Meyer Lansky – who had come to the United States in 1911 after a pogrom in his home town, Grodno, in Russian Poland – acted as the Jewish mobsters' accountant, and also dealt in illegal drugs. The Jewishness of these gangsters was never hidden; it was at a Bar Mitzvah that

Lansky first met Arnold Rothstein, considered by some as the first major American drug dealer. When Rothstein died in 1928 – shot in the stomach by someone to whom he had lost money at cards – his empire was taken over by his Jewish lieutenant, Louis Lepke, who operated an opium-manufacturing plant in Brooklyn. In dramatic contrast to the life and work of Jewish criminals, Louis Marshall, the Jewish judge who in 1903 had sought to mitigate the plight of Russian Jews, intervened in 1922 to prevent Harvard imposing a quota on Jewish students, and campaigned against Henry Ford's anti-Semitic newspaper the *Dearborn Independent*, obtaining a formal apology from Ford in 1927.

One of the most famous American Jews of his time, whose name became a household word, was the escape artist Harry Houdini. Born in Budapest (as Erik Weiss), his father was a rabbi who had emigrated to the United States when his son was only a few months old. As well as his magic tricks, which included making an elephant disappear, Houdini was a vociferous public opponent of mind-readers and mediums, insisting that they were charlatans who deceived those who were vulnerable. He was willing, however, to make a plan with his wife Beatrice that whoever died first would try to get in touch

'The World's Greatest Magician'. *Harry Houdini preparing for an underwater escape. He chose the stage name Houdini to remind his audiences of the great French magician, Robert-Houdin, who had died in 1871, three years before his own birth. Houdini was the founder of both the Society of American Magicians and the London Magicians' Club. One of his exploits involved escaping from an 'escape-proof' police van in Russia. He refused to divulge his secrets, which went to the grave with him.*

with the other. He died in 1926; shortly before her death seventeen years later she announced that the experiment had failed.

In 1924, Russian-born Serge Koussevitzky became head of the Boston Symphony Orchestra, a position he held for twenty-five years. A champion of new music, and of American composers, he premiered works by Aaron Copland, Samuel Barber and William Schuman. Later he established the Berkshire Music Centre at Tanglewood. In 1927 Oscar Hammerstein wrote the libretto for *Show Boat*. That same year the Warner brothers transformed the whole art of film by producing the first talking picture, *The Jazz Singer*, which included Irving Berlin's song 'Blue Skies', and starred Al Jolson, who had been born Asa Yoelson in Russia. When Jolson died he left ninety per cent of his fortune to charity, insisting that it should be divided equally among Jewish, Protestant and Catholic institutions.

Jewish intellectual and scientific achievement spanned all national borders. The biochemist Casimir Funk, born in Warsaw, and working in Berlin and London before the First World War, when he discovered vitamins, continued his work in the United States after 1915. He was a pioneer in researching male and female sex hormones, diabetes and the hormone insulin. Working in Copenhagen, Niels Bohr, whose mother was Jewish, won the

Broadway's cantor. *Al Jolson wearing his 'black and white minstrel' make-up. His father, a synagogue cantor, gave him and his brother voice lessons as soon as they could talk, hoping they would follow in his footsteps, but they ran away from home in their teens to try their luck in show business. Jolson made his first stage appearance in Israel Zangwill's play* Children of the Ghetto. *Then, on the Vaudeville circuit, he adopted the 'blackface' minstrel act for which he became famous.*

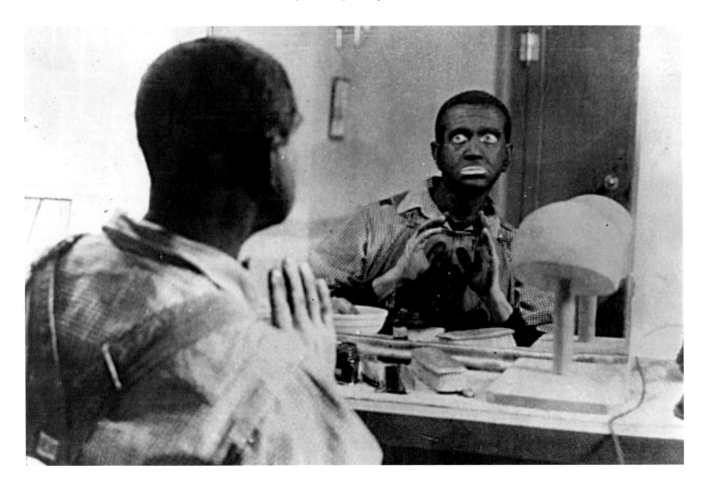

Champion. *Harold Abrahams lunges for the line (left) at the British Amateur Athletics championship, 1924. Recalling his Olympic victory in the same year, he later wrote that one reason 'why I hardened myself to win was that there was a certain amount of anti-Semitism in those days... I felt I had become something of an outsider'. In 1936 he refused to boycott the Berlin Olympics, believing that he could better help German Jews through his contacts in the sporting world, and he broadcast for the BBC from the opening of the Olympics, in Hitler's presence.*

Cheering them on. *Arpad Blody and Walter Frankl in 1928 (right), at the Ha'koach Sports Club championship in Vienna, an annual Jewish sporting event. Frankl, on the right, won several Austrian national championships in the 1920s. Koach is the Hebrew word for strength.*

Nobel Prize for Physics in 1922. Five years later, in Paris, the philosopher Henri Bergson, descended from a Hassidic family, won the Nobel Prize for Literature. In his later years he was attracted to Catholicism, which he considered to be the 'fulfilment' of Judaism, but refused to be converted because of the prevalence of anti-Semitism in Europe, including Catholic anti-Semitism. 'I want to be among those who will be persecuted', he said. When the Vichy French authorities offered him the status of 'honorary Aryan' he refused. Instead, at the age of eighty-two, he insisted on standing in line with his fellow-Jews to be registered, an effort which hastened his final illness.

The 1920s also saw a flourishing of sporting activities among Jews. The Bar Kochba Club, the first Jewish national sports club in Germany and Central Europe, which had been established in 1898, was so successful in the 1920s that many Jews left their non-Jewish athletic clubs to join it. By the end of the decade it had 5,000 members. Also during the 1920s, Maccabi Sports Clubs were established throughout Europe, with fierce competitive zeal being shown every four years at the Maccabi Games, or Maccabiah – known among Jews as 'the Jewish Olympics', and recognised by the International Olympic Committee. In 1928 the Maccabi Games were held in Vienna; four years later a specially built stadium in Tel Aviv, the first stadium in Palestine since Roman times, was ready to host it. Ideologically inspiration came from the words of Theodore Herzl's deputy, Max Nordau – a physician – who in 1898

had told the second Zionist Congress that 'gymnastics and physical training are exceedingly important for us Jews, whose greatest defect has been a lack of discipline'. Nordau believed, as he told his fellow Jewish delegates, that 'nature has endowed us with the spiritual qualities required for athletic achievements of an extraordinary quality. All we lack is muscle, and that can be developed with the aid of physical exercises.' Nordau's philosophy was clear and bold: 'The more Jews achieve in the various branches of sport, the greater will be their self-confidence and respect.'

It was at the Olympic Games that Jewish athletes made their most impressive mark. At the Paris Olympics in 1924 a British Jew, Harold Abrahams, won the 100-metre dash, the first European to win an Olympic sprint title. An American Jew, Jackie Fields (born Jacob Finkelstein), won a gold medal for boxing while only sixteen years old at the same games. He later said of his youth in Chicago: 'Being in the ghetto you had to fight.' A Finnish Jew, Elias Katz, also won a gold medal in 1924 as a member of his country's 3,000 metre cross-country team, as well as a silver medal in the 3,000 metre steeplechase. That same year Victor ('Viki') Barna, a Hungarian Jew, played his first game of table tennis – at a Bar Mitzvah party. Within the next five years he was to win five singles titles and seven world team championships.

The beginning of the 1920s saw the climax of the boxing career of Benny Leonard (born Benjamin Leiner). The son of Orthodox Jews, he had become the world lightweight boxing champion in 1917. As a young boy in New York he won local Jewish plaudits when he attacked with his bare fists a group of non-Jewish boys who were beating up an elderly Jewish woman in the street;

Spreading the word. *The Hungarian-born Samuel Fischer, who founded Fischer Verlag in 1886 in Berlin, the publishing house that numbered Thomas Mann, Herman Hesse and Sigmund Freud among its authors.*

Foreboding. *Franz Kafka. Born to an assimilated Jewish family in Prague, he studied Hebrew and Jewish history, contemplated settling in Palestine, and expressed concern about an impending Jewish catastrophe. He died in 1924, aged 41, and his posthumously published allegories,* The Trial *and* The Castle, *speak for the lot of the individual in the totalitarian decades that followed.*

he quickly became known as 'the champion of Eighth Street'. He retired in 1924 after eight years as world champion. 'My mother was so happy,' he recalled. 'I was twenty-nine, practically a millionaire, and without a scratch.' This was the same mother who, when he had told her that he wanted to become a boxer, had exclaimed: 'A Prizefighter you want to be? Is that a life for a respectable man? For a Jew?' So as not to upset his mother, he never fought on a Jewish holiday. His open Jewishness, and his success in the ring, made him the most famous Jewish personality in America; an editor of Hearst newspapers once said of him: 'He has done more to conquer anti-Semitism than a thousand textbooks.'

German-born Phil Wolf, a member of the American Bowling Congress, won his third American bowling title in 1928 playing for a Chicago team. He was noted for his 'cold demeanour' in wearing down his opponents. Charlotte Epstein, known as 'the mother of women's swimming in America', fought successfully for the inclusion of women's swimming at the 1920 Antwerp Olympics. The success of her efforts on behalf of women athletes also led to the inclusion of women in subsequent Olympic track and field events. At the 1928 Amsterdam Olympics a German athlete, Helene Meyer, whose father was Jewish, won a gold medal at fencing.

For Jews in the Americas, Britain and western Europe, the 1920s were a decade of growth and opportunity. For Central and Eastern European Jewry they were also years when progress and prosperity seemed on the horizon, but there were also clouds. Shortly before his death in 1924, the Czech-Jewish writer Franz Kafka wrote of the life of the Jew in the second decade of the twentieth century: 'Not one calm second is granted to the Western Jew. Everything has to be earned, not only the present and the future but also the past – something after all which perhaps every human being has inherited – this too must be earned; it is perhaps the hardest work.'

CHAPTER FOUR

CHALLENGE AND RESPONSE

1930-1939

FOR MUCH OF THE JEWISH WORLD THE 1930S BEGAN with a sense of relief. The Arab attacks in Palestine in 1929 had not been renewed. The Jews of Europe were participating in national life at the highest levels. In the United States the children of immigrants who had come at the turn of the century were emerging as fully-fledged Americans. In almost every country where Jews lived it seemed the dawn of a golden age. Even in the Soviet Union, where the Communist regime allowed no independent manifestations of Jewishness, there were successful Jewish doctors, engineers, inventors, musicians, even generals: all recognised as being Jewish, even if the regime frowned on Jewish worship and Jewish national aspirations.

In Palestine the steady growth in Jewish national institutions gave credibility to the Zionist claim that it was possible for Jews to behave as any other people, with strong educational and medical programmes, trade unions to protect the workers, savings banks, insurance and pension schemes, and self-defence units. Under the benign eye of the British, the numbers of Jewish immigrants increased each year. Poland still provided the largest single source of immigrants, but no country in the Jewish world was excluded. Each newcomer brought some skill, if only the physical strength of his or her hands, a vital necessity in each new kibbutz: and these were being set up every few months, sometimes three or four in a single month.

Among the newcomers in Palestine in 1930 was Nehama Leibowitz. In her parent's home in Berlin, unusually for the time, modern Hebrew was the daily language. Settling in Jerusalem she became a teacher at a teachers' training college for Orthodox women, teaching Bible for the next sixty-three years; both before and after the establishment of the State of Israel in 1948 she also gave weekly Bible lessons over the radio. Her brown suit and brown beret became a familiar feature to generations of students at the seminar, and also to those whom she taught throughout Israel. When, in 1983, she received an honorary doctorate at Israel's Bar-Ilan University, she refused to wear the

Welcome home. *Members of Kibbutz Ein Harod in the Jezreel valley, on horseback, greet new arrivals from Germany at the nearby railway station – on the Haifa-Damascus railway line – in February 1934.*

traditional cap and gown: instead, it was in her beret and brown suit that she received the award.

A climax to the achievements and also a token of the normality of Jewish life in Palestine came in 1932, when the Maccabiah, the Jewish Olympics, were held in Tel Aviv. Five hundred Jewish athletes participated, including contingents from twenty-three countries. Many of the visitors remained in Palestine after the games, and went on to become permanent residents. Henceforth all the Maccabiahs were held in Palestine – later Israel. But in that same year, Norman Bentwich, who had been Palestine's first Attorney General and had become professor of international relations at the Hebrew University, was heckled by militant students for advocating the idea of a bi-national state during his inaugural lecture.

In Greece the Jewish community was inspired by the success of Jewish enterprise in Palestine. Members of Jewish sports clubs in Greece mirrored the different Zionist political groupings that were striving to win adherents from the ranks of Jewish youth: Labour Zionist, Revisionist and Religious Zionist. In many smaller towns, such as Yoannina, Jews made their livelihoods unhampered by anti-Semitic prejudice, but there was consternation in Salonika when in 1931 a law was passed forbidding children with Greek nationality attending foreign schools before they had completed their elementary education. The twelve Alliance Israelite schools, which almost all Salonika Jewish children attended, were funded by and controlled from France.

Lithuania witnessed a flourishing of Jewish life. Zionism was strong and there were Hebrew-language schools in a dozen towns. In the capital, Kovno, the Revisionist movement was stimulated in 1933 when Jabotinsky visited the town and handed over the Betar flag to his young uniformed followers. Two years later he returned to Kovno, urging emigration to Palestine. In Lithuania, as all over Europe, Britain and the United States, special Hakhshara camps were set up to train youngsters for life in Palestine. Woodcutting, ploughing, growing grain, fruit and vegetables, harvesting – training for secretarial work – were all part of their preparation.

In Germany, the beginning of the 1930s marked a high point of Jewish emancipation and participation in national life. One youngster, Klaus Hugo, later recalled: 'We were Jewish, but had a very liberal upbringing, so until Hitler came to power I never realized I was Jewish. My family had been in Germany for five hundred years or so. My father considered himself one thousand per cent Prussian, and had been a much-decorated cavalry officer.' His father, who was wealthy, had many friends in exploration and aviation, and had sponsored the first German fliers who went east to west across the Atlantic. Even the growing electoral support for Hitler did not deter Jewish enthusiasms. In 1932 the Bar Kochba youth club relay race passed Hitler's headquarters, the Brown House, in Munich; and uniformed Nazis looked on, unable to intervene.

Munich 1932 *Jewish athletes of the Bar Kochba Sports Club run past Hitler's Brown House. Bar Kochba was the leader of a three-year Jewish revolt against Rome in the second century AD.* [PHOTO: TIM GIDAL]

Hitler came to power in Germany on 30 January 1933, and from the first days of the Nazi regime, Germany's Jews faced boycott, isolation, segregation and violence. The portrayal of one section of society as alien, reprehensible and dangerous was undertaken with all the power and authority of the totalitarian state. The fact that there had been a Jewish presence in Germany for more than 1,600 years was no protection, nor that 12,000 German Jews had been killed on active service during the First World War, fighting as an integral part of the patriotic German forces.

149

A normal day. *Three Polish Jewish women in Bedzin in the 1930s. On the right is Rozia Koplowicz, on the left her sister Rywka. They are walking with a friend. All three women are believed to have perished at Auschwitz. This photograph is from an album containing 2,400 family photographs, confiscated by the Nazis on the eve of the deportation. In 1931 there were 21,000 Jews in Bedzin, 45 per cent of the total population. Jews owned chemical works, paint and candle factories, and, most notably, button factories.*

A one-day boycott of Jewish shops throughout Germany took place on 1 April 1933. Hundreds of Jews were arrested, taken to police stations and beaten up, while many in Nuremberg were herded into the sports stadium and made to cut the grass with their teeth. Lady Rumbold, wife of the British Ambassador in Berlin, saw the notices on the shop windows warning the public not to buy there. In many cases there were other notices as well, saying sweated labour was employed in that particular business, or caricatures of Jewish noses. One such arrest was witnessed and photographed by the Jewish photo-journalist Stefan Lorant (see illustration on p. 176), who was himself soon arrested and sent to the newly opened concentration camp at Dachau, just outside Munich. He was fortunate that, as a Hungarian citizen, he was not only able to secure his release but to leave Germany altogether, and within a few years to become the key figure in British photo-journalism, on *Picture Post* magazine. His book *I Was Hitler's Prisoner*, published in 1935, was one of the very first that described the brutal conditions inside a concentration camp. In the first three years of the Nazi regime, forty-five Jews were murdered in Germany in Dachau. At least a hundred more were killed – often beaten to death by sadistic guards – in two other concentration camps, Buchenwald near Weimar, and Sachsenhausen north of Berlin.

In 1935 the Nuremberg Laws made all German Jews second-class citizens. Signed by Hitler, the laws established a barrier between Jews and non-Jews that existed nowhere else in the modern world. Two and a half years of intense anti-Jewish propaganda and the deliberate isolation of Jews from the society of which they had been an integral part were turned, by these Laws, into a strictly enforceable apartheid. Marriages between Jews and non-Jews were forbidden. No Jewish businesses or families could employ a non-Jewish German woman under the age of forty-five. Villages competed with each other to declare themselves 'Jew-free', while a popular song claimed

> When Jewish blood spurts from the knife,
> Then all goes twice as well.

Thirteen further regulations followed the Nuremberg Laws, removing Jews overnight from all official professional life in Germany. In an article for the *Strand* magazine, Winston Churchill protested that the Jews 'were to be stripped of all power, driven from every position in public and social life, expelled from the professions, silenced in the Press, and declared a foul and odious race'. He continued, in a denunciation which provoked an immediate protest from Berlin: 'The twentieth century has witnessed with surprise, not merely the promulgation of these ferocious doctrines, but their enforcement with brutal vigour by the Government and by the populace. No past services, no proved patriotism, even wounds sustained in war, could procure immunity for persons whose only crime was that their parents had brought them into the world. Every kind of persecution, grave or petty, upon the world-famous scientists, writers, and composers at the top down to the wretched little Jewish children in the national schools, was practiced, was glorified, and is still being practiced and glorified.'

Churchill was not exaggerating; a senior member of the British Mandate Administration in Palestine, Eric Mills, who had just completed a tour of Central Europe and Germany, wrote to Jerusalem: 'While before I went to Germany I knew that the Jewish situation was bad, I had not realised as I now do, that the fate of German Jews is a tragedy. Mills reported that the 'cold intelligent planning by those in authority' in Germany against the Jews was similar to that of the Bolsheviks in Russia against their opponents, and the Turks against the Armenians in the First World War.

In the six years following Hitler's coming to power, half of the 600,000 Jews living in Germany found refuge abroad. Einstein was among more than 100,000 German Jews who were allowed to enter the United States, as were two of his fellow Nobel laureates, Otto Meyerhof, a world expert on human

An abnormal day. *Berlin, 1 April 1933. German passers-by read dual-language anti-Jewish posters urging them to ignore 'Jewish atrocity propaganda' and to buy goods 'only at German shops'. This one-day boycott of their shops was one of the first of a growing and accelerating series of privations and persecutions. The posters were translated into English for the foreign press. Hitler made no secret of this racist policy.*

LEFT GERMANY FOR THE USA.
Arnold Schoenberg, one of the innovators of twentieth-century music, champion of the atonal and twelve-note composition. He was brought up as a Christian but returned to Judaism in 1933.

LEFT GERMANY FOR FRANCE.
Lion Feuchtwanger, a popular and pro-lific novelist. His most famous book, Jew Suss, *about an eighteenth-century 'Court Jew' who ended on the scaffold, was an allegory for his times.*

LEFT GERMANY FOR THE USA.
Kurt Weill, composer and conductor, collaborator with Bertold Brecht on The Threepenny Opera. *He left Germany in 1935 with his wife, the singer Lotte Lenya.*

LEFT GERMANY FOR THE USA.
Otto Klemperer, one of the leading German conductors of his generation. Forced to leave Germany in 1933, he became Music Director of the Los Angeles Philharmonic.

LEFT GERMANY FOR BRITAIN, THE USA AND BRAZIL. *Stefan Zweig, writer. He rejected Austrian or Jewish nationalism and despaired of the present; writing biographies let him reaffirm the values of the past.*

LEFT GERMANY FOR THE USA.
Max Reinhardt, theatrical producer and director. He built several theatres in Germany, confiscated in 1933. Later he founded an acting school and theatre workshop in Hollywood.

Before the deluge. *Anne Frank (left) and her sister Margot, in Germany in 1933. Both girls were German Jews, born in Frankfurt am Main. When Hitler came to power their parents fled with them to Holland, where Anne, who was born in 1929, received all her education. In 1942, when the deportations from Holland began, the family hid in an attic in Amsterdam, but two years later were betrayed to the Gestapo and deported to Auschwitz. Anne and Margot died of typhus in Belsen concentration camp in March 1945. Anne's ambition was to become an author. Today her wartime diary is her everlasting monument.*

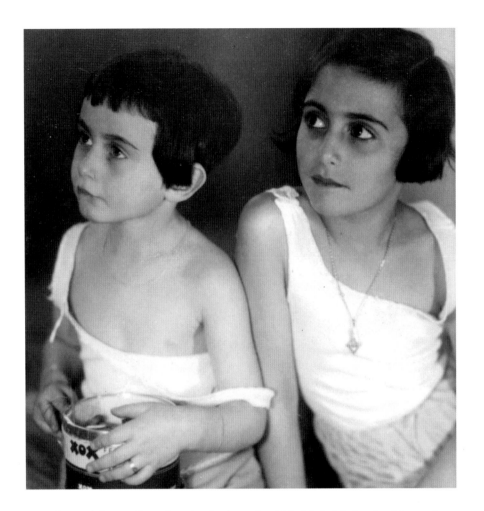

muscle, and James Franck, who had received his Nobel Prize for his work on the structure of matter. Among young German scientists who reached the United States was the nuclear scientist Edward Teller, born to a prosperous Hungarian-Jewish family, who had received his doctorate in Germany and been teaching there from 1931. When President Roosevelt called at the start of the Second World War for scientists to help defend the United States against Nazism, Teller began work on the theoretical studies of the atomic bomb.

From the world of the arts two leading German conductors, Otto Klemperer and Bruno Walter, and Artur Rubinstein, the piano virtuoso, moved to the United States, as did Max Reinhardt, one of the most innovative theatre directors in Berlin, and founder of the Salzburg Festival. Russian-born Roman Vishniac, who had worked in Berlin since 1920, and had travelled from there during the 1930s to photograph Jewish life in Eastern Europe, eventually made his way to the United States in 1940. On the outbreak of war he made his way to France where he was interned in the camp at Gurs near the Pyrenees before managing to leave for America. As a result of German racial policies, the artistic, cultural, financial, political and scientific life of the United States, as well as its warmaking potential, was being massively enhanced.

For those refugees who felt that the greatest safety lay in a land in which Jewish institutions were protected by law – as they had so recently been in Germany – a land with several vibrant Jewish towns and several hundred Jewish villages, Palestine was the preferred destination. More than 80,000 German Jews, many of them small children and youngsters – made their way to Palestine between 1933 and 1939, the beneficiaries of Palestine Certificates issued by the British Mandate authorities. The Palestine Office in Berlin, under Zionist supervision, was a main distribution centre for such certificates. From the first weeks of the Nazi regime in Germany, Henrietta Szold, who had emigrated from the United States to Palestine in 1922, organised youth emigration (Youth Aliyah) from Germany, bringing 30,000 orphans and unaccompanied children to Palestine between 1933 and 1945. Whenever possible she would sit with them in the buses taking them to their new homes, greeting each child personally.

Jewish refugees from Germany contributed to every facet of life in Palestine. The Polish-born painter Mordechai Bronstein, whose artistic success in Germany had just begun when Hitler came to power, became director of the Bezalel Academy in Jerusalem, and in due course one of Israel's best known painters. Later he changed his surname to Ardon. Another Jewish immigrant from Germany, the architect Erich Mendelsohn, designed the Hadassah Hospital on Mount Scopus and Chaim Weizmann's house in the scientific research institute at Rehovot. Among other German Jews reaching Palestine were the philosopher Martin Buber, who had continued with his teaching in Germany until he was banned, and the gynaecologist Bernhard Zondek, the developer of pregnancy testing.

More than 65,000 German Jews found refuge in Britain. Some, recent graduates, students and children, were to do their most productive work in Britain. Berlin-born Ernst Chain was a biochemist who isolated and purified penicillin – for which he later won a Nobel Prize – in time for it to be of inestimable value to the Allied soldiers in the fight against Germany, healing wounds that would otherwise have killed them. Ludwig Guttmann, who left Germany in 1939, pioneered the treatment of spinal injuries, reducing the death rate among British soldiers wounded in the spine from eighty to ten per cent. When the war ended a British Minister said, with reference to Guttmann, 'Thank you, Hitler, for sending us men like these.' The German stage and screen actress Elisabeth Bergner, much loved by audiences in Vienna and Berlin, also fled to Britain. Her first British film was *Catherine the Great*, which was suppressed in Germany because of her 'Jewish' participation in it.

Not only people but also books had to be found a safe haven from the destructive Nazi regime. The library of Aby Warburg, the art historian – who had died in 1929 – was brought to Britain: it consisted of 60,000 books and 20,000 photographs. Another German Jew, Dr Alfred Wiener, brought with

Erich Mendelsohn, *born in East Prussia in 1887, was one of the most innovative architects in Germany before 1933. He served, and saw action, on both the Eastern and Western Fronts in the First World War, where he spent his spare time making architectural sketches which verged on the sculptural, with their emphasis on streamlined curves and outlines. With Hitler's rise to power he emigrated to England, and then lived in Palestine, before moving to the United States in 1941.* [PHOTO: TIM GIDAL]

The Einstein Tower and Observatory *in Potsdam, the only realisation of the ideas in Mendelsohn's wartime sketches, was built to facilitate study of Einstein's theory of relativity. The lonely figure on the path is in fact Einstein. Mendelsohn also designed the Metal Workers' Union headquarters in Berlin and the Schocken department stores in Nuremberg and Stuttgart, making imaginative use of glass. After leaving Germany in 1933, his buildings included the seaside Art Deco de la Warr Pavilion in Bexhill, on the south coast of England, the Maimonides Hospital in San Francisco and a synagogue in Cleveland, Ohio, with a dome one hundred feet in diameter.*

him to Britain his collection of books, pamphlets, photographs and documents describing in detail the earliest years of the Nazi regime. For the next seventy years his library, re-established in London, and later part re-located at Tel Aviv University, served as a focal point of research and study.

While Hitler was rapidly consolidating his power in Germany, the Zionists in Palestine continued with equal speed to expand the existing Jewish settlements, to establish new ones, and to welcome the German Jewish refugees as a source of strength in every profession and walk of life. Kibbutz Ein Harod, in the Jezreel valley, was among those that welcomed German Jewish youngsters. On the kibbutz, farming and defence went side by side. Moshe Dayan, then aged twenty-two, worked in the fields of Nahalal, and also patrolled in the area as a member of the Jewish Settlement Police. Colonel Orde Wingate, a British officer – a devout Christian who always carried his Bible with him on military operations, and later famous as the founder of the Chindit commandos in the Burmese jungle – taught new defence tactics to the Jews of Palestine, initiating Special Night Squads that would leave the

defensive perimeter of the kibbutz and strike out across the fields to catch Arab raiders before they could attack.

Jewish religious life flourished in Palestine. A Latvian-born Rabbi, Abraham Isaac Kook, who in 1904 had emigrated to Palestine to become rabbi of Jaffa, was appointed the first Ashkenazi Chief Rabbi (there was also a Sephardi Chief Rabbi) of Mandate Palestine in 1921. An advocate of the synthesis of religious and secular studies, his influence on Orthodox Judaism in Palestine was considerable. It was his belief that Jews in the Diaspora were cut off from a 'normal' Jewish existence, and that the 'holiness of exile' – impressive though it was – should be replaced by the 'normal' holiness of life in the Land of Israel.

Tens of thousands of Jews were entering Palestine each year, from almost every country in Europe, from the Americas and South Africa. Only the Soviet Union had a policy of not allowing Jews to leave. The British Mandate authorities welcomed Jews who had some capital, or who were coming as students, or as trained farmers, or with enough capital to set up a small business. This latter category brought in middle-class enterprise and modernity. The streets of Tel Aviv became more and more bustling, and more and more European.

In 1934 more than 42,000 Jews entered Palestine, mostly from Germany and Poland. In 1935 the number of immigrants was 61,000. The Arabs protested that the arrival of so many Jews – more than 100,000 in two years – would lead to the dispossession of the Arab inhabitants. Since the 1922 White Paper the British government had been committed not to admit more immigrants into Palestine than the country's 'economic absorptive capacity' would allow. Examining this argument in its 1937 report, a British Royal Commission concluded: 'So far from reducing economic absorptive capacity, immigration increased it. The more immigrants came in, the more work they created for local industries to meet their needs, especially in building: and more work meant more room for immigrants under the "labour schedule". Unless, therefore, the Government adopted a more restrictive policy, or unless there were some economic or financial set-back, there seemed no reason why the rate of immigration should not go on climbing up and up.' Arab readers of the report refused to accept its argument, and would have been equally dismissive of Vladimir Jabotinsky's plea to the Commission: 'When the Arab claim [to Palestine] is confronted with our Jewish demand to be saved, it is like the claim of appetite versus the claim of starvation.'

Tolerance from the pulpit. *Chief Rabbi Kook speaking at his Yeshiva – religious academy – in Jerusalem. A visitor recalled: 'I remember him... defending the irreligious for their self-sacrifice in draining the swamps and giving their lives that Israel might be reborn... I remember too his famous football dictum which I heard him give, in Yiddish of course, that the game was permissible on Shabbat but not for money or for tickets...'*
[PHOTO: TSADOK BASSAN]

Confronted by persistent Arab opposition to Jewish immigration on the existing scale, the British government began to seek an upper limit on the number who could come in. Churchill, who in 1922 had given the pledge that the Jews were in Palestine 'of right and not on sufferance', opposed any limit, but was no longer in government. On 24 March 1936 he told the House of Commons that in the minds of those non-Jews like him there was 'an added emphasis upon this question of Jewish migration which comes from other quarters, at a time when the Jewish race in a great country is being subjected to most horrible, cold, scientific persecution, brutal persecution, a cold "pogrom" as it has been called ... their little children pilloried in the schools to which they have to go; their blood and race declared defiling and accursed ... I say that, when that is the case, surely the House of Commons will not allow the one door which is open, the one door which allows some relief, some escape from these conditions, to be summarily closed.'

Extraction of mineral salts *at Ashdot Ya'akov, on the Jordan river south of the Sea of Galilee. Two kibbutzim were founded here in 1933. The warm climate enabled intensive farming of citrus fruits and bananas. The name combines the Hebrew word Ashdot ('waterfalls') and Jacob – in gratitude to James de Rothschild, a British patron of settlements in the region.*

[PHOTO: AVRAHAM MALAVSKY]

MODERNIST ARCHITECTURE

in Palestine. Apartments (far left) in Tel Aviv betraying the influence of the German Bauhaus movement in their stripped-down functionalism, though making concessions to heat and sun with recessed balconies and hooded windows. An Egyptian Airlines biplane (Misr Airways) at Palestine's main airport (above), just outside Lydda. After Israeli independence it was called Lod (the Hebrew version of Lydda), and more recently Ben Gurion Airport. A Ford garage (below) offers 'Service' in Arabic, English and Hebrew.

[PHOTO OPPOSITE: ITZHAK KALTER]

[PHOTOS THIS PAGE: A. HIMMELREICH]

WORK AND PLAY. *A lunch-break during fruit picking (top left) at Ein Harod in the Jezreel Valley. Much of the fruit was for export, an important source of revenue for the kibbutz. Men and women shared the tasks side by side. A member of* a kibbutz (left) in the communal kitchen, *carrying out the duties that were shared equally among all the members. A Tel Aviv restaurant (above), where cosmopolitan standards were maintained, with waiters, tablecloths and hats for the ladies at* lunchtime – a sight that would have delighted Theodor Herzl who dreamt of *transplanting 'genuine Viennese cafés to Palestine'.*

[PHOTO OPPOSITE BELOW: WALTER ZADEK]

[PHOTO ABOVE: TIM GIDAL]

The British government still maintained that Palestine was not a suitable place for any substantial additional number of Jewish refugees. For their part, the Palestinian Arab leaders made it clear that they were opposed to Palestine being made a haven for any more European refugees whatsoever. They regarded even the existing number as too large, pointing out that in the four years since 1933 the Jewish population of Palestine had increased from 230,000 to 400,000, reaching one third of the total population. In protest against any further Jewish immigration the Arabs began a general strike on 15 April 1936. On May 7 their leaders, meeting in Jerusalem, demanded an immediate end to all Jewish immigration, a ban on any further Jewish land purchase, and an Arab majority government to replace British rule. Throughout Palestine,

Precautions. *On the day of the establishment of a kibbutz, a watchtower was erected, around which the tents and huts would then be placed, to protect them from any hostile Arab attack.* [PHOTO: WALTER ZADEK]

Defending the kibbutzim. *A unit of Jewish Settlement Police cavalry, on patrol near the settlement of Nahalal, in the Jezreel valley, December 1938, determined to forestall any attack before it could reach its objective.*

Jewish farms were attacked, Jewish houses were burnt, shops looted, and orchards destroyed. Within a month twenty-one Jews had been killed, among them women and children.

The British responded to this Arab violence by announcing that they intended 'to suppress all outbreaks of lawlessness', and six Arab rioters were killed by the British police. The Jewish Agency urged the Jews to exercise restraint, and, although eighty Jews had been killed by October, no Jewish reprisals took place. British troops, however, killed more than 140 Arabs, and thirty-three British soldiers were killed in armed clashes with them.

For the Jews it was galling to see what little effect British protection could have. During the summer of 1936 thousands of Jewish-cultivated acres were destroyed, Jews were killed while travelling in buses, and even in their homes. Levi Billig, an emigrant from England, was studying medieval Arabic manuscripts from a distant era of Muslim-Jewish harmony, when he was stabbed

Repression and revolt. *Aproned and kilted British troops from a Scottish regiment – the Cameron Highlanders – on guard at the Citadel, at the entrance to the Old City of Jerusalem (below), at the start of the Arab uprising, 10 June 1936. (left) Smoke pouring from blazing Jewish houses, set on fire by Arab terrorists at Tel Aviv (right), 15 September 1936.*

from behind while working at his desk, his books and manuscripts spattered with his blood as he died. As a gesture of solidarity with the Jews of Palestine, Arturo Toscanini –who was not Jewish – made a special visit to Palestine, where he conducted the Palestine Philharmonic Orchestra in a number of concerts. Many of its musicians were recent immigrants from Germany. Despite the riots and the dangers of travel on the roads, Jewish artistic life flourished. Gertrud Kraus, a member of the Dance Macabre modern dance ensemble, was billed as the Isadora Duncan of Palestine. New settlements continued to be set up, as more and more Jews, particularly from Germany and Poland, entered the country.

A new movement threatened to polarise the Jewish community in Palestine – the 'Yishuv'. Discontented with what he considered ineffective defence measures carried out by the official Jewish underground – the Hagannah ('defence') forces – the Revisionist leader Vladimir Jabotinsky encouraged the establishment of a specifically Revisionist underground force, the Irgun Tzvai Leumi – the National Military Organisation, known by its Hebrew initials as the IZL, or Etzel. It believed in reprisals for Arab attacks. The Jewish Agency, which administered the Jewish national institutions in Palestine, continued to press for a policy of 'restraint', and when the Irgun

Showing solidarity *Arturo Toscanini with the founder of the Palestine Philharmonic Orchestra, Bronislaw Huberman, at its inaugural concert in Tel Aviv on 26 December, 1936. Huberman, a brilliant, world-famous violinist, had raised money with speeches and concerts to fund the orchestra.* [PHOTO: WEISSENSTEIN]

began a series of retaliatory raids against the Arabs in 1936, David Ben Gurion, head of the Jewish Agency, condemned all reprisals and called Jabotinsky 'Hitler'. The Hagannah argued that retaliation killed innocent people on both sides, as well as weakening the prospect of agreement with the Arabs.

Travelling through eastern Europe, Jabotinsky reiterated his call for the mass emigration of Polish and Lithuanian Jews to Palestine. Although tens of thousands did emigrate, this was on a far smaller scale than he had hoped: he always spoke of a million and a half immigrants. Ironically, many Polish Jews, while hoping to live in Palestine at some future date, and while learning modern Hebrew in school in Poland, hesitated to take what they saw as the undue risk of moving to a land in turmoil.

In Poland itself, the conflict between fending off the indignities of anti-Semitism, and maintaining a vigorous Jewish existence, was continuous. So numerous were the Jews of Poland – more than three million when Hitler came to power – that they were known as 'the Jewish Nation in Poland'. They had innumerable newspapers and magazines, Socialist and Zionist groupings, theatrical troupes, musical groups and film companies, charitable organisations and sports clubs. In 1936 the tragi-comic film *Yidl mit'n Fidl* (Yiddle with his Fiddle), starring Molly Picon, showed scenes in village Poland and in Warsaw. Molly Picon herself was born in New York at the end of the nineteenth century, the daughter of an immigrant from Warsaw. She had given her first stage performance in 1903, at the age of five, and between the wars was the leading star of New York's Yiddish musicals. She also appeared in dozens of films, from *East and West* in 1923 to *Fiddler on the Roof* in 1970. Recalling the inter-war heyday of the Yiddish theatre she wrote: 'Yiddish is more than a language. It means warmth, family feeling, togetherness, the custom of charity.'

Starting in 1935, pogroms in Poland threatened to set back much of what had been achieved in the acceptance of Polish Jews by their predominantly Catholic fellow-Poles. In 1936 a Polish Jesuit periodical asserted the need 'to provide separate schools for Jews, so that our children will not be infected with their lower morality'. The Catholic Primate of Poland wrote in a pastoral letter to his flock: 'The Jews are fighting against the Catholic Church, persisting in free thinking, and are the vanguard of godlessness, Bolshevism and subversion.' The Jews were defended by a leading Roman Catholic, Cardinal Hlond, who declared in a pastoral letter: 'It is true that the Jews are committing frauds, practising usury, and dealing in white slavery. It is true that in schools the influence of the Jewish youth upon the Catholic youth is generally evil, from a religious and ethical point of view. But let us be just. Not all Jews are like that. One does well to prefer his own kind in commercial dealings and to avoid Jewish stores, and Jewish stalls in the market, but it is not permissible to demolish Jewish businesses, break windows, blow up their houses...' Not all Poles reacted with moderation to this somewhat mixed message. Five weeks after the Cardinal had called for restraint, three Jews were murdered by a Polish mob in the village of Przytyk in central Poland.

The 'Przytyk pogrom' sent a wave of fear through Polish Jewry. Within a week, five Jews were murdered in the village of Stawy, not far from Cracow. In several dozen villages, Jews took up sticks, knives and cudgels in self-defence, and managed to drive away the attackers. Similar defensive action had also happened in Przytyk, but the mob there, confronted by the Jewish defenders, had retreated from the centre of the village and attacked a Jewish house on the outskirts, killing its inhabitants. In August 1937 alone there were 350 attacks on Jews and Jewish property. In the three years during which these pogroms took place, seventy-nine Jews were killed. Tens of thousands of Polish Jews emigrated: to France, Belgium and Holland, and to Palestine.

In Romania, members of the fascist Iron Guard prevented Jewish students from entering the lecture halls. Synagogues and Jewish schools were looted and Jewish cemeteries desecrated. From 1934 Jewish lawyers were no longer allowed to enter the legal profession. In 1936 the Iron Guard exploded a bomb in a Jewish theatre in Timisoara: two Jews were killed and many more injured. In January 1938 Romania repealed the minority rights granted to Jews under the Minority Treaties of the League of Nations. Four months later the Hungarian government passed its first law restricting the number of Jews who could find employment in the liberal professions, the administration of the country, commerce or industry. Eleven months after these first legal restrictions, a second 'Jewish law' was passed by the Hungarian parliament forbidding any Hungarian Jew from becoming a judge, a lawyer, a schoolteacher or a member of Parliament. A bomb thrown into a Budapest synagogue shortly before this second law was passed killed one worshipper and injured dozens more. Lithuanian universities, where anti-Semitism was also to be found lurking in the higher ranks of the professorial body, decided in 1936 that not a single Jewish student be admitted that year to study medicine.

Anti-Semitism also found an outlet in Britain in 1936, when the British Union of Fascists planned a provocative march into the predominantly Jewish East End of London. The Jews gathered in self-defence, barricades were erected, large numbers of police protected the marchers, and the defenders were caught up in several violent skirmishes with the police. But the marchers withdrew, no one was killed, and the marchers had failed to enter the East

The Przytyk Pogrom. *Members of the Jewish self-defence group in Przytyk stand guard during bread distribution in the village, a few days after the Polish attack of 9 March 1936, when three Jews were killed. The incident was followed by further pogroms throughout Poland, and similar self-defence efforts.*

Polish persecution. *Jewish-owned homes and shops set on fire during anti-Jewish riots twenty miles east of Warsaw, at the town of Minsk Mazowiecki, on 6 June 1936. A Jewish self-defence group beat off their assailants here.*

End streets through which they had been determined to march. 'That night,' wrote William Fishman, a sixteen-year-old member of the Labour Party League of Youth at the time, 'there was dancing in the pubs and in the side streets of the East End.' In the following year a court in Switzerland made legal history by declaring the pre-First World War anti-Semitic book, the alleged *Protocols of the Elders of Zion*, to be 'ridiculous nonsense'.

In the Soviet Union, throughout the time of Stalin's purges, Jews among the victims included the writer Isaac Babel, the poet Iosip Mandelshtam and the soldier Marshal Tukhachevsky. One prominent Jew left unmolested was Lazar Kaganovich, the Party 'trouble shooter' whom Stalin put in charge of building the Moscow underground, each of whose main stations had, at Stalin's urging, the apparance and dimensions of a marble palace; another was Yemelyan Yaroslavsky (born Gubelman), Chairman of the League of Militant Godless, the Party organisation which campaigned on behalf of atheism and conducted propaganda against all religions.

From the outset of the Spanish Civil War in 1936, the Soviet Union, seeing in General Franco's Nationalist insurgency the dread hand of Fascism, gave active support to Republicans. Individual Soviet Jews were prominent in the Soviet contingent, among them Lev Manevitch, who was to win the highest Soviet award for bravery in the Second World War. Hungarian-born Emil Kléber (a nom de guerre taken from the French revolutionary general – his real name was Lazar Stern), who had been trained in the Soviet Union, commanded the volunteer International Brigade. From the United States, more

than a thousand Jews volunteered to fight in Spain, ten per cent of the total number of American volunteers. 'Don't you realise,' wrote one of them, Hyman Katz, to his mother, after he had been wounded, 'that we Jews will be the first to suffer if Fascism comes?' Katz was killed in action in 1938. A great many American Jews were killed at the battle of Brunete outside Madrid in July 1937. Dr Edward Barsky, a surgeon at the Beth Israel Hospital in New York, volunteered as a battlefield doctor for the Republicans. Returning to the United States after Franco's victory, hundreds of wounded volunteers were helped by the generosity of Bernard Baruch. Several hundred British and French Jews also fought for the doomed Republic. Lou Kenton, whose parents had fled to Britain before the First World War from the Russian pogroms, and who had himself fought against Mosleyites in the East End, drove an ambulance between hospitals and the front line, and distributed medical supplies on his motorbike. Alfred Sherman, who fought in three major actions, was, forty years later one of the leading architects of the policies of the British Conservative leader Margaret Thatcher.

In France, a Jew, Léon Blum, headed the French Popular Front government, despite his refusal to support the Republicans in Spain, and introduced widespread social reforms. His opponents on the far right of French politics had no hesitation in using anti-Semitism as a weapon against him. The liberal nature of Blum's government made France an attractive place for Jewish refugees from Germany.

The United States' quota of 20,000 people from any one country in any one year constituted the most generous of immigration policies. Among the more than 100,000 German Jews that made their way there was Henry Kissinger, who left Germany with his parents when he was fifteen. After President Roosevelt came to power in 1933, the New Deal – a nationwide policy of public works and creative projects to combat the effects of the Depression – was at the centre of United States policy. One of those who helped Roosevelt most closely was Felix Frankfurter, who had reached

Entente: *Léon Blum and his wife, on arrival at Croydon aerodrome, London, for a conference on 23 July 1936 between Britain, France and Belgium, to discuss German intentions in Europe. His increased spending on armaments was disliked by many of his own left wing.*
[PHOTO: G. ADAMS]

On set. *Hungarian-born film director, Alexander Korda. In 1919 he was one of the heads of the motion picture organisation in Bela Kun's Communist regime. His first major British film success was* The Private Life of Henry VIII, *starring Charles Laughton, in 1933. He gave employment to many actors fleeing from Hitler. His film* Lady Hamilton, *starring Vivien Leigh, was a patriotic rallying call for Britain in 1940, and a favourite of Churchill's. In 1942 Korda was knighted by King George VI, the first film-producer to be so honoured.*

America from Vienna in 1894, at the age of twelve. He taught at Harvard Law School for twenty-five years, was the founder of the American Civil Liberties Union, as well as legal adviser to the National Association for the Advancement of Coloured People. Another American Jew, New York born Henry Morgenthau Jr, was Secretary of the Treasury both for the period of the New Deal and throughout the Second World War.

Despite the Depression, which wiped out many Jewish businesses with the rest, American Jews flourished throughout the 1930s in the world of arts, literature, entertainment and sport. In 1930 the boxer Maxie Rosenbloom (known as 'Slapsie Maxie') won the world light heavyweight title, holding it for four and a half years. That same year the Marx brothers – Chico, Groucho and Harpo – appeared in *Animal Crackers*. Jack Benny (born Benjamin Kublesky) made his debut as a radio and film comedian. In 1933 Hank Greenberg joined the Detroit Tigers; he was later to have his place in the Baseball Hall of Fame. That same year Eddie Cantor (born Iskowitz) starred in *The Kid from Spain*. Sophie Tucker, who had been born in Russian Poland in 1884, became the leading American figure in both Yiddish and English Vaudeville, known as the 'last of the red hot mamas'. George Gershwin's *Porgy and Bess* was first produced in 1935, the year in which the clarinettist and

"SHOWBIZ." *Samuel Goldwyn (left), born Shmuel Gelbfisz in Warsaw. A film executive extraordinary, he set up his first film company in 1910 in the United States. Actress Vera Gordon on the right, director Bill Nigh, centre, and actor John Gilbert on the left, sitting in chairs inscribed with their names in Yiddish (far left), while filming* Four Walls, *the story of a Jewish boy, 1927. Julius Henry Marx, alias Groucho (bottom left), one of the four Marx brothers, the sons of German Jewish immigrants to New York. Peter Lorre, born Ladislav Lowenstein (bottom centre), a Hungarian actor who studied psychiatry in Vienna under Freud and Adler, then starred in many Hollywood films, including* Casablanca. *Jack Benny and Martha Raye (bottom right) in the film* College Holiday, *1936. Benny Goodman, 'the King of Swing', with guitarist Allan Reuss and the Benny Goodman Orchestra (right) at the Manhattan Room, Hotel Pennsylvania, New York City, 1938. Goodman took his first music lessons at his local synagogue.*

[PHOTO OPPOSITE CENTRE: ELMER FRYE]

band leader Benny Goodman (born Benjamin David Goodman) established himself as the 'King of Swing'. In 1939, as war clouds loomed over Europe, David Selznick produced the film *Gone with the Wind*. Jewish artistic life also flourished elsewhere. In Britain, Alexander Korda's film *The Private Life of Henry VIII* had its premiere in 1933. In Paris the Polish-born harpsichordist Wanda Landowska felt that she was at last ready to give her first complete performance of Bach's Goldberg Variations; she confided to her audience that she had been practising them for forty-five years.

Although each post-immigrant generation in the United States aspired to speak English, and was often embarrassed by the Polish, German, Hungarian or other 'foreign' accents of parents, grandparents, uncles and aunts, the one Diaspora language that did maintain a vibrant life when transported to America was Yiddish. Immigrants for whom it was the language of arts and literature, discourse and humour, business and leisure, gave it a new, vibrant life. The Galician-born actor Alexander Granach, who first presented Yiddish plays in New York in 1931 and emigrated there seven years later, staged a Shylock in Yiddish that was remembered for decades to come. Lithuanian-born Ben Zion Goldberg, who emigrated to the United States at the age of twelve, was for forty years, from 1920 to 1960, a daily columnist on the Yiddish newspaper *The Day*, often angering his readers by his strong support of the Soviet Union. Another Yiddish daily, *Forward*, had Isaac Bashevis Singer – later a Nobel prize winner – among its Yiddish writers.

In Australia, Pinchas Goldhar, who had been born in the Russian-Polish industrial city of Lodz at the beginning of the century, and emigrated to Melbourne, edited Australia's first Yiddish-language weekly newspaper. In Poland, one of the heartlands of Yiddish for four hundred years, the 1930s constituted the great age of Yiddish writing and journalism. Warsaw's two Yiddish daily newspapers, *Haynt* and *Moment*, reached the highest reporting and literary standards. The *Vilna Tog* (Day), which published the Yiddish lyrical poems of Chaim Grade, the Kovno *Yidishe Shtime*, which had a weekly Hebrew-language supplement, and the *Parizer Haynt* in Paris, for which the scholar, poet and jurist Arye Leib Grajewski wrote, each made Yiddish a vehicle for every aspect of modern life and culture. Only the German destruction of so much of the Yiddish-speaking world brought that vibrant linguistic aspect of Jewish life to an end.

For the Jewish world in the 1930s, language, literature and culture were all overshadowed by the persecution of German Jews and their desperate search

A set-up. *A Jew is arrested in a police raid in the Jewish quarter of Berlin, 4 April 1933. The Nazis claimed they were searching for weapons and false identity papers. In fact they were trying to justify the one-day boycott of Jewish shops four days earlier. They had alerted newspapers and radio reporters in advance of the raid. This photograph was taken by Stefan Lorant, who was later arrested and taken to Dachau concentration camp. Being a Hungarian citizen, he was soon released, and emigrated to Britain, where he applied the photo-journalistic skills he had pioneered on the* Münchener Illustrierte Presse *since 1927 to a new weekly magazine* Picture Post, *which he created with Edward Hulton.*

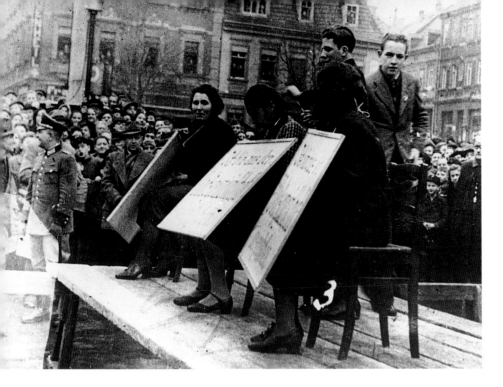

After the Anschluss. *Austrian Jewish women have their hair shorn in Linz, November 1938. The placards read, 'I am excluded from the community.'*

for new homes outside Germany. Gradually, the Jewish refugee replaced the Jewish scholar, rabbi, poet, storyteller, actor or shopkeeper as the stereotype of the twentieth-century Jew. In 1936, Sir Horace Rumbold, former British Ambassador in Germany who had become deputy head of the Commission investigating the future of Palestine, came on an immigrant's hut there in which there was a piano. It dawned on him that not long before the immigrant had performed in a concert at the Berlin embassy. When he suggested that it must have been a terrible change, the musician replied, 'It is a change, from Hell to Heaven.'

In 1938 it became the turn of Austrian Jewry to suffer. Jews had lived in Austria since Roman times, and in the medieval period had undergone persecution and expulsions, but they had always returned until, in 1867, the Austro-Hungarian government abolished all laws based on religious discrimination. For many Jews, participation in national life and prosperity followed. After the defeat and disintegration of Austria-Hungary in the First World War, the 1919 Treaty of St Germain established a shrunken Austria as an independent State, forbade its union with Germany, and guaranteed the Jews minority rights. The vast majority of Austrian Jews, more than 180,000, lived in Vienna, but in 1934 there were 760 towns and villages throughout Austria which had some Jewish inhabitants, including 1,720 in Graz, one of the centres of the Austrian Nazi movement, which was as virulent in its anti-Semitism as that in Germany; some of the most cruel concentration camp commandants and officials of the Holocaust years were Austrian-born.

On 13 March 1938, on Hitler's orders, German troops crossed into Austria. No shots greeted them, only cheers and applause. Those Austrians who opposed Nazism kept well hidden, knowing how ferocious the reprisals could be. Within twenty-four hours Hitler annexed Austria, and introduced the full apparatus of Nazi terror to cement this 'Anschluss'. All Jewish religious, communal and cultural organisations were closed down. Jewish leaders were imprisoned and some were taken to Dachau and murdered. Well-organised hooligans desecrated the Great Synagogue in Vienna, which was then taken over by the German army. Austrian Nazis stopped Jewish students entering the University of Vienna, and seized Jews on the streets, forcing them to scrub the pavements. Jews were forced to stand in front of Jewish shops in Vienna holding placards which said, 'Aryans, don't buy from Jews.' At dusk

HUMILIATIONS. *Hitler Youth (left) supervise an Austrian Jewish 'scrubbing party', forced to remove the slogans of the previous Schuschnigg government from the streets in March 1938 after the Anschluss, while the Viennese look on. Hitler Youth (above) sculpting a Jewish snowman in a Berlin park. They aren't very competent – its star should have six points, not five.*

they were rounded up and taken to some dark alley where their fellow-Austrians were allowed to beat them up.

Many Jews were forced to hand over their property to the Gestapo, an early example of how those who tormented the Jews also made money out of their harshness. Jewish professors were banned from the universities, Jewish teachers forbidden entry to their schools, Jewish scientists denied any further access to their research laboratories. There was such desperation among Jews that more than 300 killed themselves that March, and a further 267 in April.

In the immediate aftermath of the annexation Sigmund Freud, then eighty-two years old and battling cancer, was virtually smuggled out of Vienna by his psychoanalyst colleagues and sent to London. Made a member of the prestigious Royal Society, he was too ill to journey into the centre of London to sign the society's register. Instead, as a mark of respect, the register was brought to him in his new home. Freud reached London together with his youngest daughter Anna, then aged thirty-one, and herself a psychiatrist, specialising in helping young people. In 1943 she founded the Hampstead Clinics for children separated from their parents because of the war; and had eighty children in her residential care.

A young SS officer, Adolf Eichmann, who was considered by his superiors to be an expert on the 'Jewish question' and a competent functionary, was sent to Vienna in August 1938 with the task of facilitating the emigration of Austria's Jews. On average, 8,000 left each month, their non-Jewish neighbours or business rivals, and sometimes former friends, often being the beneficiaries of their life's possessions and hard-earned livelihoods, as the property of those who emigrated was transferred to non-Jews. The Jewish community leaders still in Austria opened training courses to prepare those Jews who remained for life as refugees. Several thousand youngsters were sent to a Zionist-owned farm to receive training in agriculture, before leaving for Palestine.

Of Austria's 180,000 Jews, 128,500 succeeded in emigrating, helped to do so by Eichmann. As emigration was the official policy not only authorised but encouraged from Berlin, he could carry it out with all the bureaucratic efficiency at his command. The largest number of refugees, just over 30,000, went to Britain. Almost as many, 28,600, went to the United States. Just over 9,000 were allowed into Palestine. European countries that were later to be overrun by Germany took in 24,500, many of whom were later deported – also on Eichmann's orders, in pursuit of a new policy – from the countries in which they had hoped to find a haven, to camps and execution sites where they were murdered.

In July 1938, even as emigration from Austria was gaining momentum and that from Germany continuing, many governments who had been most open-handed towards the refugees were confronted by inflamed popular prejudice against allowing in 'too many' foreigners. Meeting at the French resort town of Evian-les-Bains, on the southern shore of Lake Geneva, nation after nation expressed reluctance to take in more than a modest quota of Jewish

Blockade. *One of the Schocken department stores in Germany blockaded by uniformed Nazis, who allowed no one to enter. This photograph was taken in 1939. Salmann Schocken had already emigrated to Palestine, where in 1934 he acquired ownership of the daily newspaper*

Ha'aretz. *In 1931 he had founded a leading Jewish publishing house in Berlin, Schocken Verlag, which published the Nobel Prize-winning novelist S.Y. Agnon. After 1933 Schocken established publishing houses in Tel Aviv (Hebrew books) and New York (English).*

refugees, though Australia agreed to increase its quota. Canada was particularly reluctant, only agreeing to let in a few hundred Jews when tens of thousands were seeking to leave Europe. The British government told the Evian Conference that nowhere in Britain's Colonial Empire was there any territory suitable for the large-scale settlement of Jewish refugees. No mention was made of Palestine until the closing session, when the British representative explained that only 'very limited' immigration there could be considered. For its part, the United States insisted on adhering to its existing quotas, 27,370 refugees a year from Germany and Austria. These were not, in normal times, ungenerous, but the times were no longer normal. Given the American insistence on the letter of the law, it would have taken twenty years – until 1958 – for all the Jews still in Germany to reach asylum in the United States.

Other countries were not willing to take up the shortfall, indeed the United States' decision to maintain its quotas served as a guideline for other countries: the delegate from Peru described the 'wisdom and caution' of the United States as being a 'shining example that guided the immigration policies' of Peru itself. Only Holland, Denmark and the Caribbean republic of Santo Domingo agreed to let in refugees without restrictions.

On the last day of the Evian Conference a resolution was passed which stated that 'the countries of asylum' – such as they were – 'are not willing to undertake any obligation towards financing involuntary emigration'. Other resolutions expressed the conference's 'sympathy' towards the plight of the refugee, Jewish and non-Jewish alike. On the following day a journalist from a Swiss newspaper asked one of the Jews present, Golda Meyerson – later, as Golda Meir, Prime Minister of Israel – for her comments. 'There is one ideal I have in mind,' she replied, 'one thing I want to see before I die - that my people should not need expressions of sympathy any more.'

As Austrian Jews joined German Jews in the mass emigration to Palestine, the violence there continued. On a single day, 19 June 1938, seven Arabs were murdered by fellow-Arab terrorists for the so-called 'crime' of having worked for Jews. One of those murdered was a woman in her last month of pregnancy; another woman had been tied to a tree before being shot dead.

At the beginning of July 1938 the Government of Palestine published its official report for the previous year, warning that public security in Palestine had been 'seriously disturbed by a campaign of murder, intimidation and sabotage conducted by Arab law-breakers'. On 'a few occasions', the report also noted, this campaign had 'provoked Jewish reprisals'. It then pointed out that since 1922 the Arab population of Palestine had increased by 261,000, compared with a Jewish increase of 245,000, and that despite the heavy Jewish immigration of the early and mid-1930s, the Arab population, as a result both its own considerable immigration, and a higher birthrate, had grown by a larger absolute number than the Jewish population. The Report also referred to those Arab tenant farmers who were dispossessed of their land as a result of the sale to Jews of the land which they worked, noting that for the whole of 1937 only six Arab families had claimed to have been dispossessed: and that each had then been settled on Government land as compensation.

Arab attacks on Arabs and Jews continued through the summer. On June 24 two Arabs working in a Jewish-owned stone quarry near Haifa were wounded by Arab raiders. The wounded men were taken to hospital but two of the raiders entered the hospital in search of them, killing by mistake another Arab patient. On June 29 an Arab terrorist threw a bomb at a Jewish wedding party in Tiberias: seven Jews were wounded, including three children.

Sanctuary. *German Jewish refugees at work in a refugee camp in Holland, May 1939. When Germany conquered Holland a year later they were subjected to internment and eventual deportation, mainly to Auschwitz.*

Despite the outspoken opposition of the Jewish leadership, Jewish terrorists struck back in violent acts of reprisal. After nine Jews had been killed by Arabs in June, a single Jewish terrorist threw a bomb which killed twenty-five Arabs in Haifa. The killings and counter-killings continued: on July 21 four Jewish workers were killed at the Dead Sea; four days later, in Haifa, a Jewish terrorist threw a bomb which killed thirty-nine Arabs in the melon market there.

Inside Palestine the Jewish newspaper *Davar* denounced the Jewish reprisals as both 'shameful and calamitous', while the newspaper *Ha'aretz* declared them to be 'a criminal gamble with the fate of the Jewish community'. The Zionist leaders reiterated their condemnation: the terrorists, declared David Ben Gurion, were 'miserable cowards'. Yitzhak Ben Zvi warned that they 'were stabbing the community in the back'. The Histadrut, the Jewish Labour Organisation in Palestine, issued an official manifesto stating that reprisals were 'a disgrace and a madness'.

Arab provocation showed no signs of abating, nor did the Arab leaders issue any appeal for moderation. On July 26 two Jews were killed in Galilee and two in Jerusalem, and in the last week of July there were twenty-seven separate Arab attacks on Jewish villages. Many Jews in Europe, when anti-Semitism erupted around them, nevertheless hesitated to make their way to such a troubled land. It was only after the Munich crisis was over in October, and Britain was able to transfer another division of troops to Palestine, that the revolt died down. Prior to that, seventy massive concrete forts had been built at key points, together with an electrified fence along the northern border. Tracker dogs were imported from South Africa, while sabotage of railway lines was largely stopped by putting hostages from villages along the lines on flat-bed trucks ahead of the engines, so they would be blown up first by any explosives that had been planted.

In October 1938 Germany annexed the predominantly German-speaking Sudeten mountain region of Czechoslovakia. Long-established Jewish communities such as that of Cheb, which could trace its origins to the thirteenth century, were dissolved, and almost all the 20,000 Jews of the Sudetenland fled across the new German border to Bohemia and Moravia, the two western provinces which Hitler allowed to remain in existence as a truncated Czechoslovakia. On the eve of the German annexation, local German-speaking Nazis had burned down the main synagogue in Cheb, and also in Marienbad – the spa town in which Jewish doctors had contributed half a century earlier to the medicinal use of its curative waters.

Also in October 1938 the Polish government took a harsh step, announcing from Warsaw that all Polish Jews who had lived outside Poland for more than five years would have their passports revoked, thereby becoming 'stateless'. Some 17,000 of these Jews had lived and worked in Germany for ten, fifteen, even twenty years. The German government responded at once, announcing that all stateless Jews must leave Germany within two weeks. The date fixed for the expulsion was October 18; that evening they were ordered

to assemble at their nearest railway station with only a single suitcase, and were then taken by train across Germany to the Polish border, where they were kept for several weeks in barracks and stables. Among those who hurried to help them before they were finally allowed to enter Poland was the historian Emanuel Ringelblum, who for the previous five years had been monitoring the intensification of German anti-Jewish measures. With money provided by the American Jewish Joint Distribution Committee, he directed relief work at the border, collected testimonies from the deportees, and gathered further information on German policy towards the Jews.

Threat. *This tailor's shop in Vienna bears the warning that the owner will be sent to Dachau if the word 'Jud' (Jew) and the crude drawings of a bearded Jew and a Jew hanging on the gallows are removed.*

One of the expellees described the swift expulsion in a letter to his seventeen-year-old son, Hershl Grynszpan, who was then in Paris. Outraged by what he read, Grynszpan went to the German embassy on November 7 and shot and mortally wounded a young German diplomat. The diplomat's death on the afternoon of November 9 was used by Hitler and the Nazis to launch an immediate orgy of destruction. That very night 191 synagogues throughout Germany, Austria and the Sudetenland were set on fire, as were almost two hundred Jewish apartment houses and 7,500 Jewish-owned shops and warehouses. More than 30,000 Jews were taken from their homes and sent to concentration camps. In the streets, Jews were savagely attacked, and thirty-six were killed. A further fifty-five died later of their injuries.

Following what quickly became known as the Kristallnacht – the 'Night of Broken Glass' – the German government imposed an enormous fine on the Jews of Germany, confiscated all their insurance claims, and drove the remaining Jewish businessmen and traders out of German economic life. Some of the Jews who had been sent to concentration camps were killed, others committed suicide, and most were detained until early in 1939. The British Government received full details of these events, a senior British diplomat in Germany, Sir George Ogilvie Forbes, reporting that in an obviously ridiculous and vindictive decree, all damage done to Jewish property would have to be paid for by the Jews themselves, and they would also have to pay a massive fine. Not surprisingly, many Jews – Ogilvie Forbes reported – 'are wandering about in the streets and parks afraid to return to their homes', and he added: 'I can find no words strong enough in condemnation of the disgusting treatment of so many innocent people, and the civilised world is faced with the appalling sight of 500,000 people about to rot away in starvation.'

The Consul-General in Frankfurt, R.T. Smallbones, reported to London on November 16 on 'scenes of indescribable, destructive sadism and brutality', including householders locked into their lavatories while 'the mob entered and destroyed everything or threw everything on to the streets, where in some cases they were set on fire'. There had been 'innumerable cases of suicide' in Frankfurt and the near surroundings: 'I personally know of eleven acquaintances who have taken their lives to avoid being arrested.'

The Kristallnacht ended all hope of an improvement in the situation of the half million Jews of Germany, Austria and the Sudetenland. The situation of the Jews was also ominous in Poland, Germany' eastern neighbour, and a potential victim of German territorial aspirations. On November 20 the British Ambassador in Warsaw, Sir Howard Kennard, reported on Poland's attitude towards its three million Jews. Most Poles, he wrote, 'regard it as inevitable that in order to induce a state of mind favourable to emigration among the Jews, their position here must be made less comfortable'. Kennard added: 'Local excesses - not organised, as recently in Germany, but more or less spontaneous - are of not infrequent occurrence.'

In the immediate aftermath of the burning of synagogues, looting of homes, murders and beatings of Kristallnacht, the British government opened its doors as a matter of urgency to German Jewish children who could make the journey without their parents. Known as the Kindertransport – the Children's Transport – it saw more than 9,500 children brought to Britain in the nine months between Kristallnacht and the outbreak of the Second World War. The first train with children from Germany left Berlin on December 2, only three weeks after Kristallnacht; the first train from Vienna left on December 12. From then on, trains left at regular intervals until the day Germany invaded Poland on 1 September 1939. The last time that almost all these children saw their parents was when they waved goodbye to them on a station

The Night of Broken Glass. *On the night of 9/10 November 1938 the Nazis destroyed hundreds of synagogues and damaged thousands of Jewish shops. The scene is outside a Berlin store on the morning after.*

platform in Germany. Most of the parents were to be deported to their deaths in 1942 and 1943.

Travelling across Germany to the Dutch port of Hook of Holland – their passports stamped on the front page with the letter 'J' in red – the children were then taken by boat across the North Sea to Harwich, and from there by bus to a nearby former Butlin's Holiday camp at Dovercourt, where they were housed and fed, and found families with whom to live. Others were sent on directly by train from Harwich to Liverpool Street Station, London, where they were met by the family that had earlier agreed to sponsor them and take them in. The children were described officially by the British government as 'transmigrants', supposed to return to their homes in Germany once the 'danger' had passed. In the event, other than those who went after the war to Canada, the United States and Palestine, almost all of them stayed in Britain.

The main organisation in this act of rescue was the Central British Fund, a Jewish charity. To bring out Orthodox youngsters an Orthodox rabbi, Dr Solomon Schonfeld, travelled repeatedly from Britain to Vienna and other cities. A twenty-five-year-old Dutch-born Jew, Wim van Leer, went to Leipzig, where he persuaded the local Nazis to let him take back twenty-two youngsters to Britain. Non-Jewish organisations, including the Save the Children Fund and the Quakers, brought back several thousand young Jews, or sponsored those who had arrived with their single suitcase and no means of existence for the time being apart from the charity of others. Each Kindertransport child made his or her contribution to British life. Klaus Hugo, who began life in Britain as a schoolboy, fought against Germany as a fighter pilot with the Royal Air Force. Otto Hutter, who was fourteen years old when he left Vienna for Britain, became professor of physiology in Glasgow; in the next generation, born and educated in Britain, his son became a heart surgeon. Ursula Rosenfeld was for many years a magistrate in her adopted home of Manchester, but she can never forget her eighth birthday party a few weeks after Hitler came to power. She and her mother waited, but not a single child came. 'From that moment I realised I was ostracised.' her father was arrested after Kristallnacht and beaten to death in Buchenwald.

The pressures for yet more emigration mounted in March 1939, when German troops occupied Prague, the capital of Czechoslovakia, and Hitler annexed Bohemia and Moravia to Germany, leaving only Slovakia with notional independence. In the twenty-four hours following the annexation,

Prisoners. *Some of the 10,000 German Jews, their heads shaven, at roll call in Buchenwald concentration camp, where they had been sent in November 1938 after Kristallnacht. An additional 20,000 were sent to Dachau and Sachsenhausen concentration camps. Almost all were released before the outbreak of war, but two years later most were deported and killed.*

several dozen Czech Jews who had the necessary exit documents and were able to buy airline tickets flew from Prague to London – there was a regular daily air service between the two capitals – but lacking the documents required to enter Britain they were detained overnight and sent back to Prague the following day.

Using the Nuremberg Laws as a base – one Jewish grandparent was sufficient to define a person as a Jew – the Germans designated 118,000 former Czech citizens as Jews. With the imposition of German rule the pattern seen in Austria a year earlier was repeated: Jewish property was confiscated, Jewish shops looted, individual Jews beaten up, and synagogues burnt. Everywhere within the borders of what became known as 'Greater Germany' the Jews were the daily victims of abuse and persecution. 'Only when the Jewish bacillus infecting the life of people has been removed,' Hitler declared publicly on April 1, 'can one hope to establish a cooperation among the nations which shall be built up on a lasting understanding.'

Tens of thousands of Jewish refugees were still trying to enter Palestine. The Palestinian Arab leadership, and the Arab governments near Palestine – Iraq, Transjordan, Egypt and Saudi Arabia – continued to demand a drastic curb on Jewish immigration. In Palestine more than three hundred moderate Arabs, who were willing to accept some compromise, were murdered by those of their fellow-Arabs who, led by Haj Amin al Husseini, the Mufti of Jerusalem, demanded a complete halt to Jewish immigration. At the beginning of 1939 Jewish and Arab leaders were called from Palestine to London to discuss the British government's plan to calm Arab fears by curbing Jewish immigration. Even while the Jewish delegates were putting the case for a more open refugee policy, the British government was taking active steps to check and if possible to halt the continuing flow of 'illegal' Jewish immigrants who, fleeing from central Europe and travelling down the Danube to the Black Sea, went on by ship to Palestine, without the necessary permits to enter. This flow of 'illegals' had begun in 1934 and reached a peak in 1939, when more than thirty ships, carrying more than 16,000 refugees, sailed from the Romanian Black Sea ports through the Bosphorus, on to Greek ports and thence to Palestine.

During February 1939 all British Consuls had been instructed by London to warn shipping agencies not to allow Jews without valid immigration documents to board ship for Palestine. On February 24, however, in a telegram which was to set the pattern for future British policy, the Minister in Bucharest, Sir Reginald Hoare, informed the Colonial Secretary in London, Malcolm MacDonald, that in spite of these instructions 'I have little doubt that this exodus of Jews will continue.' The ambassador added: 'We must ourselves take effective police and naval measures to prevent the smuggling of

Illegal immigrants *are brought ashore on the Palestine coast in small boats from a* *ship that managed to avoid the British naval blockade.* [PHOTO: ROLF M. KNELLER]

unauthorised refugees into Palestine either from the High Seas or over land.' Such measures were taken at once, and were to a certain extent successful, so much so that the Foreign Secretary, Lord Halifax ,was informed by the Private Secretary to King George VI, on February 28, that the King was 'glad to think that steps are being taken to prevent these people leaving their country of origin'. King George VI's interest in stopping German Jews leaving Germany for Palestine was effective. Two days after his message the Foreign Office telegraphed to the British Ambassador in Berlin: 'There is a large irregular movement from Germany of Jewish refugees who as a rule, set out without visas or any arrangements for their reception, and then attempt to land in any territory that seems to them to present the slightest possibility of receiving them. This is a cause of great embarrassment to His Majesty's Government and also, it appears, to the American Government, and the latter have expressed a wish that you should join the American Chargé d'Affaires in Berlin in bringing this situation to the attention of appropriate German Authorities and requesting them to discourage such travel on German ships.'

The ambassador did as he was instructed, urging the German Government 'to check unauthorised emigration' of Jews from the German Reich. This was not so much dislike of Jews finding a safe place of refuge but fear of the Arabs being further upset by it. On April 20, when the British Cabinet's Palestine Committee discussed possible American government objections to stopping the 'illegals' reaching Palestine, the Foreign Secretary was able to report to his colleagues that he had discussed this question with

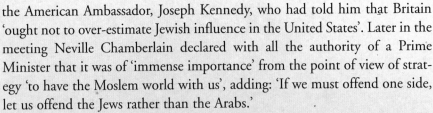

First steps. *Jewish immigrants, having landed in Palestine illegally, make their way inland over the sand dunes to a Jewish town, where they will be absorbed into the local population without the British finding out about them. They carry their worldly possessions with them.*

the American Ambassador, Joseph Kennedy, who had told him that Britain 'ought not to over-estimate Jewish influence in the United States'. Later in the meeting Neville Chamberlain declared with all the authority of a Prime Minister that it was of 'immense importance' from the point of view of strategy 'to have the Moslem world with us', adding: 'If we must offend one side, let us offend the Jews rather than the Arabs.'

By the end of April 1939 the British government had finalised a Palestine White Paper, fixing an upper limit of 100,000 on the number of Jewish immigrants to be admitted over the following five years, after which the Arabs would have an effective veto on any further Jewish immigration. The chief draftsman of this scheme, Malcolm MacDonald, was well aware of its unfairness. 'As regards the policy itself,' he told the Cabinet on May 1, 'he had admitted frankly that certain points had been inserted to meet Arab pressure and which, perhaps, would have been omitted if the matter had been looked at on strict merits.'

The new White Paper was made public on May 19. In the debate that followed in the House of Commons, Churchill, whose Palestine White Paper of 1922 had opened the doors for almost half a million Jewish immigrants, spoke with force and bitterness against what he regarded as both a betrayal of the Balfour Declaration and a shameful act of appeasement: 'I could not stand by and see solemn engagements into which Britain has entered before the world set aside for reasons of administrative convenience or - and it will be a vain hope - for the sake of a quiet life.'

During the course of his speech Churchill drew attention to the large Arab as well as Jewish immigration into Palestine since the beginning of the Mandate, drawn to Palestine by its new-found prosperity. Many Arabs resident in Palestine in 1939 had come from Morocco, Algeria, Tripoli and Yemen. This led Churchill to tell the House of Commons: 'So far from being persecuted, the Arabs have crowded into the country and multiplied till their population has increased more than even all world Jewry could lift up the Jewish population... We are now asked to submit, and this is what rankles most with me, to an agitation which is fed with foreign money and ceaselessly inflamed by Nazi and Fascist propaganda.' Of the proposed Arab veto on all Jewish immigration after 1944, Churchill declared emphatically: 'Now, there is the breach; there is the violation of the pledge; there is the abandonment of the Balfour Declaration; there is the end of the vision, of the hope, of the dream.'

Parliament had to decide; the final vote was 268 to 179 in favour of the new White Paper – known henceforth to the Jews as the 'Black Paper'. With the gates of Palestine closing, even greater efforts were made to find havens elsewhere. Indeed, six days before the White Paper was published, as part of the daily efforts of German Jews to find somewhere, anywhere, that would take them in, a German ocean liner, the *St Louis*, had set sail from Hamburg. Of the 930 Jewish refugees on board, 734 held United States immigration quota numbers that would allow them to enter the United States in three years' time. Their hope was that, on reaching the Caribbean, they would find some, or several countries willing to take them in until, in 1942, their American permits would become valid. Cuba agreed to take in twenty-four of them, but no more. Four South American countries, Colombia, Chile, Paraguay and Argentina, each of whom had accepted German Jewish refugees earlier, refused to agree to take in a single refugee from the *St Louis*. On June 6, while the ship was steaming off the coast of Florida, within sight of the Miami waterfront, the refugees appealed by radio telegram direct to President Roosevelt but received no answer. Four days later the American government informed them that they could not land.

The *St Louis* returned across the Atlantic, to the Belgian port of Antwerp. As a result of widespread publicity and anguished appeals from on board ship, none of the refugees had to return to Germany. Three countries, France,

Temporary haven. *Some of the passengers on the* St Louis *return to Europe after being rejected by the New World, reaching Antwerp on 17 June 1939, less than three months before the outbreak of war. Their smiles tell that they must have heard they will be taken in by Britain or other European countries.*

Belgium and Holland, took in 619 of them. A further 287 were allowed in to Britain. Within a year only those who had gone to Britain were outside German rule. Of the others, several hundred were murdered in the Holocaust, doomed when Belgium, France and Holland were conquered by Germany in 1940.

Throughout the summer and autumn of 1939, following the British Parliament's approval of the Palestine White Paper, illegal immigration to Palestine intensified, as did the British government's efforts to halt it. On August 4, as punishment for the illegal immigration of more than ten thousand Jews so far that year, the British government decided that no immigration quota would be issued for the next six-monthly period, from October 1939 to March 1940. It was essential, the Minister responsible, Malcolm MacDonald, told the Cabinet, 'that we should adhere firmly to this decision' which was already making the Jewish leaders realise 'that they would have to use their influence to stop illegal immigration in order to secure the resumption of legal immigration'. In addition, MacDonald explained, 'Very strong representations had been made in particular to Romania, Poland and Greece, and the first results of this action had been good. Romania and Greece had taken action which should secure much stricter surveillance, and while the good effect of our representations might not last, since the power of Jewish money was great, for the present at any rate the results were good.' This reference to 'the power of Jewish money' was ill-chosen. In reality the situation of European Jewry in 1939 was precarious and weak, and the funds of the Jewish charitable institutions helping refugees were nearly exhausted.

On August 17 news of another desperate situation, this time for the Jews of Slovakia, reached the British Foreign Office. Some Slovaks, encouraged by the Germans, 'do all they can to rob and plunder Jewish property and persecute the Jewish people'. Other Slovaks, 'unable to show their hatred of the Germans, vent their wrath instead upon the Jews'. More than 85,000 Jews were affected by the new Slovak mood. Since the previous March, when Hitler allowed Slovakia to break away from Czechoslovakia and become an independent State, all but a tiny proportion of Slovak Jews had been excluded from all the professions and from the universities. Many Jewish shops and businesses had been forced to close. Many Slovak Jews were joining the 'illegal' movement to Palestine: 'Their nerves

Protest. *On the day after the British announced severe restrictions on Jewish immigration to Palestine in May 1939, there were anti-British demonstrations throughout the country, as here in Tel Aviv, outside the headquarters of the office of the collective settlement.* [PHOTO: HANS PINN]

can stand no more' the report explained. 'Fear of the unknown in other countries is more pleasant to them than present persecution and feeling that they are trapped.'

The British government's hostility towards Jewish refugees making their way to Palestine was not only because of Arab opposition. A mild underlying dislike of Jews also played its part, not necessarily anti-Semitism of the sort that had led to such grave hardship for the Jews inside Greater Germany and in Slovakia, but what a senior British civil servant described at the beginning of 1939 as 'a vague dislike of anything with a Jewish label'. On 30 July 1939 Neville Chamberlain commented on the German persecution of the Jews in a private letter: 'I believe the persecution arose out of two motives; A desire to rob the Jews of their money and a jealousy of their superior cleverness.' His letter continued: 'No doubt Jews aren't a lovable people; I don't care about them myself; – but that is not sufficient to explain the Pogrom.'

A number of diplomats paid no attention to the restrictions and restrictive tone emanating from London. In Berlin, Frank Foley gave as many Palestine certificates to Jews as he could. In the Lithuanian capital, Kovno, another British official, Thomas Preston, did likewise. Chinese diplomats in several European capitals issued visas which enabled Jews to leave Europe, cross Siberia by train, and travel to Shanghai. Before the outbreak of war in September 1939, the city of Shanghai took in 25,000 refugees from Germany. The German pattern of life was established in the orient. German-style cafés, restaurants, bakeries, small hotels and bookshops were set up by the newcomers for their fellow-Jews.

With each territorial expansion of Germany, more Jews came under German rule, so that by the summer of 1939, despite the emigration of more than a quarter of a million Jews, there were still half a million remaining under the harsh gaze of Nazism, uncertain of what their future would be. Most were eager to leave, and sought whatever avenue of escape seemed open. Then, on 23 August 1939, the Jewish world was shaken to the core by the news of a secret agreement, the Nazi-Soviet Pact, which had been reached between Hitler and Stalin a few days earlier. This effectively sealed the fate of Poland's three million Jews, for it made possible a German invasion of Poland, unchallenged by Russia, hitherto the only country with a strong anti-Nazi

At the quayside. *Helmut Stern, a violinist from Berlin and his family at Harbin on sledge rickshaws, with Manchurian onlookers. They had left Berlin after Kristallnacht, sailing first to Shanghai. In 1949 they emigrated to Israel. Dr Ho Feng Shan, Chinese Consul-General in Vienna, saved the lives of thousands of Austrian Jews by issuing visas to them.*

policy which had a common border with Poland, and a large army. Britain and France, who had both offered Poland guarantees of help in the event of a German attack, would be powerless if Russia were to turn a blind eye to a German invasion. They might declare war on Germany, but their ability to counter a German assault on Poland was minimal.

The news of the Nazi-Soviet Pact reached Geneva while the twenty-first Zionist Congress was in the mid-session. Arthur Ruppin, one of the delegates from Palestine, wrote in his diary: 'The news exploded like a bomb.' In his final words to the Congress on the evening of August 24, Chaim Weizmann told the delegates, many of whom had come specially from Poland for the meeting 'If, as I hope, we are spared in life and our work continues, who knows – perhaps a new light will shine upon us from the thick black gloom. The remnant shall work on, fight on, live on, until the dawn of better days. Towards that dawn I greet you. May we meet again in peace.' The official protocol of the Congress recorded how at that point: 'Deep emotion grips the Congress. Dr Weizmann embraces his colleagues on the platform. There are tears in many eyes. Hundreds of hands are stretched out towards Dr Weizmann as he leaves the hall.'

Some of the delegates from Poland managed to make their way home. Others decided to stay in Switzerland, or made their way to France and Britain. No Jew could know in the autumn of 1939 which way the Nazi military juggernaut would turn, which Jewish community or communities might be in danger, or how imminent that danger might be. It was Hitler who would decide that. Having signed his pact with Stalin, he was in supremely confident mood. On 1 September 1939 a boat left the Hook of Holland for Harwich and a new life for the several hundred German Jewish children on board. That same day, as these children were on their way to safety, the German army invaded Poland.

Kindertransport. *German Jewish children reach the British port of Harwich. As a result of the widespread outcry at Kristallnacht, Britain took in more than 9,000 children from Germany and Austria, known as Kindertransport ('Children's Transport') or just Kinder. Margaret Thatcher's parents took in a Kindertransport child.*

CHAPTER FIVE

THE SECOND
WORLD WAR

1939-1945

THE EVENTS OF THE SECOND WORLD WAR WERE TERRIBLE
for many nations; tens of millions of soldiers, sailors, airmen and civilians were killed. But no people suffered more than the Jews. At the beginning
of 1939 there were just over sixteen million, half of them living in Europe. By
the end of 1945 six million of Europe's eight million Jews had been murdered.
It was to take more than half a century before the Jews were again to number
sixteen million. The fate of the Jews of Europe was an integral part of the
Second World War, the annihilation of Jews and of Judaism a main objective
of Hitler and his regime.

In the fighting which followed the German invasion of Poland on 1
September 1939, 6,000 Jewish soldiers were killed in action in the Polish
army. From the first days of the war, individual Jews and groups of Jews were
murdered by the German conquerors in more than forty Polish towns and villages. As an example of what was in store for the Jews of Poland, on 9
September 1939, in the town of Bedzin, the Germans set fire to the Great
Synagogue and, as the flames spread to the Jewish quarter, cordoned off the
area and shot dead anyone who tried to flee from the flames: more than a
hundred Jews were killed.

As the German army advanced deeper and deeper into Poland, a quarter
of a million Polish Jews escaped to the Soviet Union; most of them survived
the subsequent German invasion of Russia by travelling as far east as they
could, largely to Soviet Central Asia. Some were sent by Stalin to labour camps
in Siberia, where hundreds died. Several hundred Jews, most of them doctors,
were also among the Polish officers who were captured by the Russians at the
time of the Russian occupation and annexation of eastern Poland, and killed
on Stalin's orders at Katyn and two other prisoner-of-war camps.

Even before the new German-Soviet border had been fixed, the Germans
were planning to drive the Jews out of hundreds of towns and villages in the
newly annexed territories. On 21 September 1939 it was decreed that all communities with fewer than five hundred Jews were to be dissolved, and that all
Jews were hereafter to live in certain restricted areas in the larger cities, or in

With spade and star.
Jews assembled by the Germans in Russia for forced labour, 1941.
It is unlikely that any of those in this photograph survived.

a special area set aside for them in a deprived region in the centre of Poland, the so-called 'Lublinland reservation'. Even Jews waiting at Hamburg with tickets and visas for the next ship to the United States – then neutral – were deported across Europe to Lublinland. By the end of the winter of 1939-40, lacking proper housing, food or medical help, hundreds of these deportees to Lublinland had died. Others worked in harsh conditions, savagely beaten by guards in forced labour camps, and again many died.

On 30 October 1939, the head of the SS, Heinrich Himmler, had fixed the following three months as the period during which all Jews must be cleared out of the rural areas of western Poland. In the Poznan region, fifty communities were at once uprooted. From Lodz, hundreds of women, children and old people were deported eastward by train in sealed freight-cars, mostly to the Lublin region. In the cities to which the deported Jews were sent, overcrowding was severe. Poverty followed swiftly for tens of thousands of families, already stripped of their possessions, and without a livelihood. On 12 December 1939 two years' forced labour was made compulsory for all Jewish males between the ages of fourteen and sixty. At first, Jews were seized

Forced labourers *being taken away by truck from the Warsaw Ghetto, to work outside, 1941. This photograph was one of a series taken by a German soldier, Ulrich Keller. Jews were forbidden to have cameras in the ghetto.*

in the streets in order to fill the camps. Later there was organized conscription. Many died in the camps from brutality and exhaustion.

On 10 May 1940 the German army attacked Belgium, Holland and France. Jews fought in each of the defending armies. With the German victory, no immediate measures were taken against Jews, but gradually even their rights under occupation were taken away. The wearing of a yellow Star of David was made compulsory, creating a deep and disturbing sense of isolation. In Holland, many German Jews who had found refuge there before the German conquest were sent to an internment camp at Westerbork. Among them were several hundred Jews who had tried to reach the United States on board the *St Louis* and been refused entry.

In May and June 1940, as the German army drove through France, safe havens were found for many hundreds of Jews in the United States. Diplomats of neutral countries helped to secure several thousand visas that made it possible for Jews to leave Europe. These 'Righteous diplomats' – as they are now known – included an American, Varian Fry, working in southern France, who helped at least 1,500 Jewish artists and intellectuals to flee Nazi rule. On the French side of the border with Spain, a Portuguese diplomat, Aristide de Sousa Mendes, handed out several thousand visas as the German army drove towards the border. In the Lithuanian capital Kovno, a Japanese diplomat, Chiune Sugihara, and his Dutch colleague Jan

A clothing workshop *in the Warsaw Ghetto, 1941, another of Ulrich Keller's photographs. Work in the ghetto was a guarantee of at least a minimum amount of food. These greatcoats were being made for the German armed forces.*

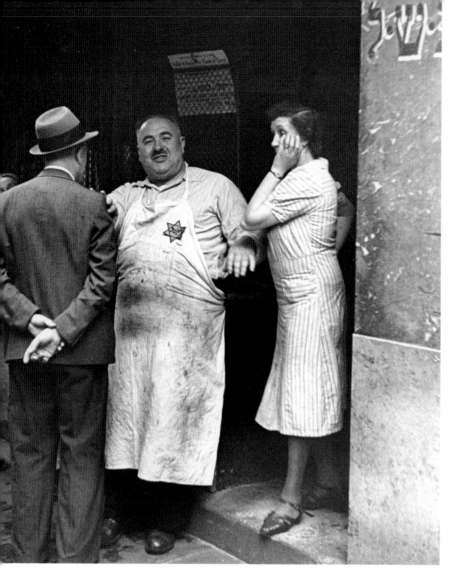

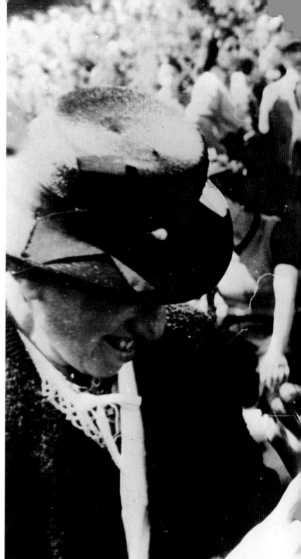

THE YELLOW BADGE, *in the shape of the Star of David, or 'David's Shield'. Intended by the Germans as a badge of shame, as well as to identify Jews wherever they might be, as early as 1933 a German Jewish editor, Robert Weltsch, had declared: 'Wear it with pride!' A butcher (above) wears the badge on his apron, at the entrance to his shop in the Jewish quarter of Paris. A Dutch Jewish woman (above centre) in 1942. David Moffie (right), the last Jewish student to receive a doctorate at the university of Amsterdam during the Second World War, wearing the Star of David at the degree awarding ceremony. He was later deported to Auschwitz, but survived the war.*

THE STAR IN BELGIUM

A wedding after the occupation began (above) at which the bride and groom, their families and their guests, are all wearing the Star of David. Rajala Lederman and her daughter Annette in a Brussels street (left) shortly before Annette was placed in hiding. Rajala was later killed at Auschwitz, as was her husband. But Annette and her sister Margo survived in hiding, and went after the war to the United States.

Amsterdam, 1941, *the entrance to the Jewish quarter, an area set up by the German occupation authorities, within which all the city's Jews were confined, and from which many were deported to a transit camp at Westerbork, in north-east Holland, and then to Auschwitz.*

Zwartendijk, gave transit visas through Japan and the Dutch East Indies to more than 2,000 Jews, most of them refugees from Poland. Taking the Trans-Siberian Railway to Japan, these refugees then made their way to Shanghai, Australia or the United States. Also in Kovno, the British Consul, Thomas Preston, helped to provide 400 'illegal' certificates in addition to 800 legal ones for Jews who were then able to make their way through Russia and the Black Sea to Palestine.

Hitler had conquered Norway in May 1940. Five months later more than 1,000 Norwegian Jews, and 300 German-Jewish refugees who had been given sanctuary by the Norwegians before the war, were forbidden to practice in the professions. That month, 15,000 German Jews living along the River Rhine were deported to internment camps in the French Pyrenees. These camps were run by French guards loyal to the Vichy regime and conditions in them were harsh: more than 1,500 Jews died in them.

Within a month of the conquest of Poland, the German occupation authorities began to confine the Jews there to a particular area of each town, known as the ghetto, the name of the Jewish quarter in medieval cities. Sometimes the area chosen by the Germans for the ghetto was the already predominantly Jewish quarter. Often, however, it was a poor or neglected part of the town, away from the centre. Jews from the rest of the town were then forced to leave their homes, and to move into this area, where even the basic amenities were not always available. Not only the Jews of each of the towns, but also the Jews expelled from western Poland, and from many rural Jewish communities, were forced to move into the new ghettos. At Piotrkow 8,000

The internment camp *at Gurs, in the French Pyrenees. It was administered by French officials. 15,000 Jews were interned there, including, from October 1940, 4,000 German Jews. There are 1,200 graves in the camp cemetery. In March 1943 almost 2,000 were deported from Gurs to the death camps in German-occupied Poland. A thousand survived in Gurs until liberation.*

local Jews were joined by an equal number of deportees. In each ghetto food supplies and medical provisions were restricted. Intense overcrowding, hunger and disease led to widespread suffering, and death. In the Lodz ghetto, 5,000 Jews died from starvation in the first six months of 1941.

The Warsaw ghetto was the largest of all the ghettos established by the Germans in occupied Poland. The section of the city chosen was one in which more than 280,000 Jews were already living. A wall was built around the area, the Jews being made both to build and pay for it. As soon as it was built, the thousands of Jews who lived elsewhere in Warsaw were forced to leave their homes, abandon almost all their possessions, and move into the ghetto. One Warsaw Jew, Chaim Kaplan, described in his diary how many Poles drove Jews out in advance, before the fixed date, and then took over their apartments.

Early in 1941, 72,000 Jews were expelled from towns throughout the Warsaw region and driven into the ghetto, bringing the total number of

A round-up in Paris. *French policemen and German officers herd Jews on to a bus, 20 August 1941, as the first stage of their internment and forced labour. Within a year most of them had been deported to Auschwitz.*

A ghetto bridge, *(overleaf) one of three specially built in Lodz to link the two sections of the ghetto. Jews were not allowed in this street, although it ran through the ghetto, because trams ran down it which they were forbidden to use. The German soldier on the right records it on cine film.*

203

refugees there to 150,000. Terrible over-crowding, minimum rations, and almost no contact with the outside world was the fate of 400,000 people. Under the ration scales imposed by the Germans, all Germans in Warsaw were entitled to 2,310 calories a day. Foreigners – such as Scandinavian businessmen working for German firms – were entitled to 1,790 calories, Poles to 934, and Jews to 183. Even for these totally inadequate rations, Jews had to pay twice as much as Poles, and nearly twenty times as much as Germans. From 22 February 1941 any Pole selling food to a Jew outside the Warsaw ghetto was automatically sentenced to three months' hard labour, while at the same time the ghetto ration was reduced to three ounces of bread a day. Within six months, by June 1941, more than 13,000 Jews died of starvation there. Smuggling, for which the penalty was death if caught, became the only way to ensure survival. Many of the smugglers were young Jewish boys and girls.

Ghettos were also set up in Cracow, Lublin and Kielce. From Vienna, more than 5,000 Jews were deported to these eastern ghettos or to slave labour camps in German-occupied Poland. Attempts to render conditions as bearable as possible were made in each ghetto by the Jewish Councils. These had been set up by the Germans to carry out German orders, and to administer the ghettos internally. In Warsaw, as elsewhere, the Council provided what relief it could, often clandestinely, and arranged cultural activities, concerts and education. Jewish theatre and Jewish music continued; School classes were held in secret. Painters continued to paint and to teach painting. Singers continued to sing and to teach singing. But the Germans were also continually taking Jews from the ghetto for forced labour, where some benefitted from greater rations but where all were faced by the cruelty of their taskmasters and the risk of death for some infraction of harsh rules, or from exhaustion.

The year 1941 saw no abatement of the severity of German policy towards the Jews. In Amsterdam, more than 400 Jews were seized in the

Young smugglers *in the Warsaw ghetto (above), climbing over the ghetto wall, in the daily search for food.*

Accursed power. *Jewish police (opposite) in the Warsaw ghetto. The Germans ordered the Jews to police themselves, then used the ghetto police in round-ups for forced labour and even deportation. Jewish police who refused to participate in the deportations were themselves deported. Some of the Warsaw ghetto police were feared, others did what they could to make life in the ghetto less unbearable. Almost all were later murdered by the Germans. One Jewish police chief in Warsaw was assassinated on orders of the Jewish Fighting Organization, which co-ordinated resistance in a dozen ghettos.*

streets and deported to the stone quarries of Mauthausen concentration camp, where they were killed. In Paris, several thousand foreign-born Jews were seized and interned in May 1941. Outside Paris, at Suresnes, 133 Jews were shot for resistance. In Bucharest, outside the area of German control, anti-Semitic violence led to the killing of 120 Jewish men, women and children who had been hunted down by armed Romanian gangs.

Jews continued to fight the Axis in different ways. Inside German-occupied Europe, escape routes were organized to enable Allied pilots and air-crew, after they had been shot down, to return through Spain to Gibraltar and

Warsaw ghetto. *Jews outside a funeral parlour, 1941, wearing white armbands with the Star of David, their faces a study of dignity under duress. Not long after this photograph was taken all Jews with fur coats and fur collars had to hand them over to the Germans, to be sent to the Russian front to supplement the soldiers' inadequate winter clothing.* [PHOTO: WILLY GEORG]

A Jewish partisan, *(right) Mosa Pijade with the Yugoslav partisan leader, Marshal Tito. An art teacher in Belgrade, Pijade was imprisoned from 1925 to 1939 for Communist agitation. After the war, as President of the Serbian Republic within Communist Yugoslavia, he took a leading part in the separation of Belgrade from Moscow.*

Britain. One of the first of these escape lines was organised by a Jew, Victor Gerson, who volunteered to be parachuted behind German lines in France in 1940 specifically for that purpose. Hundreds of airmen were able to return to Britain via his escape route, known as the 'Vic' line. During the British attack on Vichy French forces in Syria in 1941, Jewish soldiers fought alongside the British. It was during this campaign that Moshe Dayan lost an eye. Later, as Chief of Staff of the Israeli army, his eye-patch became his hallmark.

When the German army invaded Yugoslavia in April 1941, Jewish soldiers were among those who fought and died defending their Yugoslav homeland. The German victory was swift, and within a month a further 70,000 Jews were brought under Nazi tyranny. In Serbia, within a few months, almost all the 3,000 Jews of the Banat region, just north of Belgrade, had been taken by the SS to a concentration camp at Tasmajdan near Belgrade and shot – some in the camp itself, others by the banks of the river Danube. In Croatia, where a Fascist regime persecuted the Jews without Nazi encouragement, the Croat Fascist Ustachi murdered tens of thousands of Jews throughout the region, though 3,000 escaped over the mountains to the Italian-controlled coastal zone. Also, as a result of intervention by the Roman Catholic Church and the Papal Nuncio on behalf of Croat Jewish partners in mixed marriages, 1,000 survived the war.

In Serbia, 15,000 Jews were deported to a concentration camp at Zemun, near Belgrade, where they were murdered by a German SS unit in specially adapted gas vans. Of Serbia's 23,000 Jews, 20,000 were killed, leading the local Nazi chief to inform Berlin in boastful tones that the 'Jewish problem' had been 'totally solved' – 'the only community in which this has been achieved'. Bosnia was also overrun by the Germans. Just over a 1,000 Jews managed to flee over the mountains into Italian-occupied territory. The Jewish community of Sarajevo had been built up during the sixteenth century by Jewish refugees from Spain, 'Sephardi' Jews who spoke their own language, Ladino, and as merchants and traders helped to link Bosnia with the outside world. After the Austrian annexation of Bosnia in 1878, hundreds of Ashkenazi Jews from Vienna, Prague and Budapest joined the local communities. Disaster struck from the first days of the German occupation, with the burning down of the synagogue by German troops and local Muslims. Almost all Bosnia's 15,000 Jews were later deported to concentration camps controlled by the Croat fascist Ustachi. As with the Croatian

Jews, so with the Bosnian Jews: fewer than a thousand survived the war.

From the first days of the German conquest of Yugoslavia, Jews were active in the Yugoslav resistance. The first secret radio in Zagreb was operated by two Jewish brothers. In Belgrade, several Jews were among those executed by the Germans in the first mass execution of Yugoslav partisans. In the years ahead more than 2,000 Jews fought in the ranks of Tito's partisans: a specifically Jewish partisan unit of 250 men and women lost more than 200 in the fighting. Some of Tito's closest partisan comrades were Jews, among them Mosa Pijade – later a Vice-President of Yugoslavia – and Dr Papo, head of the partisan medical services. The radio operator of the first British mission to be parachuted into Yugoslavia to join Tito was a Jewish volunteer from Haifa, Peretz Rosenberg.

On 22 June 1941 the Germans attacked the Soviet Union. It was a turning point in the Second World War, pitting two totalitarian powers against each other. It was also a turning point for the two million and more Jews of eastern Poland and western Russia – the new war zone. From the first days of the German advance, in an intensification of the killing of Jews on a scale hitherto unknown in German-occupied Poland, specially trained SS killing squads followed closely behind the German forces. By the end of July they had murdered many tens of thousands of Jews in cities, towns and villages. In August, in the Russian city of Kamenets-Podolsk, 14,000 Jews who had earlier been deported there from Ruthenia – the eastern region of Czechoslovakia annexed by Hungary just before the war – were marched by German SS and armed Ukrainian units some ten miles from the town, ordered to undress, and were then murdered by machine-gun fire. At the end of September, at Babi Yar, a ravine just outside Kiev, more than 30,000 Jews were murdered during the course of three days, the SS being helped by volunteer Ukrainian militiamen. Also in September, German forces entered Estonia, where all 1,000 Jews who had not managed to escape to the Soviet Union were seized and murdered. In Vilna – the 'Jerusalem of Lithuania' and a centre of vibrant Jewish creativity for several hundred years – the SS seized 20,000 Jews and took them to the Ponar woods eight miles outside the city, a favourite pre-war picnic place, where they were ordered to undress on the edge of a ravine, and shot. Germans and Lithuanians participated in the killing. All but ten or twenty of the Jews who managed to escape from the ravine – having been left for dead under the corpses that fell on top of them – were hunted down and killed by a unit of Germans and Lithuanians set up specially for that purpose.

From the outset of the German invasion of the Soviet Union, the SS killing squads were helped by local volunteers: Estonians, Latvians, Lithuanians and Ukrainians all participated. In the Lithuanian capital, Kovno, several hundred Jews were brutally murdered by so-called Lithuanian 'partisans' even before German troops arrived. In Romania, which had joined in the invasion of the Soviet Union, 6,000 Jews were forced by Romanian Fascist Iron Guard militia into two trains and sent in sealed carriages from Jassy on a 250-mile journey southward, without food or water: 2,530 died on the journey, the dead being taken off the train at each station.

An execution *in German-occupied Russia. At the edge of a pit in which many Jews have already been shot and killed, a German soldier, watched by fellow soldiers, members of the German Labour Service drawn from older age groups and boys of the Hitler Youth, executes a Jew in full view of the photographer, Vinnitsa, Ukraine, 1942.*

As the German army drove eastward, hundreds of thousands of Russian Jews fought in the defence of the Soviet Union, on land, in the air, and at sea. On the Moscow front a Jewish general, Lev Dovator, only thirty-two years old, commanded a sector of the capital's defence system. On a crucial day of the battle, in November 1941, when the Germans were desperate to surround Moscow, he led his Cossack cavalry against the German forces holding a river bank, driving the Germans away. He was killed as he reached the German-held shore, and posthumously honoured as a Hero of the Soviet Union. Another Jewish general, Jacob Kreiser, commanded the Moscow Proletarian Infantry Division in December 1941. For his tactical skill and personal bravery he too was made a Hero of the Soviet Union. Subsequently he fought on four Soviet war fronts, helping drive the Germans from both the Crimea and the Baltic. The first Soviet woman pilot to be killed in action, Lydia Litvak, was Jewish.

In hiding. *Felix Zylbersztajn, who survived the Holocaust after being given sanctuary in a Belgian convent. This photograph was taken in the convent in February 1943, at a time when more than a thousand Belgian Jews – mostly of Polish origin like Felix – were being sent to Auschwitz every month.*

Jews were active in the Soviet partisan movement which sprang up behind the German lines in Russia. One of the first partisans to be executed by the Germans was a seventeen-year-old Jewish woman, Masha Bruskina, who was publicly hanged in Minsk for helping escaped Russian soldiers. On 26 September 1941 the SS rounded up 8,000 Jews in the town of Swiecany for execution. Several hundred managed to escape, breaking through a Lithuanian police cordon and making their way forty miles eastward to dense woodlands. There they survived on their wits, attacking German troop and supply routes whenever they could. On 25 October 1941, when the SS killing squads reached the towns of Tatarsk and Starodub, Jews who had managed to acquire weapons greeted them with salvos. To stop such resistance, the SS called in regular German army units to help them crush the revolts and the two Jewish communities were destroyed, like those around them.

The new German conquests in the East enabled yet another phase of the Holocaust to begin: starting on 16 October 1941 the Germans deported 22,000 German, Austrian and Czech Jews by rail to the former Soviet cities of Riga and Minsk, where almost all of them were murdered. Among those deported and killed were more than five hundred Jews from Luxembourg. Starting on 24 November 1941, tens of thousands of other German, Austrian and Czech Jews were deported to a ghetto that was specially set up in a former Austro-Hungarian, and later Czech garrison town, Terezin, called in German, Theresienstadt. The town's 3,700 Czech inhabitants were forced to leave, and 96,000 Jews were then crammed in.

The fate of the Jews under German rule had yet one more stage to reach – what the SS called the 'Final Solution' – deportation to camps set up solely for the purpose of mass murder. On 8 December 1941 just over 2,000 Jews were taken to Chelmno, the first of these death camps in German-occupied

Poland. They were put into a large lorry in groups of a hundred and more, which was then driven into the nearby woods. By the time the lorry reached a natural clearing in the woods, those inside it were dead, killed by the exhaust fumes which had been funnelled back into the lorry. Their bodies were then thrown into specially dug pits. The camp commandant judged this experiment a success, and it was repeated two days later, when more than a thousand Jews were killed. It then continued on a daily basis, the commandant boasting 'one day, one thousand' as his killing rate. In the coming months, Jews were brought to Chelmno from all the surrounding towns and villages, including the Lodz ghetto.

On 20 January 1942 – forty-six days after the first gassings at Chelmno – a gathering of senior German officials met at a villa on the Wannsee, near Berlin, where they discussed the fate of the surviving Jews of Europe. The convener of the meeting, SS General Reinhard Heydrich, told the gathering that he had just been appointed 'Plenipotentiary for the Preparation of the Final Solution of the European Jewish Question' and that in the course of implementing it, 'Europe will be combed from East to West'. Adolf Eichmann, the SS officer in charge of the Jewish Affairs section of the Gestapo, then presented a statistical table to show that as many as nine million Jews were still alive in Europe. These included 131,800 in Germany and 2,680,000 in German-occupied Poland. Eichmann also noted that there were

Two by two. *Children from the Lodz ghetto being led to the trucks waiting to take them to the death camp at Chelmno, fifty miles away, 23-30 September 1942. In that week 16,000 Jews were deported from Lodz to Chelmno. Not one of them survived.*

330,000 Jews in Britain who lay beyond German power, and thousands more in the neutral countries of Europe, including Ireland, Spain, Switzerland and Sweden. Eichmann did have one encouraging report for his fellow-German bureaucrats: virtually all the Jews in Latvia and Lithuania had already been killed, 229,052 in all.

The gathering at Wannsee discussed ways to draw as many Jews as possible into the deportation network. Even as they spoke, the deportations to Chelmno death camp continued. During the early months of 1942, three further death camps were set up elsewhere in German-occupied Poland. To the camp at Belzec, Jews were brought from both West and East Galicia – including the cities of Cracow and Lvov - and from towns and villages throughout Germany. Of the 600,000 Jews deported to Belzec, there were only two survivors. Also murdered there were 1,500 Christian Poles, whose 'crime', in German eyes, was to have tried to save Jews from deportation.

At the death camp of Sobibor, hundreds of thousands of Jews from central Poland were murdered, while Jews from Warsaw and central Poland were killed at Treblinka. From the Warsaw ghetto, in the first month of the deportations, 66,701 Jews were murdered at Treblinka on arrival. No one was spared. Children and babies were deported to Treblinka, as to all the death camps, and killed without compunction, including the orphans under the charge of Janusz Korczak, then sixty-three years old. He insisted, despite a German offer to exclude him from deportation, on accompanying the youngsters to their fate, and trying to comfort them.

Auschwitz – originally a punishment camp for Poles, where thousands of Poles were killed – was being extended during the spring and summer of 1942 to enable hundreds of thousands of Jews to be brought there, both from German-occupied Poland and from all over Europe, and to be murdered. A new camp was set up a mile and a half from the Auschwitz camp, at Birkenau. The first deportation of Jews to Birkenau took place on 26 March 1942, from Paris. The deportees – tattoed with a number on their forearm – were Jews who had been living in France when war broke out, but had been born outside France, mostly in Poland. The German register of the deportees shows that some were born as far away as Constantinople, Haifa, Tunis and Marrakech.

The first gassings at Auschwitz took place on 4 May 1942. Earlier experiments, carried out by the SS on Soviet prisoners of war, showed that a commercial pesticide, Cyclon B, was the most effective method of mass murder in gas chambers, four of which were were being built at Birkenau. When, three weeks later, Reinhard Heydrich was murdered in Prague by Czech patriots, the reprisals included the killing of several thousand Czechs – among them the men, women and children of the village of Lidice – and the deportation of 3,000 Jews from Theresienstadt to Auschwitz, where they were gassed.

During the summer of 1942, several thousand Jews were also taken from Theresienstadt to Treblinka, Sobibor and Belzec, and murdered there. An even

News about the old world. *In a Jewish cafeteria in New York, complete with neon Star of David, Orthodox Jews listen to a radio broadcast by President Roosevelt, 12 September 1941. The United States was not yet at war, but Roosevelt was speaking out against the evils of Nazism.*

[PHOTO: WEEGEE]

larger eastward deportation of Theresienstadt's Jews took place to yet another death camp, Maly Trostenets, near Minsk, where more than 23,000 were murdered. During the next two years, a further 44,000 of Theresienstadt's Jews were deported to Auschwitz and killed, while 33,000 Jews died of starvation while still inside Theresienstadt, among them Albert Flatow, who had won four gold medals for Germany in the first modern Olympic Games, held in Athens in 1896. A leading figure in German gymnastic circles, Flatow had been expelled from the national gymnastic organisation in 1933 because he was a Jew. He was seventy-three years old when he died.

News of the scale of the killings reached Britain and the United States in the form of a comprehensive summary of the executions in Eastern and Western Galicia, smuggled from Warsaw to London by members of the

A deceptive moment. *Jews being loaded onto a train for Treblinka at Siedlce railway junction, 22 August 1942, watched by a Ukrainian volunteer guard. Some 7,000 Jews had been travelling on the train for two days, without food or water. This photograph was taken by an Austrian soldier, Hubert Pfoch, who was on his way through the same junction to the Eastern Front. He noted that a few moments after he took this picture the guard killed a Jew with a single blow of his rifle butt. Pfoch counted fifty corpses on the platform after the train left.*

socialist Bund, and widely publicised. In May 1942, at a meeting in the Biltmore Hotel, New York, Chaim Weizmann expressed his anguish that according to a 'calm, statistical estimate' a quarter of Central European Jewry would have been 'liquidated' by the end of the war. Another speaker, Nahum Goldman, head of the Zionist Emergency Council, believed that even Dr Weizmann's figures might be too optimistic: Goldman felt that no more than 'two or three million' Jews would be found to have survived. According to Goldmann's statistic, up to six million might be murdered before the war ended, not a quarter but three-quarters of European Jewry.

The SS killing squads continued their operations throughout 1942. On 2 March 1942, 5,000 Jews were taken from the Minsk ghetto to a newly dug pit on the outskirts of the town, and machine-gunned. No ammunition was 'wasted' on the hundreds of children seized that day: they were thrown into the pit alive, to die of suffocation under the bodies of the adults machine-gunned after them. As in many of the ghettos in German-occupied Russia, attempts were made by the Jews of Minsk to resist the round-ups. The

Germans responded by full-scale military attacks on the ghettos, and the execution of the resistance leaders.

The systematic pattern of deportations accelerated during the summer of 1942. The first deportation from Holland to Auschwitz took place on 15 July: by the end of the war 106,000 Jews had been deported from Holland and killed; only 20,000 survived. On August 4 more than 1,000 Jews who had been rounded up and held in an internment camp at Malines, in Belgium, were deported to Auschwitz. The Archbishop of Malines, Cardinal van Roey, was among several Roman Catholic leaders who protested, but the Germans ignored him. By the time of liberation, 25,631 Belgian Jews had been deported, of whom only 1,244 survived. But more than 25,000 others were hidden by the local population in private homes and Christian orphanages, and so saved. Of the thousand Belgian Jews who fought with the local resistance, 140 were killed in combat.

In German-occupied Poland the will to resist was strong. On 19 September 1942, while 5,000 Jews were being murdered by a German police battalion in the Polish town of Parczew, several hundred managed to escape to the nearby forest. There they formed a 'family camp', protected by a Jewish resistance group led by Yehiel Grynszpan, and joined by escapees from other towns. Three months later, several hundred of those in the forest were hunt-

Men, women and children *being loaded onto open freight wagons for the journey by narrow-gauge railway to the death camp at Chelmno, in German-occupied western Poland. On reaching the camp, all the deportees were murdered.*

ed down and killed by German troops. Others died of starvation and disease, and the terrible cold of two successive winters. Later the remnants were helped by a Polish partisan battalion commanded by a Jewish officer, Alexander Skotnicki, and as many as 200 survived the war.

The most successful Jewish family camp was in the forests of White Russia, where the three Bielski brothers, Tuvia, Asael and Zus, led a 150-strong Jewish partisan group which not only harrassed German lines of communication but protected more than 1,200 women and children who had escaped from the ghettos of the region. The Bielskis established their own hidden flour-mill, bakery, kitchen, metal workshop, hospital and school. Further east, when all 3,000 Jews of Tuczyn, in the Volhynia, were rounded up by the SS, 2,000 managed to escape. In the months ahead, the German hunts for them were ferocious, local Ukrainians gave no help, and only fifteen survived the war.

There were many instances of help being given to the Jews to avoid destruction. Although 77,000 Jews were deported from France to Auschwitz and killed, many Church leaders in France spoke out against the deportations, and many local people did what they could to hide Jews. At the French Protestant village of Le Chambon-sur-Lignon, the villagers, inspired by their pastor André Trocmé, gave sanctuary to more than 3,000 Jewish adults and children, then helped disperse them to other hiding places, and took many to safety across the border to neutral Switzerland. André Trocmé's cousin Daniel, who was caught hiding Jews, was sent by the Germans to Buchenwald, where he died. In Holland, where several thousand Jews were hidden by the Dutch, 250 families in the town of Nieuwland acted collectively to take in Jews, and feed, house and hide them until liberation.

The SS continued the deportations without respite. October 1942 saw the greatest number of Jews deported and murdered in any month of the war, 300,000 in all, five per cent of the total Holocaust death toll. During the round-ups, children, and those too old or sick to make their way to the railway stations, were shot dead in the streets: this was the fate of Dov Ber Fichtencwejg, my own great grandfather, then in his early nineties. The intensity of the deportations and killings in November 1942 was almost as great as the previous month. That same month, a Jewish resistance group in French Algeria gave crucial help to the Allies at the time of the North African landings, which marked the turn of the tide of war in the Mediterranean. At Stalingrad and El Alamein, battles which ended in victory for the Allies, Jewish soldiers were among the front-line fighters, and the dead. Off Crete, a Jewish Petty Officer, Thomas 'Tommy' Gould, won the Victoria Cross when he removed an unexploded bomb from his submarine.

A special Jewish Commando had fought in the Eritrean /Ethopian campaign against the Italians. When it was disbanded in 1942 twenty-eight of its members, all of them fluent German-speakers and many of them pre-war

'AMBROISE AND VIOLETTE'

Jewish agents (above) who operated clandestine radios in German-occupied France, as members of the British Special Operations Executive, SOE. Denise Bloch – 'Ambroise' – (top) was nearly captured by the Gestapo in 1942 as a member of the French Resistance, but managed to cross the Pyrenees and make her way back to England. Re-entering France in March 1944 to work with the Resistance before the Normandy Landings, she was captured and executed in Ravensbruck concentration camp early in 1945. Muriel Byck – 'Violette' – (below) was dropped by parachute south of Orleans in April 1944 and, after a few weeks of intense activity and narrow escapes, died of meningitis on May 23.

CLANDESTINE FIGHTERS.

SIG members (above) on leave in Tel Aviv, from left to right, Dov Cohen, recruited from the Irgun, Rosenzweig, Maurice Tiefenbrunner (Tiffen) and Walter Essner, a German, former prisoner of war, ex-Afrika Corp soldier, who helped to create SIG's German identity before betraying its first big operation. He was later 'shot while trying to escape'. For their story see pages 218-20.

refugees from Germany, joined a clandestine group known by the initials SIG (possibly standing for Special Intelligence Group). They wore German uniforms, did German drill, and during their training were woken by surprise in the small hours to ensure they spoke German straight away. In June 1942 they assisted the fledgling Special Air Service in a raid on two North African airfields to blow up planes being used to attack Malta. They drove captured German trucks, loaded with French soldiers who, they pretended, were prisoners of War under their care. Unfortunately some of them were betrayed by two former German prisoners of war who had been recruited into the group to help train its members. In September 1942 four or five of the surviving SIGs were employed in a similiar subterfuge. They crossed the desert and entered German-held Tobruk undetected, but the British forces coming by sea could not be landed, so the operation failed. All SIG members eventually managed to return to the safety of Allied lines.

Humiliating 'sport'. *Greek Jews, rounded up in the port city of Salonika, beaten and humiliated by their German guards. Almost 10,000 men were kept standing in the hot summer sun for the whole of 11 July 1942, before being released at the end of the day. A year later the whole Jewish population of Salonika was deported to Auschwitz.*

By the end of February 1943 as many as eighty per cent of Polish and western Russian Jewry had been murdered. On March 3, the SS turned their attentions to the former Greek regions of Macedonia and Thrace, which Bulgaria had occupied, and to Eastern Thrace, which was under direct German rule. Within three weeks 12,000 Jews had been deported to Treblinka – in twenty trains – and murdered there.

On 10 March 1943 the German government asked the Bulgarians to begin the deportation of all 50,000 Bulgarian Jews. The King of Bulgaria, Boris, opposed any such deportation. His son's godfather, Angelo Roncalli, then Papal Nuncio in Turkey – later Pope John XXIII – urged that the German request be ignored. Bulgarian farmers let it be known that they would lie down on the railway tracks if deportations began. At an emergency session a week after the German demand, the Bulgarian parliament voted against any deportations. None took place. King Boris, summoned to Berlin by Hitler, refused to change his mind: just as the Hungarian Regent, Admiral Horthy, who was likewise summoned to see Hitler – in Salzburg – refused to deport any of the 665,000 Jews then under Hungarian rule.

Cheated of two targets, the SS moved rapidly to find and destroy another. On March 15 the deportation began of the Jewish community of Salonika, the principal city of northern Greece. After five months, 43,000 of the once vibrant 56,000-strong community of Salonika had been murdered in Auschwitz. It was the greatest single tragedy to befall Sephardi Jews since the expulsion from Spain in 1492. A thousand miles from Greece, on the first day of the deportations from Salonika, a fifty-two-year-old woman, Trude Neumann, died of hunger in Theresienstadt. She was the daughter of Theodor Herzl, founder of the Zionist movement. From 1918 she had been a patient in a mental institution in Vienna: in 1942 all the patients were deported to Theresienstadt, where almost all of them died.

In German-occupied Poland there had been a final deportation from the Cracow ghetto starting on March 13, not this time to Belzec, but to Auschwitz. Of the 2,000 Jews rounded up for deportation, 700 were shot dead in the street. Several hundred Cracow Jews were also sent to the nearby slave labour camp at Plaszow, where the SS commandant Amon Goeth was a much-feared sadist. A German Roman Catholic factory owner, Oskar Schindler, was able to save a thousand Cracow Jews from being sent to Plaszow by persuading the Gestapo to allow him to employ them in his factory on the outskirts of Cracow, making kitchen and other utensils for the German army. Another non-Jew, Julius Madritch, originally from Vienna, had a clothing factory in the nearby city of Tarnow, and persuaded the Gestapo to let him take 232 Jewish men, women and children from the Cracow ghetto to work for him. When Amon Goeth went specially to Tarnow to get these Jews transferred to him, Madritch was able to bribe him to let them stay. In Berlin itself, where 7,752 Jews were deported that March to Auschwitz, another non-Jew, Otto Weidt, who ran a small brush factory in the centre of the city, took several hundred blind and deaf mute Jews under his protection, insisting to the Gestapo that the work these Jews did was essential for the German war effort. He also provided food and false documents for fifty-six Jewish workers who were in hiding. Despite frequent Gestapo searches, twenty-seven of them survived the war.

Deported across Europe. *11,000 Jews from the Bulgarian-occupied regions of Greece and Yugoslavia were rounded up on 3 March 1943, then carried more than 800 miles in railway wagons and by Danube barge to the death camp at Treblinka. Less than a dozen survived.*

Marched through burning streets *of the Warsaw ghetto in the last two weeks of May 1943, even as the Germans were crushing the final stages of the ghetto revolt, thousands of Jews were taken to the railway sidings nearby and sent by train to the death camp at Treblinka. One of the photographs pasted into a special album by the commander of the German forces, SS General Stroop.*

In April 1943 the Germans decided to renew the deportations from Warsaw which had been suspended after a spate of Jewish resistance four months earlier. When a German military force entered the ghetto on April 19 with tanks and artillery as well as machine guns, the Jews fought back. The Germans withdrew, then moved into the ghetto again, systematically destroying buildings, while Jews hiding in cellars and sewers were driven out by smoke bombs and hand grenades. For two weeks the battle raged, until, on May 8, the Germans reached the underground headquarters of the organiser of the revolt, Mordechai Anielewicz. After a fierce struggle, Anielewicz and more than a hundred of his fighters were killed and their headquarters overrun: today a memorial stone marks the spot.

In triumph, the German SS General Jürgen Stroop reported to Berlin: 'The Warsaw ghetto is no more'. During the revolt and in its aftermath more than 56,000 Jews were killed: many were burned alive inside the buildings, some were shot dead as they emerged, while others were rounded up – even while the fighting still raged around them – and deported to Treblinka, and to three slave labour camps south-east of Warsaw where they were killed during a three-day period in the first week of November in what the Nazis designated a 'harvest festival'.

In the immediate aftermath of the Warsaw ghetto revolt as many as 15,000 Jews escaped to the 'Aryan' side of the city, where they went into hiding, many of them protected by Poles at great risk to themselves, though some were betrayed and handed over to the Gestapo. Among those betrayed and then killed was Emanuel Ringelblum, the historian of the fate of the Jews of Poland. There were Jewish uprisings in many other ghettos on the eve of the final deportations, both before and after the Warsaw ghetto revolt. All were crushed, but not before the defiance of the victims had shown the strength of the human spirit.

Two Jewish fighters *captured by the Germans on 27 April 1943, the ninth day of the Warsaw ghetto uprising. When the uprising began Joseph Goebbels wrote: 'Of course, the fun won't last very long. But it shows what is to be expected of the Jews when they are in possession of arms.' Another photograph from General Stroop's album.*

Women fighters *captured by the Germans during the Warsaw ghetto uprising. From General Stroop's album.*

The only 'permanent' Jewish inmates in the death camps were the slave labourers who were being forced to burn the bodies of the murdered Jews. They themselves could not expect to live for long: every month or so the whole labour force would be shot, and replaced by new deportees. On 2 August 1943 the slave labourers at Treblinka rose up in revolt, led by a doctor, Julian Chorarzycki, and an engineer, Alfred Galewski, both of whom were killed in the fighting In the death camp at Sobibor the 150 members of a similiar squad dug a tunnel out of the camp and tried to escape: the tunnel went under the camp perimeter but emerged into the minefield that surrounded the camp. All 150 were caught and executed.

On August 16, as deportations began of 40,000 Jews from the Bialystok ghetto, east of Warsaw, there was an armed uprising, led by Mordechai Tenenbaum and Daniel Moszkowicz. The Jews had a number of rifles and pistols, even a few machine guns, but the Germans used artillery and tanks to crush them. In the aftermath of the uprising, 1,260 children under the age of thirteen were rounded up and deported to Theresienstadt. After a month, volunteers were asked for, to accompany them to neutral Switzerland – rumour said they were then to be sent from Switzerland to Palestine. Fifty-three doctors and nurses offered to accompany them. Their destination was in fact Auschwitz, where all the children and most of their helpers were killed.

The Germans continued to comb Europe for Jews to deport. In the first week of October 1943 it was to have been the turn of the Jews in Denmark to be deported, among them many pre-war refugees from Germany. During the night of October1/2, in a gesture of extraordinary defiance, Danish sea captains and fishermen ferried not only 5,919 Jews, but also 1,301 part-Jews – designated Jews by the Nazi racial laws – and 686 Christians married to Jews, across the narrow stretch of water between Denmark and neutral Sweden, where they found sanctuary for the rest of the war. When the Germans arrived to search for Jews they found only 500, most of them old people. They were deported to Theresienstadt, but the Danish government persisted in asking regularly about their fate, and 423 of them survived the war.

In September 1943, as the Allied armies landed in southern Italy, Mussolini was overthrown and Italy withdrew from the war. The German army immediately moved into northern Italy, advancing until it confronted the Allied armies south of Rome. The SS, following in the wake of the German troops, began without delay the deportation of Italian Jews to Auschwitz, starting on September 16, and continuing throughout October and November. In all, 8,000 were deported to Auschwitz and killed. But Italians gave hiding places to thousands more, including 477 Jews who were given shelter inside the Vatican, and 4,238 more in the monasteries, convents and Roman Catholic institutions in the capital. As a result, more than 5,000 of Rome's Jews could not be found by the SS, which had to be content with the arrest and deportation of just over 1,000.

Despite the overwhelming German military superiority, revolt and resistance remained a Jewish imperative, wherever it was possible. At Sobibor a revolt of the slave labourers on 14 October 1943 was led by a Russian Jew, Alexander Pechersky, and a Polish Jew, Leon Felhendler. Of the 600 labourers 200 were shot by the SS and Ukrainian guards while running out of the camp, or were killed while crossing the camp minefield. Of the 400 who got away, 100 were later captured and killed. Of the 300 who then remained, more than 200 died of typhus while in hiding, or were killed – as soldiers – fighting in the ranks of the Soviet Army. Only eighty-four survived the war, among them Pechersky – who lived in the Soviet Union to a ripe old age – and Felhendler, who was murdered by anti-Semitic Poles immediately after the war.

The German search for Jewish victims continued even when the war was beginning to go against them. On 15 March 1944 – exactly a year after the start of the deportations from Salonika, and as the Red Army was moving inexorably forward towards the German border – the SS began a round-up of all 10,000 Greek Jews in Athens, Epirus, Thessaly and the Peloponnese, the heartland of ancient Greece, hitherto under Italian occupation. Four thousand were able to flee into the countryside and the mountains, where they were given shelter by local peasant farmers, and where many joined Greek partisan units. More than 1,000 were able to escape by boat across the Aegean to neutral Turkey. Many survived as a result of an instruction issued by the head of the Greek Orthodox Church, Archbishop Damaskinos, who told all monasteries and convents in Athens and the provincial towns to take in any Jews who knocked on their doors. But more than 6,000 Greek Jews were caught and deported to Auschwitz that spring. Hundreds died during the eight-day rail journey in sealed cattle trucks.

Among the Jews who joined Greek partisan groups were forty who took part in blowing up the Gorgopotamo bridge, breaking German road and rail communications with the north. A Greek rabbi, Moses Pesah, commanded a resistance group in the mountains of Thessaly. Among the non-Jews who helped Jews escape deportation was Princess Alice of Greece, a great-granddaughter of Queen Victoria, and the mother of Prince Philip. She hid several Jewish families in her home in Athens.

Safe haven. *Four months before the German invasion of the Soviet Union, the teachers and students of one of eastern Europe's leading religious academies, the Mir Yeshiva, obtained visas from Chiune Sugihara, the Japanese consul in the Lithuanian capital Kovno, and were able to make their way across Russia to Japan, then*

On 19 March 1944, five days after the round-up of Greek Jews, the German army entered Hungary. Its aim was to prevent the Hungarian government from making a separate peace with the Soviet Union and withdrawing from the war. With the German troops came a special SS unit headed by Adolf Eichmann who, a month later, ordered Hungary's 750,000 Jews, including those in Ruthenia and Northern Transylvania which Hungary had annexed in 1939 and 1940, into ghettos. Eichmann then prepared a schedule of deportation from Hungary to Auschwitz, and by mid-June – as reported by the SS to Berlin with their usual precision – a total of 289,357 Jews had gone. In two towns, Miskolc and Satoraljaujhely, where the Jews tried to resist boarding the trains, several hundred were shot dead on the platforms.

Even as the massive influx of Jews from Hungary, the most intense of all the deportations, was keeping the four gas chambers and crematoria at Birkenau working night and day, the SS search for Jews took them to the extremities of German control. On June 14 – eight days after Allied landings in Normandy, which spelt doom for Germany – the 1,800 Jews of Corfu were rounded up, and put on board a ship for mainland Greece. The SS also wanted to put the 257 Jews of the nearby island of Zante on the same ship, but the head of the local Greek Orthodox Church, Archbishop Chrysostomos, and the Mayor, Lukos Karrer, refused to obey the order to bring the Jews of the island to the quayside. Instead, he arranged for all able-bodied Jews to be given sanctuary in the remote mountain villages. The archbishop told his flock: 'If the deportation order is carried out, I will join the Jews and share their fate.' The Gestapo on the island managed to seize sixty Jews – old people and children – and take them to the quayside, but the boat's captain informed them that his boat was already so crowded that it would not stop for any more deportees.

on to Shanghai, which had no restrictions on Jewish entry, and had already taken in 25,000 Jewish refugees, mostly from Germany and Austria. This was the only eastern European Yeshiva to survive the Holocaust intact. After the war it transferred to Brooklyn.

From Hungary, 437,402 Jews had been deported and almost all of them killed. Then, in the last week of June, the truth about their fate, and comprehensive details about the previous two years of mass murder at Auschwitz, reached the West. It had been brought from Auschwitz itself, initially to Slovakia, by four Jewish escapees: two Slovak Jews, Rudolf Vrba and Alfred Wetzler, who had been at Auschwitz for almost two years and had escaped shortly before the arrival of the first trains from Hungary, and a Polish and a Slovak Jew, Czeslaw Mordowicz and Arnost Rosin, who had been in the camp during the first few days of the gassing of Jews from Hungary. Their reports were combined, smuggled by courier to neutral Switzerland, and then sent by urgent diplomatic telegrams to London and Washington. The outcry was immediate: President Roosevelt, Winston Churchill, the King of Sweden and Pope Pius XII each demanded an immediate end to the deportations. The Hungarian Regent, Admiral Horthy, a devout Roman Catholic who had earlier resisted Hitler's pressure to deport Jews from Hungary, bowed to international and Papal pressure. Summoning the senior German representative in Hungary, SS General Viessenmayer, Horthy ordered a halt to the deportations: they stopped within forty-eight hours of his demand. The surviving Jews in Hungary, more than 100,000, mostly living in and around Budapest, were saved from deportation.

Palestine during the Second World War saw a continuing expansion of Jewish enterprise and Kibbutzim while, to maintain secrecy, and to prevent British raids in search of arms, two Hagannah headquarters were set up, in small apartments in Tel Aviv five minutes' walk from each other. The Hagannah did, however, cooperate with the British over all war activity: it was a Hagannah unit of twenty-three men that set off under a British officer to attack the Italian oil refinery in the Lebanese port of Tripoli: they were never seen again.

Grim news. *A news stand in Tel Aviv (opposite), May 1940, with Hebrew, Yiddish, Polish and French newspapers. One of them,* La Bourse Egyptienne, *announces the flight of French troops from Arras, in north-eastern France. A Hebrew paper tells of 'half a million people' fleeing the advancing German forces in France. Within two weeks the Germans had occupied Paris.* [PHOTO: A. HIMMELREICH]

An exercise break *for students (left) at an agricultural school for immigrant women at Ayanot, just south of Tel Aviv. Founded in 1930, it mostly taught citrus cultivation. The school became co-educational in 1947.*
[PHOTO: ZOLTAN KLUGER]

In 1941, as the German army advanced into Egypt, threatening the Suez Canal, a new kibbutz, Dorot, was established in the Negev desert ten miles east of Gaza, which, if the British were to withdraw from Palestine, could form a front line of defence by the Hagannah of the Jewish settlements throughout Palestine. At Ben Gurion's urging, a group of youngsters, their suppplies loaded on twelve camels, made their way to the northernmost tip of the Red Sea, opposite the Jordanian port of Akaba, where they hoped to set up a Jewish presence on the water's edge, but the British had made the area a closed military zone. The group managed, however, to draw some detailed maps, most helpful five years later, when the port of Eilat was established. Among the teenagers was Shimon Peres, later three times Israel's Prime Minister.

While the Hagannah found common cause with the British, a small Jewish terrorist group attacked British soldiers and police. When its leader, Avraham Stern – who gave the group its name, the Stern Gang – was killed, his place was taken by Yitzhak Shamir, later Prime Minister of Israel. A larger terrorist group, the Irgun, led by Menachem Begin, a Polish-born Jew who reached Palestine during the war, called on the Jews to revolt against the British, and likewise carried out acts of terror, which were strongly denounced by Ben Gurion and the Jewish Agency. After attacks on several British police stations, in search of arms for its members, the Irgun announced that it would not attack the British until the war with Germany was over. It was two members of the Stern Gang who, in 1944, murdered the British High Commissioner in Egypt, Lord Moyne – and his driver – blaming Moyne for his earlier opposition to widespread Jewish immigration to Palestine. They did not know that he was about to meet Weizmann, at Churchill's suggestion, to discuss the possibility of a future Jewish State in Palestine. So outraged was the Jewish Agency at Moyne's murder that it gave the British the names of 700 Irgun members, and their known locations. Most of them were arrested. For its part, the Stern gang promised the Jewish Agency not to try to assassinate Churchill while Moyne's murderers were on trial: both were later executed.

British, American, Polish and Canadian Jews fought in all the D-Day armies. In one of the cemeteries near the Normandy beaches are the graves of 335 Canadians killed on the day of the landings, among them two Nova Scotia Highlanders on whose headstones the Star of David is carved: Private J. Gertel, aged twenty-two and Private B. Goldsmith, aged twenty-four.

On July 23, the SS rounded up all 2,000 Jews on the former Italian island of Rhodes, in the Eastern Mediterranean. They were a Ladino-speaking Sephardi community. Haluk Ulukmen, the Turkish Consul-General on the island – which had been Turkish until conquered by Italy before the First World War – was determined to save as many Jews as possible from deportation, and presented the local German commander with a list of fifty Jews whom he claimed were Turkish nationals, insisting that they be released. Not wishing to antagonise neutral Turkey, the commander agreed. But the remain-

REACHING A NEW HOME:
861 Polish Jewish children, 719 of them orphans, who had fled to safety in Russia when Hitler invaded Poland in 1939, reached Palestine on 18 February 1943 (right and far right). They had left Russia in 1942 with 24,000 Polish and Jewish soldiers and refugees whom Stalin allowed to join the Allied armies in the Middle East. Travelling through Teheran, where they were housed in a temporary camp (above), they were known as 'The Teheran Children'.

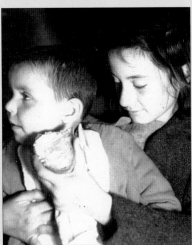

ing 1,950 Jews were taken by ship from Rhodes to Salonika, joined by more than a hundred Jews from the smaller island of Kos, and transported with them to Auschwitz, where 1,700 of the Jews from Rhodes and 120 of the Jews from Kos were killed.

In France, as the Allied forces were advancing on Paris, the SS ordered the arrest of all Jewish orphans in the Paris region. Within four days, 500 had been rounded up, and on 31 July 300 of them were among the 1,300 Jews in the last of more than seventy deportation trains to leave Paris for Auschwitz. On reaching Auschwitz, 800 of the deportees were killed, including all the young orphans. Three days later, as Allied forces advanced into northern Italy, a final train brought 222 Italian Jews to Auschwitz from Verona.

Denied any further deportations from Hungary, the SS turned its attention to the Lodz ghetto, the last one in which large numbers of Jews were still alive, working in factories providing clothing for the German army – almost all the German army, navy and air force caps, with their swastikas and insignia, were made there. Starting on August 6 and continuing for more than three weeks, 70,000 Jews were deported to Auschwitz and killed. France, too, continued to be a source of victims, even as the Allies were poised to drive the Germans out altogether. On August 17, a single carriage attached to one of the last German trains to leave Paris before the Allies arrived, took fifty-one Jews to Auschwitz and their death.

Throughout 1944, and reaching a climax in August, Jews were active in resistance movements in France, Greece, Yugoslavia, central Poland and northern Italy – where the Jewish partisan leader Rita Rosani was caught by the Germans and killed. In the Balkans, more than a dozen Jewish parachutists from Palestine were dropped behind German lines with the double task of harming the German war effort and helping any Jews whom they might encounter. Seven of them were captured and killed, including Italian-born Enzo Sereni, who was shot in Dachau, and Hungarian-born Hannah Szenes, who was parachuted into Yugoslavia and captured after she had crossed into Hungary. Taken to Budapest, she was tortured and killed.

On the Russian Front, where the German army was being driven back through the Baltic States and eastern Poland, an entirely Jewish military force, the 16th Lithuanian Division, was in action. In Britain, Churchill supported the creation of a Jewish Brigade Group, to fight with its own Star of David

Jewish partisans *in southern France, armed with British-supplied Sten guns, August 1944. Jewish resistance fighters played a major part in the liberation of two French towns, Mazamet and Castres, before the arrival of the Allied forces.*

insignia. In Slovakia, a Jewish battalion took part in the national uprising. Rudolf Vrba, one of the Auschwitz escapees, was among the Jews who fought to liberate the country. In Warsaw, more than a thousand Jews who had been in hiding since the ghetto revolt sixteen months earlier, including a Jewish battle unit commanded by Shmuel Kenigswein, took part in the Polish national uprising. A Jewish woman, Shoshana Kosower, who led Polish units through the sewer system, was awarded the Polish Cross of Valour.

On 3 September 1944 the last deportation train left Holland for Auschwitz. Among more than a thousand deportees were Anne Frank and her family, German Jews who had found refuge in Holland before the war, and been hidden by a Dutch Christian. He and they had been betrayed. When the train reached Auschwitz three days later, 549 of the deportees, including all seventy-nine children under the age of fifteen, were immediately gassed. Anne Frank, sent to the barracks at Auschwitz, survived, but died in Belsen in 1945, a few months before the camp was liberated. At Auschwitz itself there was a brief halt to the daily killings when, on October 7, a group of Jews being

Jewish partisans *in central Slovakia, where they were active in the Slovak national uprising against the Germans which broke out on 26 August 1944.*

forced to work near the gas chambers, obtained explosives from Jewish women working in a nearby munitions factory, and blew up two of the four crematoria. All those who took part in the revolt were tracked down and killed, as were the women who had helped them. The only survivor was a Jew from Salonika, Isaac Venezia, who managed to get back into the camp. He was later among the hundreds of Jews who died of starvation at the concentration camp at Ebensee, in Austria, in the final days of the war.

In Hungary, despite the halting of deportations to Auschwitz in July, the Jews of Budapest were again at risk when, on October 15, a Hungarian Fascist regime came to power and anti-Jewish violence erupted in the streets. Tens of thousands of Jews were given protective documents and put into safe houses by the foreign diplomats in Budapest. The Swedish emissary Raoul Wallenberg – sent to Budapest on the authority of the American War Refugee Board in Washington – issued 15,000 such documents. The Swiss Consul, Charles Lutz, personally signed 7,800. Thousands more were issued by the Director of the

Jews reach Auschwitz *from Beregszasz, a Czech Ruthenian town which had been occupied by Hungary in 1940. They were among 10,000 Jews from the town and surrounding villages who were murdered at Auschwitz on the last day of May 1944. A few moments after this photograph was taken, all women with children, and all old men and women, as well as the disabled, were separated from the able-bodied men and women and sent to the gas chambers. This photograph and the next were taken by a German SS sergeant as part of an album he prepared of a single deportation.*

Budapest office of the Red Cross, Friedrich Born, and by an Italian citizen, Giorgio Perlasca, who had been given charge of the Spanish embassy in Budapest. At least 200 Jews were saved by the intervention of an Armenian doctor, Ara Jeretzian, who sheltered them in the hospital where he worked and in an emergency clinic which he set up in a private home, providing food and, when needed, false documents.

Auschwitz was in its final days as a place of mass murder. On October 28 the librarian of the Jewish Museum in Prague, Tobias Jakobovits, and his staff, whom the Germans had kept at work assembling, exhibiting and cataloguing Jewish books and artefacts with a view to showing future generations the 'lost world' of European Jewry, were deported there and killed. On October 31 more than 8,000 Slovak Jews were brought to the camp; they too were killed. Then, with Soviet troops having entered southern Poland, the SS ordered the gassing to stop. From Budapest, 50,000 Jews who could no longer be sent to Auschwitz were sent on foot towards Austria. Raoul Wallenberg personally gave

In the wood at Auschwitz, *a hundred yards from two of the gas chambers, Jews from the Beregszasz deportation train who have been marched from the railway siding, are kept waiting, shortly before being taken, all unsuspecting, to their deaths. Another photograph from the S.S. sergeant's album.*

A death march, *inmates of Dachau pass through a German village, photographed clandestinely from an upstairs window, early April 1945. The SS were determined to go on with their mission of extermination to the very end, driving Jews away from the advancing United States troops, even if it meant exposing the reality of persecution to ordinary German eyes.*

Swedish protective certificates to 4,000 of them, and they were saved, but 10,000 Jews perished on the march, many of them shot down in cold blood.

By mid-January 1945, Soviet forces were within a few miles of Auschwitz. The SS ordered the evacuation of the camp and of the dozens of slave labour camps around it; more than 30,000 Jews were put in trains and sent to camps inside Germany, or were marched away on foot. Hundreds were shot each day when they stumbled and fell, or were unable to get up in the morning to resume the march. From every slave labour camp, Jews were forced westward, taken to new camps and factories, where they worked – often underground – as part of a desperate last effort by the Germans to maintain war production.

In March 1945 the Jewish Brigade Group took its place with the Allied forces in Italy. Five and a half thousand Jews, their Star of David a proud identification, went into action against a war-hardened German adversary which had hitherto regarded that same Star of David – imposed on Jews throughout German-controlled Europe – as a symbol of servitude and contempt. After two months of fighting in Italy, the Jewish Brigade Group reached the Austro-Yugoslav border. Eighty-three of its men had been killed in action.

On 15 April 1945 British soldiers liberated Belsen. Two weeks later, the Americans liberated Dachau. What the liberators saw – the mounds of cruelly emaciated bodies, and thousands of the dying and desperately ill – brings to mind Kipling's poem about the sailors who, in the First World War, collected from a Scottish beach the bodies of those killed after an explosion on a British battleship: 'They have touched a knowledge outreaching speech…'

As many as 100,000 Jews were still captives of the SS in concentration camps yet to be liberated. On April 28, as a result of the negotiating skills and persistence of a Swedish aristocrat, Count Folke Bernadotte, 7,000 Jewish women prisoners were taken by truck and bus from Ravensbruck concentration camp, north of Berlin, to Sweden.

The war was ending, the horrors of the concentration camps had been revealed, but to the last days the SS continued to murder Jews – on the death marches and in concentration camps. One such camp was Ebensee in Austria, to which thousands of Jews had been marched in the last weeks of the war. One of the last awards of the highest Soviet war honour, Hero of the Soviet Union, was to a Jew in Ebensee, Lev Manevitch, who on 4 May 1945, starved and emaciated, warned his fellow prisoners there, many of them survivors of Auschwitz, not to go into a tunnel to shelter from air raids. He knew that the order to do so was a Nazi deception. 'No one will go' he cried out in several languages. 'They will kill us'. The prisoners recognised the urgency of his appeals and refused to go into the tunnel. On the following day the camp was liberated, but Lev Manevitch was too weak to survive. Four days after his act of defiance, he died.

The moment of liberation. *Jews in their bunks at Buchenwald, photographed by one of the first American soldiers to enter their barrack, April 1945. The face, seventh from the left, next to the upright in the middle row, is that of Elie Wiesel, winner of the Nobel Peace Prize in 1986. In writing of Buchenwald in his memoir,* Night, *he recalled looking at himself in a mirror for the first time after liberation: 'A corpse gazed back at me. The look in his eyes, as he stared back at me, has never left me.'*

On 7 May 1945 the war in Europe came to an end. The Holocaust was over. Six million European Jews were dead, among them a million and a half children. In the immediate aftermath of these horrors, a Jew who had been in the Warsaw ghetto wrote to a friend in Palestine: 'I am sending you a photo of my adopted daughter. Look well at her and remember that such children were flung into the burning ovens. Just imagine that my little Tulcia is one of the few who was saved, and that hundreds of thousands of children like her were lost in the gas chambers when they were torn away from their parents. If you have a pathological imagination you may be able to picture this yourself, but if you are a normal person you will never be able to bring this chapter of horrors to life in spite of all your imaginings.'

237

CHAPTER SIX

REHABILITATION, STATEHOOD AND RENEWAL

1945-1960

F OR JEWS EVERYWHERE, THE DEFEAT OF HITLER
constituted a moment of relief and rejoicing, but it was a brief respite for
a much-weakened people. Not only for the Jews, but for millions of others,
rehabilitation was the urgent need: Poles, Czechs and Germans had been driv-
en from their homes as the borders of eastern Europe changed. An American
Jew, Herbert Lehman, later a United States Senator, was put in charge of the
United Nations Relief and Rehabilitation Administration – UNRRA. Food,
shelter and medicine were the first need, and then a new home. More than
1,600,000 Displaced Persons – DPs – were registered with UNRRA, 250,000
of whom were Jews who had survived the ghettos, concentration camps and
death marches.

One of them, Polish-born Ben Helfgott, who was liberated from
Theresienstadt, later recalled the day when he left there by train for Prague, a
free man – he was fifteen years old. 'It was like being in heaven. I had a pass.
I could travel free. Prague was the first civilised city I had been in for six years.
There were lots of soup kitchens there, where they were giving food to former
camp inmates. The city was teaming with survivors who were coming from
all parts of liberated Europe. I met two other survivors who took me with
them to where they were staying: a deserted apartment.' Every morning at ten
o'clock, Ben Helfgott hired a boat and went rowing until twelve. 'It gave me
an opportunity to build myself up. Then every day, I went from kitchen to
kitchen until four o'clock to eat to my heart's delight. And then, each evening,
I went to the cinema. I still had some of my sugar and rice from a German
storeroom, which I was either bartering or selling. I remember enjoying the
beer, the lovely beer.' In August 1945, Britain took in 732 teenage survivors
of the concentration camps, one of them Ben Helfgott. They began their

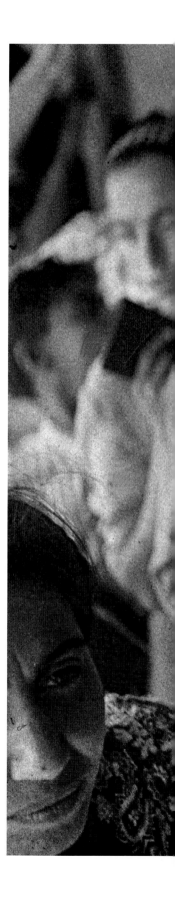

New immigrants

*from Arab lands reach the new town of Kiryat Shmonah in northern Israel. Founded in
1950 on the site of an immigrant camp, the name, 'City of Eight', commemorates the eight
Jews, among them Joseph Trumpeldor, who were killed defending the nearby settlement of Tel
Hai in 1920. The woman in front holds the key to her new home.*

[PHOTO: DAVID RUBINGER]

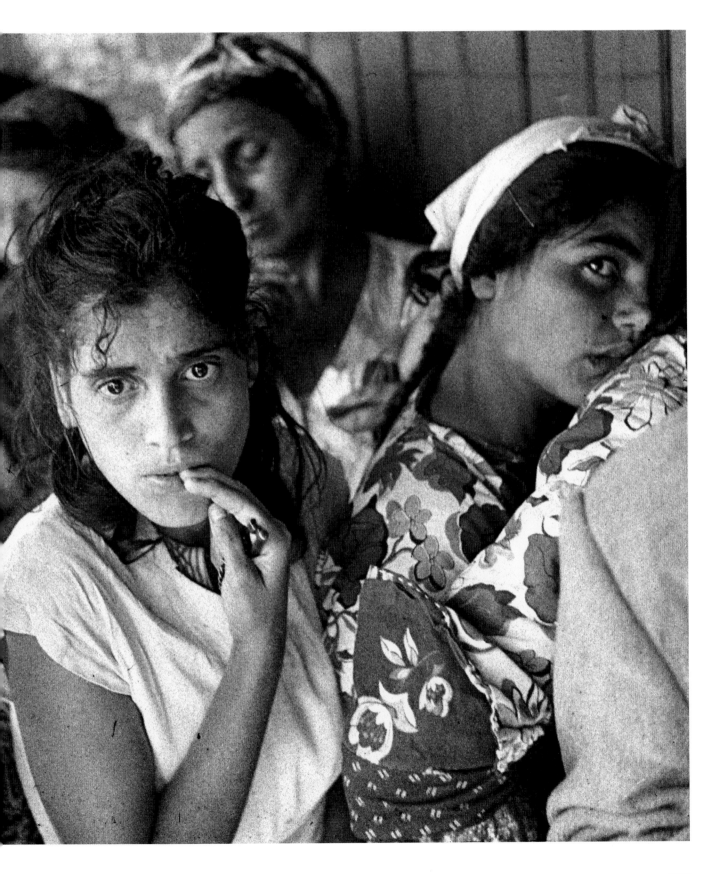

rehabilitation in the idyllic setting of the Lake District. Britain also allowed 13,000 survivors to enter Palestine. The first group from Buchenwald reached Haifa only two months after Germany's surrender.

Behind the new Iron Curtain, individual Jews came to prominence within the Communist system, and thus were leaders of repressive regimes. Other Jews worked within the Communist rules in the hope of benefiting their fellow citizens.

In Poland, in war-scarred Warsaw, the Yiddish theatre re-opened in November 1946, presided over by Ida Kaminska, who had managed to flee to Soviet Central Asia during the war. Reflecting on the decision to re-open the theatre in Warsaw, where virtually all the Jewish population had been killed by the Nazis, she wrote: 'We had the wish to make a monument to the murdered Jews and the government helped us.' At the re-opening, the theatre was packed. Among the several thousand Jews who had returned were many who wanted to show that their lives, and their culture, could continue.

The Jews who were living in post-war Poland hoped to rebuild their lives where they had lived before the war. Poland had been their country, the Polish language their language, a Polish town their home town, a Polish school their school. But a continuing, strong stimulus to emigration came from an upsurge in violent attacks on Jews throughout the country. Among Jews murdered by Poles in the first year of peace was Chaim Hirszman, one of only two survivors of Belzec. In the village of Kosow-Lacki, only six miles from Treblinka, ten Jews were killed after they had tried to return to their homes in the village. In all, 1,500 Jews were murdered by Poles in the twelve months following the end of the war. The largest single such killing was at Kielce on 4 July 1946, when forty-two Jews were murdered. Several were in the town only temporarily, hoping to make their way out of Poland and across Europe, as the first stage of the journey to Palestine. The activities of those known as 'dentists', in the chaotic days immediately following the end of the war, were symptomatic of some Poles' attitude to the Jews. They dug up thousands of skulls in Jewish cemeteries throughout Poland, looking for gold teeth.

Many thousands of Polish Jews left for western Europe and Palestine. In October 1945, when Ben Gurion visited DP camps in France and Germany, his message was clear,

No respite. *Unwanted, exhausted, survivors of a post-war pogrom in the Polish town of Kielce (above), July 1946, wait for transport out of Poland. Most of them made their way to Palestine.*

Demanding an open door *to Jewish immigration to Palestine, British Jews (opposite), assembled by the Zionist Federation, including survivors of the Holocaust, march through London along the Embankment to a rally in Trafalgar Square, 7 July 1946. The second banner reads: 'The boys from the concentration camps'. A year earlier they had been flown to Britain from central Europe by the Royal Air Force. Among those in the procession was a Jewish holder of the Victoria Cross, Petty Officer Thomas Gould.*

defiant and hopeful: 'The Jewish People will have their National Home. It will be a struggle. It will be hard. We will confront the enemy intent on destroying us. But we will win. Have no doubt about that. The Jewish flag will fly over the Land of Israel, and no one will stop this from happening.' As a result of Ben Gurion's visit to Europe, members of the Jewish Brigade Group, veterans of the final months' fighting in Europe, accelerated their efforts to find survivors, especially in Poland, Romania and Hungary.

In the Polish city of Lodz, several hundred Jews from different towns in Poland gathered after the war to study and plan for their future. 'For one year we made every effort to pick up the broken shards of our lives out of the ashes,' Tess Wise recalled, 'but it was a futile effort, because every day brought new proof that we were not welcome. Anti-semitic attacks and pogroms were the order of the day.' The seven surviving members of her family, of which there had been eighty members before the war, made a decision to travel to the American Zone of Germany.

In Munich, a university established by UNRRA became a magnet for those Displaced Persons who were determined to educate themselves. 'The period in Munich was balm to my heart,' Tess Wise recalled. 'There were hundreds of refugee students forming one big sad family, all rooting for one another – planning a future our parents had dreamed about for us before and during the war: to be doctors, engineers, dentists and scientists.'

Wherever survivors gathered, they tried to prepare themselves for a productive life. Jack Brauns, a survivor of the Kovno ghetto and Dachau, was determined to become a surgeon – and eventually did so, in the United States. In the summer of 1945 he had been smuggled out of Austria to Italy by truck in a British army uniform provided by the Jewish Brigade, together with Zew Gdud – who later took the name William Z. Good – one of the very few survivors of the death pits at Ponar. Gdud went to Rome and enrolled in the faculty of medicine there. Brauns did the same in Turin. While studying, he lived at the Casa dello Studente, a villa which the American Jewish Joint Distribution Committee leased for four years for survivors who were embarked on higher education – their high school education having been cut short during the ghetto and concentration camp years. Brauns later recalled: 'Casa dello Studente became our new family for the duration of our studies and helped us in the transition into society as free men and women. It was the bridge that helped us enter a free society with all its challenges and benefits.' Each of the fifty students at the Casa dello Studente made their contribution to society in years to come in many lands, including Israel, the United States and Australia. One of them, Joseph Gutherz, had escaped from Dubno in 1941 just before the Germans arrived and had survived the war in the forests. In 1945 he had managed to cross from Austria into Italy, but only at his ninth attempt. Later emigrating to the United States, he became a cantor – in Dubno he had been in the synagogue choir. Thus the Jewish traditions of eastern Europe continued. His son Tom was to become a rabbi in Virginia.

The post-war search for normality, education and a life free from discrimination and danger also began to evoke once more the desire for some of life's little luxuries. In 1946 in New York, Estée Lauder began marketing

Studying for the future *in Turin. Jack Brauns, a survivor of the ghetto and the concentrations camps, left Austria for Italy determined to become a surgeon.*

Soldiers of the Jewish Brigade *take survivors of the Holocaust from Displaced Persons' camps in post-war Germany across the border into Austria and Italy, 1946. Here, on Italian soil, they made plans to continue by sea to Palestine from an Italian port. Often intercepted off the shore of Palestine by the British, thousands were then interned in Cyprus until the establishment of the State of Israel two years later.*

skin-care products. She liked to make it known that she had been born a Catholic in a Hapsburg castle in Austria-Hungary and had grown up as a Countess. She was in fact Jewish, born Josephine Esther Mentzer in Queens, New York. In 1953 her 'Youth Bath' became the best-selling perfume in the world. In 1998, her cosmetics empire was valued at more than six billion dollars.

When the Second World War ended there were 554,329 Jews in Palestine, thirty per cent of the total population. It was a Zionist imperative to try to raise that number, and to reduce the numerical disparity between the half million Jews and one million Arabs. At least 100,000 survivors wished to go to Palestine, but the British Labour Government only allowed 13,000 to do so. Confronted by a virtual halt to Jewish immigration to Palestine, the Jewish Agency set about trying to bypass and avoid the British restrictions and preventative measures. A vast clandestine organisation was set up to smuggle Jews out of Europe and into Palestine. Known as the Bricha ('Escape'), its emissaries, coming from Palestine, worked closely with the soldiers of the Jewish Brigade, then part of the Allied occupation forces in Germany and Austria. Routes out of Europe were prepared, using Rotterdam, Antwerp, Marseilles, Genoa and Bari as the main ports. At Cape Sounion, in Greece, the Jewish

Agency opened a training camp for Jews whom it intended to smuggle into Palestine: they were taught both agriculture and armed self-defence.

In Palestine, the Irgun Zvai Leumi mounted a campaign of terror against British troops. On 22 July 1946 it blew up the wing of the King David Hotel in Jerusalem that was used by the British administration, killing ninety-one Britons, Arabs and Jews. Among the Jewish dead was Julius Jacobs, a Mandate official and also secretary of the Jerusalem Music Society: in 1918 he had served in the Jewish Royal Fusiliers Battalion under General Allenby. Following the King David explosion, the commander of the British forces in Palestine, General Sir Hugh Barker, issued an order forbidding British soldiers to 'fraternise' with Jews. A member of the Irgun, and former British fighter pilot, Ezer Weizman – a nephew of Chaim Weizmann – was instructed to assassinate the general. His mission failed: half a century later he was President of Israel.

On 29 July 1946, a week after the King David explosion, the United States government asked Britain to allow 100,000 Jews to enter Palestine from Europe, and to begin the move within a month. The British government

Agricultural training. *Survivors of the Holocaust being trained by Jews from Palestine at a farm near Cape Sounion in Greece, 1945.*

declined, but the illegal immigration continued: 51,700 'illegals', intercepted between August 1946 and December 1947 on the high seas or as they tried to land, were sent to Cyprus. There they were detained behind barbed wire, guarded by British soldiers, including some who, less than two years earlier, had been among the liberators and saviours of Belsen, and did not relish their new task. But on 6 October 1946, the day of Atonement, a day of prayer and fasting, when observant Jews usually do no manual or other work, eleven kibbutzim were established in a single night, pushing Jewish settlement southward into the Negev, which the Jewish Agency was intent on securing as part of any future Jewish State.

When the Twenty-Second Zionist Congress opened in Basle on 9 December 1946, in the same hall used for the First Congress in 1897, there was much talk of resistance to British rule. Ben Gurion, who urged the Congress to demand full statehood without delay and to be prepared to take up arms to fight for it, electrified many of the younger delegates, among them Moshe Dayan and Shimon Peres, two future Israeli leaders.

Intercepted by the British, *more than four thousand illegal immigrants, survivors of the Holocaust, were taken back from the coast of Palestine to France on three ships. After they refused to disembark in France the British sent them to Germany, where they were taken to an internment camp in the British Zone. The refugees shown here are in the hold of one of the three ships, the freighter* Runnymede Park, *at Port de Bouc, France, on 22 August 1947, after refusing to disembark.*

THEIR SPIRITS UNBOWED,
Jews dance the lively, exuberant Hora (above) in front of one of the huts in the internment camp at Poppendorf, after being intercepted off the coast of Palestine and brought back to Germany. More Jews arrive at Poppendorf (right). Checking the documents of new arrivals at Poppendorf (far right). Many refugees had no identification papers. Some refused to give the authorities any personal details.

Under Ben Gurion's new active policy the Hagannah set up arms caches throughout the country. Shimon Peres was put in charge of mobilising manpower. Teddy Kollek – later Mayor of Jerusalem – went to the United States to raise funds to buy arms. Independent of the Hagannah, two groups, the Irgun and the Stern Gang, were committed to taking direct military action against the British. The British searched settlements and homes for hidden arms and munitions, imprisoning and even flogging those found in possession of weapons. In retaliation, on 29 December 1946 the Irgun seized a British army major and three sergeants and flogged them. On New Year's Day 1947 the Irgun attacked a British police post, killing a policeman. The British government, unwilling to embark on an all-out war, decided in secret on 22 January 1947 that if it could not get an agreed solution between Arabs and Jews it would hand over the problem to the United Nations.

On 15 February 1947 Britain announced publicly that the United Nations must decide the future of Palestine. Meanwhile, British naval patrols

A Cyprus detention camp *where survivors of the Holocaust, who had been prevented from landing in Palestine, were forced to wait until the establishment of the State of Israel before being released.*

continued to intercept immigrant ships. On April 14 three Jews were killed on board one such ship, the *Guardian*, as the British made plans to deport the 2,552 'illegals' on board to Cyprus. In the House of Commons, Churchill, then Leader of the Opposition, called these interceptions a 'squalid war'. On April 16 the British executed four members of the Irgun being held in prison in Acre. A week later two members of the Stern Gang who had been found guilty of terrorist acts committed suicide in the Central Prison in Jerusalem just before they were to have been executed.

Jews, desperate for normality amid the strife, flocked to the Edison Cinema in the centre of Jerusalem on May 1 when the American-Jewish composer Leonard Bernstein introduced his Jeremiah symphony. When Bernstein travelled to Galilee, one of the heartlands of Jewish settlement in Palestine, a crowd of 3,500 Jews gathered from twenty and more settlements to see him conduct. The *Boston Morning Globe* reported: 'Because of Government road restrictions, many of them would have to spend the night until dawn lying in trucks or in the open fields. It was as if heaven had sent them his genius to help them forget their troubles.'

Reunited after five years, *a Jewish refugee, who had gone on hunger strike when the British refused to allow the ship he was on to sail from Italy for Palestine, is reunited with his wife in Haifa, 27 May 1946. She had reached Palestine earlier. Until a week before she believed that her husband had been killed by the Germans. In fact he had escaped deportation and fought as a partisan in Poland.*

On 15 May 1947 the United Nations set up a Special Committee on Palestine (UNSCOP) to decide on the future of Palestine. The British continued to try to stop illegal immigration. When the Hagannah ship *Exodus 1947* was intercepted in July off the coast of Palestine with 4,500 refugees on board, it was taken into Haifa port by the Royal Navy. Its passengers, transferred to another ship, the *Empire Rival*, were sent back to Europe. Members of UNSCOP who were in Palestine witnessed the transfer of the refugees and were shocked. The refugees, sent to Port de Bouc in southern France, refused to disembark. The ship continued to Hamburg, from where, on September 8, the refugees were forced to disembark on the hated soil of Germany and taken by train, its windows barred, to a detention camp at Poppendorf.

Even as the United Nations' emissaries debated the future of Palestine, Britain faced continued Jewish violence. Three more Irgun members were captured and sentenced to death for their part in acts of terror against British troops. In an attempt to avert their execution, the Irgun seized two British sergeants. The British refused to bow to such intimidation, and executed the Irgunists. As a reprisal, on July 31 the Irgun killed the two British sergeants, left them hanging in an orange grove, and booby-trapped the ground beneath their bodies. British troops, incensed, murdered several Jews in Palestine. Anti-Jewish sentiment flared in Britain. It extended even to my own London school where, aged ten, I was beaten up. The Jewish Agency, and Ben Gurion personally, condemned the Irgun for its acts of violence, calling them 'spectacular acts to gratify popular feeling'.

Reaching the Promised Land. *Holocaust survivors come ashore near the Jewish town of Nahariya, north of Haifa, 2 February 1948. Seven hundred had made a perilous winter voyage in an old freighter. The captain managed to avoid the British blockade and then deliberately ran his ship aground so that the passengers could disembark. Almost the entire population of Nahariya rushed to the beach to help the immigrants ashore.*

On 31 August 1947, UNSCOP announced its solution for Palestine: the country would be partitioned into two independent States, one Arab and one Jewish. There would also be a special United Nations administration for Jerusalem and Bethlehem. This plan, known as the Partition Resolution, was debated at the United Nations in New York on 29 November 1947, and accepted – by thirty-three votes to thirteen, with ten abstentions. Britain was among the countries which abstained. The Soviet Union, the United States, Australia, New Zealand, Canada, France, Holland, Poland and Sweden were among those voting in favour. A Jewish State, albeit only in part of Palestine, was imminent.

The Jewish Agency accepted partition, and the exclusion of Jerusalem, in return for a Jewish State, the long-awaited dream. The Palestinian Arab leaders rejected any form of statehood, wanting to rule the whole of Palestine, including the Jewish areas. Violence was immediate, an Arab crowd attacking and burning down the Jewish-owned shops in Jerusalem's Commercial Centre; dozens of Jews were killed in the following weeks. Hans Beyth, who

British armoured vehicles *and soldiers prevent Jews from reaching the Jewish shops that were being looted by Arabs in the Commercial Centre, Jerusalem, on 3 December 1947, four days after the United Nations vote in favour of the establishment of a Jewish State in Palestine.*
[PHOTO: DAVID RUBINGER]

Searching for arms, *British soldiers arrest members of the Hagannah Jewish defence force, 15 December 1947.*

during the previous two years had been responsible for the absorption into Palestine of 20,000 young survivors of the Holocaust, was killed shortly after he had welcomed a group of children who had just been released by the British from the detention camps in Cyprus. That December, Elias Katz – who in 1924 had won an Olympic gold medal in Paris as a member of Finland's 3,000-metre cross country team – was set upon by three Arabs and killed. He had been preparing to travel from Palestine, where he had lived since 1933, to London for the 1948 Olympics, as a coach for the first all-Jewish team ever to participate.

The Hagannah continued to oppose reprisals, despite Jewish anguish at so many armed attacks on unarmed civilians, while the Irgun and Stern gang continued their policy of indiscriminate reprisals. On 9 January 1948 the British announced that in the previous six weeks the death toll was 1,069 Arabs, 769 Jews and 123 Britons. On the following day a recently created 'Arab Liberation Army' crossed the border from Syria and attacked a Jewish settlement in Galilee. The attack was beaten off by the settlers, helped by a British armoured unit. In the first and second weeks of January a thousand armed Arabs attacked the Etzion Bloc Jewish settlements in the Hebron Hills. Thirty armed defenders drove them off, leaving 150 Arabs dead. But the Bloc was besieged, and a relief column of thirty-five armed men was sent to help: all were caught and killed.

On the night of 22 February 1948 a bomb, driven to the scene by two British army deserters who were working for the Arabs, was set off in Ben Yehuda Street, in the heart of Jewish Jerusalem. Fifty-two Jews were killed; most of them were asleep in their beds when the bomb went off. Shaken, but undeterred, the Jews of Palestine began to plan for the day on which Britain would leave, making preparations to defend the areas allocated to them under

Searching the ruins *in the immediate aftermath of the Ben Yehuda Street bomb (left), in the centre of Jewish Jerusalem, 22 February 1948, when fifty-two Jews were killed and ninety-seven injured.*

Weapons emerge *from an arms cache (right) hidden by the Hagannah in a grocery shop.* [PHOTO: ROLF M. KNELLER]

the United Nations plan, and also to secure the Jewish areas of Jerusalem, which the United Nation had designated a separate entity under neither Jewish nor Arab control. On March 1 a Provisional Council of State was established, headed by Ben Gurion. Eleven days later a bomb was driven by an Arab driver into the courtyard of the Jewish Agency building where the Council was located. There it detonated, killing thirteen Jews, including Dr Leib Jaffe, one of only five men then alive who had been a delegate at the First Zionist Congress in Basle.

Britain still ruled Palestine, but armed Arabs had forced the Hagannah to abandon the coastal highway south of Jaffa, cutting off several Jewish settlements in the Negev and Gaza. Then, on March 22, the Arabs cut the road to Jerusalem, laying siege to the city's Jewish quarters and population. A force of 1,500 Hagannah soldiers, three times as large as any earlier Hagannah unit, escorted convoys to and from the city. The arrival on the night of April 1 of two hundred rifles and forty machine guns by air from Czechoslovakia gave the convoys the means to defend themselves. On April 3 a further five hundred rifles, two hundred machine guns and five million rounds of ammunition reached Tel Aviv by ship from the Adriatic, hidden in a cargo of potatoes and onions. The British saw nothing.

On April 6 an armed convoy to Jerusalem reached the city without loss, for the first time. In the week that followed, a full-scale battle was fought between the Hagannah and Arab forces at Kastel, a strategic hill overlooking the road two miles outside Jerusalem. During the battle the Arab commander, Abdel Kader al-Husseini, was killed. That day Irgun and Stern gang forces attacked Deir Yassin, an Arab village on another strategic hill even closer to the city. More than one hundred Arabs were killed, most of them villagers, many of them women and children. Ben Gurion and the Hagannah High Command immediately condemned the killings, expressing their 'deep disgust and regret'. The Arabs were not assuaged: in retaliation they attacked a convoy of a hundred doctors, nurses and patients who were on their way to the Hadassah Hospital on Mount Scopus. Seventy-seven of those in the convoy were killed. That night, before news of the convoy massacre reached the coast, Ben Gurion was in Tel Aviv at the first performance of the National Opera.

In Galilee the Arab Liberation Army attacked the Jewish settlement of Mishmar Ha-Emek, overrunning it several times but finally being driven off. Among those killed in the fighting was Moshe Dayan's brother Zorik. On April 12, the last day of the battle, several hundred survivors of Belsen reached Tel Aviv, having been at last released from the British detention camps in Cyprus. They had spent more than a year behind British barbed wire. Many volunteered at once for the Hagannah, whose special strike force, the Palmach, captured the predominantly Arab town of Tiberias on the Sea of Galilee on April 18. The Arab Liberation Army, based in the town, had used it to block the main Jewish link with the Jewish settlements in Upper Galilee. The Arab citizens of Tiberias, more than two thousand, fled eastward to Transjordan. They were among the first of what were to be hundreds of thousands of Arab refugees.

The next city to fall under Hagannah control was Haifa, evacuated by the British on April 21. Yet more Arabs fled, mostly to Lebanon. Others, however, remained in the city, encouraged to do so by the Jewish mayor, with the result that to this day Haifa has a sizeable Arab population. In several villages near Haifa, as in several other parts of the country, Jewish policy was different – to frighten the Arabs into leaving. On April 21 the Director of the Lands Department of the Jewish Agency's national fund, Yosef Weitz, wrote privately: 'Our army is steadily conquering Arab villages and their inhabitants are afraid and flee like mice. You have no idea what happened in the Arab villages. It is enough that during the night several shells will whistle over them and they flee for their lives. Villages are steadily emptying, and if we continue on this course – and we certainly shall do so as our strength increases – then villages will empty of their inhabitants.' In the last week of April, on Ben Gurion's orders, several deserted Arab villages in the hills leading to Jerusalem were blown up, their buildings dynamited one by one.

The British, withdrawing area by area, were determined not to intervene as the Arab-Jewish conflict intensified. The British commander in Safed, however, indicated his personal preference in the dispute when he handed the keys of the police fort and three other strongpoints to the Arabs. The Jews there were besieged, but on May 10 the Palmach won control of the town.

Fighters for independence. *Yigal Allon (right), commander of the Palmach strike force of the Hagannah, and his Chief of Operations, Yitzhak Rabin, near the Egyptian town of El Arish, in the Sinai, during Israel's war of independence. After pressure from the United States, Israeli forces later withdrew from Egyptian soil.*

Both left their mark on Israel. Allon was later Minister of Labour, Minister of Immigrant Absorption, Minister of Education, and Foreign Minister. Rabin was to become Israeli Chief of Staff, Ambassador to Washington, and, twice, Prime Minister, signing a peace treaty with Jordan. [PHOTO: DAVID RUBINGER]

Thousands more Arabs fled, northward into Lebanon. Entering the Arab town of Beisan on May 12, the Hagannah found the town deserted; 3,000 Arabs had fled across the River Jordan, encouraged to do so by a whispering campaign, devised by the Palmach commander Yigal Allon, that vast Jewish reinforcements were on their way.

That day, May 12, the United States proposed a three-month cease-fire between Jews and Arabs. The idea was that the United Nations would take over when the British left – in two or three days' time – and that the Jews would not declare statehood until agreement had been worked out between them and the Palestinian Arabs. Summoning an emergency meeting of the Provisional Council, Ben Gurion urged his colleagues to reject the American plan, and proposed instead an immediate declaration of statehood. Five members of the ten-man Council, fearing that the moment statehood was declared the Arab nations bordering Palestine would attack and win, wanted to postpone statehood and accept a ceasefire. The Operations Officer of the Hagannah, Yigael Yadin, summoned to the meeting by Ben Gurion and asked to speak honestly about the military prospects, said that in military terms 'the other side has a significant edge', but that it had been proved 'many times' in the past 'that the numbers and the formations are not always decisive.' The Hagannah, Yadin added, possessed a high level both 'of training and determination'. Ben Gurion then spoke of new arms supplies arriving from Europe, of new manpower coming from Cyprus, and of the mass conscription of Jewish youth in Palestine. 'If we can increase our forces, widen training, and increase our weapons, we can resist and even win.'

Ben Gurion's voice and emphasis were decisive: when he took a new vote in the Council only two of the seven other members wanted to accept a ceasefire and postpone statehood. The Council then discussed what the new State should be called. Suggestions included Zion, Ziona, Judaea and Herzliya. The Council finally decided on the name 'Israel'.

On May 13, as the last British troops prepared to leave Palestine together with the Mandate administration, a joint Hagannah and Irgun force captured Jaffa. Of the 70,000 Arab inhabitants of the town, 67,000 fled southward to Gaza, some by boat, some by car and truck, but most of them on foot, taking with them only what they could carry. In western Jerusalem, as the Hagannah was overrunning each of the Arab suburbs, the Arabs captured the Etzion Bloc south of the city, after a prolonged battle. Fifteen of the defenders were killed after their surrender, while being lined up for a photograph with their captors.

The United Nations was voting on May 14 on making Jerusalem an international city. First Guatemala, then Australia and finally the United States put forward resolutions to that effect. But the Arab States insisted that the whole city should be under Arab rule, despite its Jewish majority. Ben Gurion did not want to risk further delays during which something short of Jewish statehood might be decided upon in New York, or the Jews formally denied the Jewish areas of Jerusalem, most of which had already been cleared of their Arab inhabitants. On 14 May 1948, at five o'clock in the afternoon, Palestine time – on the eve of the Sabbath, after which the Orthodox Jews leaders would not have been able to travel to the ceremony, and while the United Nations was still discussing the internationalisation of Jerusalem – Ben Gurion presided over the signing of Israel's Declaration of Independence in Tel Aviv. Two thousand years of prayer and spiritual longing had been fulfilled; fifty years of political Zionism had triumphed. There was dancing in the streets of Tel Aviv and Jerusalem. But everywhere in the country soldiers were on the alert. News of the massacre of the Jews in the Etzion Bloc cast a grim pall, as did the fact that 1,200 Jews had already been killed since the United Nations Partition Resolution less than six months earlier.

Menachem Begin, *leader of the Irgun pre-independence underground army, inspects his men. They had been active in armed revolt against the British since the end of 1943. With Israel's independence they became an integral part of the Israel Defence Forces. Three months after independence he formed a political Party, Herut ('Freedom'), which remained in opposition for almost thirty years. In 1977 he became Prime Minister, signing a peace treaty with Egypt.*
[PHOTO: FRED CSASZNIK]

Immediately independence was declared, five Arab armies crossed the border into former Mandate Palestine: the Lebanese army from the north, the Syrian, Iraqi and Transjordanian armies from the east, and the Egyptian army from the south. At Ben Gurion's insistence the Jewish Agency's Hagannah and Palmach, and the Revisionists' Irgun, were merged into a single Jewish army – the Israel Defence Forces, known as the IDF. In an Egyptian bombing raid on Tel Aviv on May 14, a hundred Jews were killed. In the days ahead, Egyptian troops overran the two Jewish settlements south of Gaza, captured a third – Yad Mordechai, on the Gaza-Tel Aviv road – and advanced to within twenty-five miles of Tel Aviv. Another Egyptian force reached the southern outskirts of Jerusalem, while the Arab Legion, having cut the road from Tel Aviv to Jerusalem, occupied the former British police fort at Latrun. Three attempts were made by the Israelis to reopen it, but each attack was beaten off. Among the wounded was Avigdor Arikha – later one of Israel's finest painters, and Ariel Sheinermann – later, as Ariel Sharon, one of Israel's most controversial generals and a future Prime Minister.

In besieged Jerusalem, the battle for the Jewish Quarter of the Old City lasted two weeks, until, on May 28, it surrendered to the Arab Legion. Among its defenders was a twenty-two-year-old English girl, Esther Cailingold, who was mortally wounded. After her death a letter was found under her pillow, in which she wrote to her parents. 'We had a difficult fight. I have tasted hell, but it has been worthwhile, because I am convinced the end will see a Jewish State and all our longings. I have lived my life fully, and very sweet it has been to be in our land.'

From the first days of independence, volunteer fighters reached Israel from abroad. They were known as Mahal, an acronym for the Hebrew words Mitnavdei Hutz La'aretz ('Volunteers from Abroad'). One of those volunteers, John Barrard, who had served in the South African Air Force in the Second World War, worked to make Israel's tiny air force serviceable: first the small planes that had been used for crop-dusting and flying clubs, which could fly mail and medicine, and then the former German Messerschmitts brought from Czechoslovakia. The first Israeli air force Messerschmitt went into action on 29 May 1948. Another Machal volunteer was an American colonel, David 'Mickey' Marcus, a graduate of the United States Military Academy at West Point, who had parachuted into Normandy on D-Day, and had seen Dachau a few days after its liberation. Marcus fought in the battles for Latrun, after which he planned and constructed a by-pass road through the hills to Jerusalem – known as the 'Burma Road' after the Second World War British supply route through Burma to China. This road enabled the Israeli army to break the siege of Jerusalem, and to rush arms and ammunition to the city, to ensure that the Jewish areas in western Jerusalem remained in Jewish hands.

On June 11, during the first of two ceasefires agreed between Israel and the Arabs, Colonel Marcus left his tent after dark, wrapped in a white sheet, and was challenged by a sentry to give that night's password. In the dark the

Esther Cailingold, *a young British Zionist who was one of 7,000 Jews killed in the war of independence. This photograph was used in 1947 in the official permit that enabled her to enter Jerusalem's Street of the Prophets, where she was a teacher at the Evelina de Rothschild School. The street was then in a special Royal Air Force Zone.*

[PHOTO: ASHER CAILINGOLD]

white sheet made him seem to be an Arab intruder. Marcus hesitated and the sentry shot him dead. His body was taken back to the United States, escorted by Moshe Dayan, and he was buried with full military honours at West Point, his headstone bearing the words: 'A soldier for all humanity'. He was later portrayed by Kirk Douglas in the film *Cast a Giant Shadow*.

During the first truce, an immigrant ship, the *Altalena*, arrived off the coast of Israel with nine hundred immigrants, most of them Revisionists, and with a considerable cache of arms, including 5,000 rifles and 270 light machine guns. The Revisionists felt their loyalties to Menachem Begin, and to the maintenance of their hitherto independent Irgun forces, for which these additional munitions were essential if they were to retain their own authority. Ben Gurion wanted the munitions sent to the Jerusalem Front where, if the truce failed, a major battle with the Arabs would have to be fought to open up the corridor from the coast, and to defend Jerusalem's Jewish suburbs.

Those on board the *Altalena* tried to land their arms and munitions thirty miles north of Tel Aviv. As they began to do so, Ben Gurion ordered the ship to be fired on. Six Irgunists and two Israeli soldiers were killed before the ship sailed away – to Tel Aviv. There, on Ben Gurion's orders, carried out by one of his senior commanders, Yitzhak Rabin, the ship was bombarded from

A photographer at war. *David Rubinger in the front line (above) during Israel's war of independence. He was later to photograph all Israel's twentieth-century wars.*

[PHOTO: DAVID RUBINGER]

The end of the siege. *A food convoy reaches Jerusalem, 15 April 1948 (opposite), the first to do so for just over two weeks, ending fears of starvation among the city's 100,000 Jews. Consisting of 131 trucks, it brought 500 tons of food. A second convoy followed two days later, with 280 trucks, and 1,000 tons of food, including flour, sugar, milk, fruit and vegetables.*

[PHOTO: ROLF M. KNELLER]

The Altalena incident, *21 June 1948.*
Jews fire on Jews as the new Israeli
government takes a tough line with the
Irgun to prevent a break-away armed force
being established. Preparing to evacuate a
wounded man (left) from the Tel Aviv sea
front. Three Hagannah soldiers wait
behind a wall. On the ambulance the star
of David is the equivalent of the Red Cross.
The Altalena *on fire (right) off Tel Aviv as*
crowds gather to watch.

[PHOTO LEFT: ROBERT CAPA]

the shore, and burned out, watched by hundreds of onlookers on the beach. Begin, who had joined those on board, was forced to jump into the sea with them and swim ashore. Ben Gurion was emphatic that he would allow no separatist fighting force, no clandestine or privately controlled store of arms, no soldiers whose allegiance was not to the Israel Defence Forces. 'Jewish independence will not endure,' his government declared, 'if every individual group is free to establish its own military force and to determine political facts affecting the future of the State.' The attack on the *Altalena* was a traumatic moment for the new State. To this day many Revisionists – their Party coming to power twenty-nine years later under Begin's leadership – have not forgiven Ben Gurion for ordering the ship to be bombarded.

Gradually the Arab armies were pushed back, but Israeli control was not restored in the Jewish quarter of the Old City of Jerusalem, in the Etzion Bloc south of Jerusalem, in the suburbs of Atarot and Neve Ya'akov north of the city, or in several kibbutzim at the northern end of the Dead Sea, all of which were overrun by Transjordan. The kibbutzim in the Gaza Strip were overrun by Egypt. On 11 March 1949 a column of Israeli troops reached the British fort of Umm Rash Rash – later the town of Eilat – at the head of the Gulf of Akaba, and raised the flag of the new State, a Star of David. This gave Israel an outlet to the Red Sea. That same day, the War of Independence came to an end with the signing of an armistice with Transjordan on the Greek island of Rhodes. Seven thousand Israeli soldiers had been killed in action, by far the largest number of war dead in any of Israel's wars. For a nation of only 650,000 people it was a heavy toll.

When the war ended, Jerusalem was a divided city, the division marked by concrete walls, barbed wire and the desolate spaces of No-man's Land. Arab East Jerusalem, like the Jordan Valley and the hill country of Judaea and Samaria, was occupied by Transjordan – which changed its name to Jordan, then being in control of both sides of that river. Under Jordanian rule, the

Jewish Quarter of the Old City was allowed to fall into ruin, and no Israeli Jews were allowed to visit the holiest Jewish site in Jerusalem, the Wailing (or Western) Wall. The Hebrew University and the Hadassah Hospital on Mount Scopus were in an Israeli enclave to which access was all but impossible: both institutions had to be found new homes in West Jerusalem, which remained in Jewish hands.

Egypt occupied the Gaza Strip, the Palestinian Arabs there, like those in the West Bank and East Jerusalem under Jordanian rule, being denied by their Arab rulers the statehood which the United Nations had voted them in the Arab-populated areas of Palestine, but which they – wanting more – had rejected.

The State of Israel had to repair the ravages of war, secure its borders – which were the ceasefire lines of battle – and formalise the institutions of statehood, many of which had been devised and evolved during the Mandate years. The new government also felt a responsibility for Jews in the Diaspora who were under the frown of hostile governments. Sent to Moscow in September 1948 as the Ambassador of the four-month-old State, Golda Meir was astounded when several thousand Russian Jews, despite the Soviet disapproval of Jewish demonstrations of any sort, gathered in Archipova Street, outside the synagogue, to greet her. The photograph of the occasion later appeared on an Israeli banknote.

The five years following independence saw a massive influx of Jews to Israel, a poor country determined to fulfil what it regarded as its obligations to all who made it their home. Romania, under Communist rule since 1945, had initially refused to let its Jews leave, but in December 1949 relented, encouraged to do so by generous payments from the Government of Israel, and suddenly a further 100,000 Jews and more were on the move. Many of them had spent the war years in ghettos and slave labour camps, and on the death marches. The American Jewish Joint Distribution Committee - The Joint - which had been founded in 1914 to help Jews displaced in the First World War, played a crucial role in enabling these Jews to be brought to Israel, using funds, diplomatic skills and tightly knit organisation, to ensure that the work of rescue was effective.

With the creating of the Jewish State, almost all of Bulgaria's Jews made their way there without let or hindrance: 37,260 in all. Theirs was a community that had actually increased in numbers during the Second World War. From Turkey, which had been neutral in the war, 34,547 Jews went to Israel in its first thirty months of statehood, more than a third of Turkish Jewry. From Yugoslavia, 7,661 Jews made their way to Israel. Smaller numbers of Jews came from Britain, Canada, the United States, South Africa and Australia – highly motivated, well-educated young professionals, many of whom committed their energies to manual labour on a kibbutz.

The majority of the immigrants reaching Israel in the five years after inde-

On the sand dunes *of Bat Yam, south of Tel Aviv, houses for new immigrants near completion, just behind a tented immigrant camp which will soon cease to exist. Those living in the tents have managed to make tiny vegetable gardens behind wooden stakes to keep out the blowing sand. Bat Yam's population in 1948 of 1,000 had grown by 1953 to 10,000.* [PHOTO: A. HIMMELREICH]

pendence were from Arab and Muslim lands. The largest number, 126,000 came from Iraq. In October 1948 many wealthy Iraqi Jews were arrested, Zionism was declared a crime, many Jews were imprisoned and some were hanged. A mass exodus followed, leading in 1950 to an official Iraqi decree confiscating the property and bank accounts of all Jews leaving for Israel.

The next largest mass emigration to Israel from a Muslim land was that of 67,000 Moroccan Jews, then 48,000 from Yemen, and a further 6,500 from nearby Aden. Their community was an ancient one, tracing its origins to Biblical times. Jews from Yemen had made their way to Palestine, a few hundred each year, in Ottoman and Mandate times. But with Israel's independence there had been anti-Jewish riots in Yemen, and several Yemeni Jews had been killed. Suddenly tens of thousands of Jews were on the move, making their way to assembly points organised by the Joint, where doctors and

MOTHERS AND CHILDREN,

New immigrants, living in the Fast Hotel, Jerusalem (far left), once a smart address in the centre of the city, but from 1948 to 1967 – only a few yards from the Israel-Jordan cease-fire line – dilapidated and occasionally the target of a sniper's bullet. Immigrant children at play outside their temporary huts (above) erected on the site of a former British army barracks in Jerusalem. Outside her prefabricated hut, a new immigrant (left) bakes bread according to the ancient methods of her Moroccan village.

[PHOTO TOP: DAVID RUBINGER]

[PHOTO BELOW: DAVID HARRIS]

[PHOTO OPPOSITE: WERNER BRAUN]

Regeneration. *Prams competing for pavement space at an open air café in Tel Aviv are a symbol of renewal and rebirth, although the poster behind strikes a smbre note. It announces a memorial meeting at the tomb of eleven Lehi (Stern Gang) fighters killed in an attack on a British Mandate railway workshop.* [PHOTO: ROBERT CAPA]

nurses from Israel did what they could to prepare them for the journey. The operation was given the name 'Magic Carpet' because, Egypt having closed the Suez Canal to all Israeli shipping and thus barred the normal way from Yemen by sea, Israel had instead to mount an airlift. It was a flight of 1,500 miles in planes crowded to capacity.

'Sometimes I used to go to Lydda', Golda Meir later recalled, 'and watch the planes from Aden touch down, marvelling at the endurance and faith of their exhausted passengers. "Had you ever seen a plane before?" I asked one bearded old man. "No," he answered. "But weren't you very frightened of flying?" I persisted. "No," he said again, very firmly. "It is all written in the Bible, in Isaiah, They shall mount up with wings of eagles." And standing there on the airfield, he recited the entire passage to me, his face lit with the joy of a fulfilled prophecy - and of the journey's end.'

Golda Meir had been entrusted by Ben Gurion with the task of going to the United States to find the money needed to create minimally acceptable housing for the mass of new immigrants. Her theme on her fund-raising visit was that the money was needed 'not to win a war but to maintain life'. As she told her American Jewish listeners at her first official public appearance in the United States: 'What we want to do is to give each family a luxurious apartment of one room; one room which we will build out of concrete blocks. We won't even plaster the walls. We will make roofs, but no ceilings. What we hope is that since these people will be learning a trade as they build their houses, they will finish them, and eventually, one day, add on another room. In the meantime, we will be happy, and they will be happy, even though it means putting a family of two, three, four or five into one room. But this is better than putting two or three families in a single tent.'

Iran was another country which, with the emergence of the Jewish State, saw mass emigration. Among the 39,000 Iranian Jews who emigrated were two young boys, Shaul Mofaz, who became Israel's Chief of Staff in 1999, and Moshe Katzav who was elected President of Israel in the year 2000. Other Jewish communities that had lived in Arab lands for many centuries also came in large numbers to Israel after independence, including 35,000 from Libya and 30,000 from Tunisia. From Syria, where twelve Jews had been killed in August 1949 when a bomb was thrown into a synagogue, 26,000 Jews emigrated to Israel, while more than 3,000 came from both Afghanistan and Algeria.

From India, 12,000 Jews reached Israel from a Jewish community known as the B'nei Yisrael ('Children of Israel') whose origins, while clearly ancient,

Rebuilding. *Young women at work in a stone quarry at Ein Harod, in the Jezreel Valley, home to many German immigrants in the late 1930s.*

were unknown. Among other Indian Jews who made their way to Israel after 1948 were 3,000 Baghdadi Jews, living mostly in Bombay and Calcutta, and 2,500 'Black' Jews living in and around Cochin, in southern India.

Between 1948 and 1960 the astonishingly large number of 491,555 Oriental Jews had emigrated to Israel, making them the largest single community in the country. The new immigrants almost outnumbered the Jewish population at the time of independence, raising it from just over half a million in 1948 to more than a million by 1960. Israel has doubled its population as a result of immigration in less than twelve years.

Most new immigrants were taken to agricultural settlements and to new towns which were established specially for them. Others began their new life in tents and shacks. In the most war-battered sections of Jerusalem, on the Israeli side of the Jordan-Israel divide, as well as in the suburbs of Talbieh and Bakaa, new immigrants were given homes in buildings from which middle-class and wealthy Arabs had fled on the eve of the War of Independence. Small prefabricated huts were soon built in the hundreds of thousands. The third phase, the building of concrete apartment blocks, took up to two decades. In 1955 a new town was established in the Negev hills. It took its name, Dimona, from a town mentioned in the Bible as belonging to the tribe of Judah. Its task was to provide homes for the labourers working in the Dead Sea phosphate works, and in the textile mills established in the town. More than half of Dimona's population were new immigrants from North Africa;

269

Milk and fruit. *Milking a cow on a kibbutz (left), its tail tied up to stop it slapping the milkmaid in the face. Bananas (right) introduced in pioneering days earlier in the century had become a staple crop.*

[PHOTO OPPOSITE: DAVID SEYMOUR]

[PHOTO RIGHT: DAVID RUBINGER]

ten per cent were new immigrants from India. Riots broke out in 1959 in Haifa over the slow pace of change for poor Sephardi immigrants from North Africa and Iraq. These spurred Ben Gurion into adding another Sephardi member to his government and to make changes in the economy and educational system to benefit the *Edot Mizrah*, the Oriental Communities.

In 1950 a Law of Return had guaranteed the right of every Jew, wherever he or she might live in the world, to enter Israel as an immigrant and become a citizen immediately on arrival. Yigael Yadin's archaeological work encouraged the newly arrived Israeli youth, as well as those born in the country – the 'sabras', named after the cactus fruit, prickly outside, soft inside – to see a direct link between themselves and the ancient Israelites and Jews of Roman times. Between 1955 and 1958 Yadin excavated King Solomon's fortress of Hazor. His discoveries are among the treasures of the Israel Museum in Jerusalem. In 1948, as Chief of Operations, he had deployed troops and seen battles fought at many of the sites where later he was to supervise the search for Israel's links with its historic and Biblical past.

An old land was being uncovered and a new land created; more than four hundred Arab villages had been blown up after their inhabitants fled in 1948, and the ruins bulldozed away. Isdud, one of several towns from which the Arabs had fled in 1948, became a Jewish town – Ashdod – populated mostly

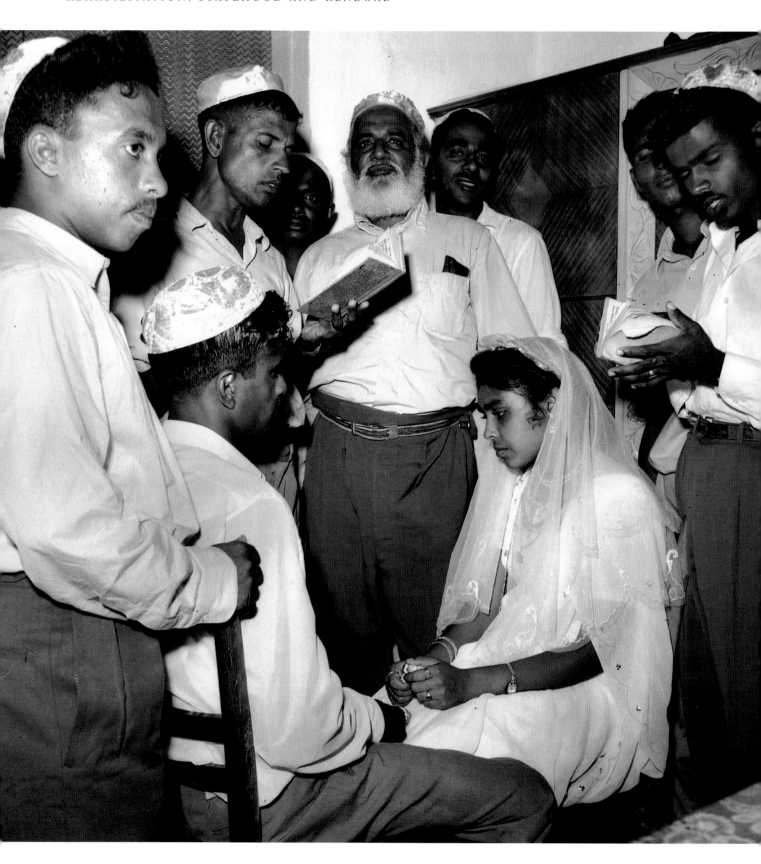

Indian Jews, *immigrants from Cochin, celebrate a wedding in 1958 at Nevatim, southern Israel, a kibbutz in which 400 Cochin Jews settled. Between 1953 and 1955 more than 2,000 Cochin Jews emigrated to Israel.*

[PHOTO: MICHA BAR-AM]

by new immigrants from North Africa, and growing rapidly in size. Lydda and Ramla, from which the Arabs had been driven at the height of the War of Independence, also became Jewish towns – Lod and Ramle. The latter, in which 3,000 Arabs remained after the war, became home by 1960 to 20,000 Jews, among them many immigrants from India, and established an Arab-Jewish Friendship League, priding itself on good relations.

On the Gulf of Akaba, Eilat became an important port for goods from the Far East, India and East Africa. Without it, ships bound for Israel, and forbidden by Egypt to use the Suez Canal, would have had to make the long voyage around the Cape of Good Hope. Eilat flourished as a port and, in due course, as a holiday resort, one of its main benefactors being a British hotelier, David Lewis, who named the suites in one of his hotels there after the British Zionists who had been so active in the early days of Zionism.

Life in Israel during its first decade and a half was kaleidoscopic, as Jews emigrated from all over the world. A wide spectrum of food, clothing, music, and language reflected the diverse countries of origin. Secular and religious Jews from very different backgrounds had to learn to live side by side. When Orthodox Jews protested against the proposed mixed swimming pool in Jerusalem, those who wanted to swim without separate sections in the pool counter-demonstrated. To try to bridge the gulf between the three main streams of Jewish life – orthodox, reform and secular – the Israeli Cabinet, headed by David Ben Gurion held regular Bible discussions.

Jews in the Diaspora could be proud of the establishment of a Jewish national entity for the first time in two thousand years, though there were always those who argued that the role of the Jewish people had become that

A demonstration *in 1958 by ultra-Orthodox Jews against the building of a swimming pool in Jerusalem. A young boy sounds the ram's horn as a note of alarm against mixed bathing.*

[PHOTO: DAVID RUBINGER]

of contributors to other cultures, serving as the salt and leaven for other peoples. In the fifteen years following the Second World War, the world continued to benefit from the work of Jews who had been driven out of Nazi Germany.

In Britain, individual Jews made their mark on every aspect of post-war life. Budapest-born Dennis Gabor, who had left Berlin for London in 1933, invented a television tube that made colour television sets for the home a practical possibility – he was later awarded the Nobel Prize for Physics. Viennese-born British art historian Ernst Gombrich published his pioneering *Story of Art* in 1950, and *Art and Illusion* a decade later: both books were central to the growth of art history as an academic and as a popular subject. At the London School of Economics, Viennese-born Karl Popper taught a generation of students the value of liberty. At King's College, London, Rosalind Franklin was doing work which made possible Crick and Watson's discovery of DNA.

Many of London's taxi drivers were Jewish, as were many of those who worked in the jewelry trade. Hairdressing also attracted Jews: in 1954, Vidal Sassoon, of Baghdadi Jewish origin, who had left London in 1948 to fight in the Israeli War of Independence, returned to London and opened his first hairdressing salon in Bond Street. Many of the Baghdadi Jews living in Bombay and Calcutta who had not gone to Israel to live went to London,

A Bible meeting in Cabinet. *The Prime Minister, David Ben Gurion (second from the left) and his Cabinet colleagues, as well as the President of Israel, Yitzhak Ben Zvi (in white suit) at one of the regular meetings called by Ben Gurion to explore the links between modern Israel and the ancient Jewish heritage.* [PHOTO: DAVID HARRIS]

274

A joyous moment. *Rabbi Immanuel Jakobovits, with his bride Amelie Munk, scion of a distinguished rabbinical family, 1949. Born in Germany in 1921, the son of a rabbi, Jakobovits reached Britain as a refugee before the war. A leading authority on Jewish medical ethics, he served as Chief Rabbi of Ireland, first rabbi of the Fifth Avenue Synagogue, New York, and Chief Rabbi of the United Hebrew Congregations of the British Commonwealth.*

Respecting God's name. *Orthodox Jews bury old prayer books which cannot be thrown away or destroyed, as they contain the words of God.* [PHOTO: WERNER BRAUN]

where they formed a cohesive community. Many Iraqi Jews did likewise, among them Nathan Saatchi, who became a leading figure in the British textile industry – in which he was active until the age of 90 – and his four sons, two of whom, Maurice and Charles, became leading figures in the world of advertising and mass-marketing.

One country which suppressed all creative manifestations of Jewishness, and virtually forbade all Jewish emigration, was the Soviet Union, whose hostility was reflected in the policies of all the Communist States of Eastern Europe. Under Communist regimes, to which individual Jews had contributed a great deal as leaders and ideologues, there were also penalties for being actively Jewish, or supportive of Israel. Most of the Jews of Czechoslovakia were survivors of Theresienstadt and Auschwitz. But although the new Communist rulers who came to power in 1948 included several Jews, this did not lead to any improvement for Jews as a community. Indeed, Jewishness was to prove a liability even for Rudolf Slansky, born Rudolph Schlesinger, the Secretary-General and effective head of the Czech Communist Party. In 1951, as a result of pressure from the Soviet Union, he was arrested by his former colleagues, imprisoned, fettered to the wall while in prison, accused of espionage at a Stalinist show trial, and executed.

Stalin, increasingly paranoid, saw a 'Jewish conspiracy' all around him. In 1952 he ordered the murder of several leading Jewish writers, among them Peretz Markish, who had earlier written a laudatory Ode to Stalin.

As well as taking action against Jewish writers, Stalin asked many prominent Jews to sign a letter denying the existence of anti-Semitism in the Soviet

Union. Almost all of them refused, among them – to Stalin's considerable anger – General Jacob Kreiser, one of the Soviet Union's most senior generals. Kreiser was immediately stripped of his command. Stalin's death a few months later saved him, and the other courageous non-signatories, from a severe fate, almost certainly death. Ironically, when people used to accuse Stalin of being anti-Jewish, he would reply, 'How can I be, my best friend is a Jew – Kreiser.'

The first President. *Chaim Weizmann, who became President on the establishment of the State of Israel in 1948, relaxes on the terrace of his home in Rehovot. Active in Zionist circles since the beginning of the*

century, he died in 1952. His house had been designed by the German-Jewish architect Erich Mendelsohn.

[PHOTO: ROBERT CAPA]

Stalin's death in 1953 was an immense relief for the Jews of the Soviet Union, among whom rumours had been circulating that he had been making plans for their mass deportation to Siberia or Soviet Central Asia. But despite the death of the dictator, the rigours of Communism remained, and with them the hostility to specifically Jewish aspirations. Boris Pasternak was not allowed to publish his novel *Dr Zhivago*, about the Russian Revolution which had to be smuggled out of the Soviet Union to be published in the West.

The 'unfinished business' of the Holocaust, as Hugo Gryn, a survivor of Auschwitz, rabbi and much admired radio debater for the BBC, later called it, reached a milestone in 1952 when the Federal Republic of Germany – West Germany – signed an agreement with the State of Israel for reparations payments to survivors. The right-wing Herut Party, led by Menachem Begin, called on the government not to accept 'tainted' money, but Ben Gurion, under whose authority the agreement had been negotiated, had an over-whelming parliamentary majority. Many survivors who lived elsewhere than Israel received compensation direct from the Federal government, but some did not, and no money at all was allocated to those who had been slave labourers. East Germany declined to make any payments at all, so it was to take another half century, and the fall of Communism, before any reparations payments were made to those survivors, at least 10,000, who lived in the former Communist bloc.

Some Jews returned to both West and East Germany after the war, rebuilding the Jewish communities in several cities, numbering some 40,000 within fifteen years of the war, scarcely five per cent of their pre-war numbers. In 1946 the Bavarian Ministry of the Interior appointed a Jew, Philip Auerbach, as State Commissioner for the care of people who had been persecuted on the basis of race, religion or political convictions. In 1950 a Central Council of Jews in Germany was established. German-language Jewish weekly newspapers were published in Munich and Dusseldorf, and Jewish schools set up in Frankfurt and Munich.

Several Jews rose to prominence in the political life of post-war West Germany. Herbert Weichmann, whose family had been murdered by the Nazis, became Mayor of Hamburg and President of the Federal Upper House, in which capacity he was acting President of Germany whenever the President was out of the country. He regularly attended synagogue and emphasised his Jewishness at every opportunity. Joseph Neuberger, who had returned to Germany from Israel, became Minister of Justice in North-Rhine Westphalia. In Austria, Bruno Kreisky, who had spent the war years in exile in Sweden, took part in the negotiations with the Soviet Union which led to the creation of a neutral, independent Austria, was then Foreign Minister, and finally Chancellor.

Jewish involvement in political life in France reached a high point in 1954, when the Prime Minister, Pierre Mendès-France, ended French involvement in the harsh war in French Indo-China (later Vietnam). In the following year, having failed to win parliamentary support for the independence of Morocco and Algeria, he resigned. Another French Jew, René Mayer, who later became Prime Minister, was a keen pioneer 'European', and for two years Chairman of the European Coal and Steel Authority, a forerunner of the European Union. In Ireland, in 1956, Robert Briscoe, the son of an immigrant from Lithuania, and a former member of the Irish Republican Army (the IRA) in the fight against Britain for Irish statehood, became Lord Mayor of Dublin. When he visited New York, he distributed green skull caps, saying he was an Irish-Jew, 'one of the Lepre-cohens'.

After the overthrow of King Farouk of Egypt in 1952, Israel suffered from a growing number of attacks by Arab raiders across its southern border. The raiders, known as fedayeen, were mostly Palestinian Arabs, refugees who had fled from Israel in 1948 and were living in refugee camps in the Egyptian-occupied Gaza Strip. Throughout the winter of 1954-55, individual Jews were attacked and killed while walking along the roads or ploughing their fields. On 28 February 1955, in retaliation for these raids, Israeli troops attacked an Egyptian army base near Gaza. Thirty-eight Egyptians were killed. The response of the fedayeen was to shell the Jewish settlements across the border. In July 1956, while raid and counter-raid continued, and Egyptian artillery shelled settlements in the Negev, the Egyptian President, Gamal Abdel Nasser, nationalized the Suez Canal. It was an act which brought down on him the military wrath of Britain and France, whose leaders, and those of Israel, gathered at a secret meeting outside Paris and co-ordinated an Anglo-French attack on Egypt with an attack by Israel across the Sinai desert. The campaign was short, lasting only six days, but it left 172 Israeli soldiers dead.

In the aftermath of the Suez war, Nasser expelled the Jews from Egypt: 56,000 made their way to Israel, tens of thousands more to Britain, France and the United States. Among those who went to Israel was Elie Cohen; he was hanged in Syria nine years later as an Israeli spy. Among those who went to Britain was Claudia Douek who – as Claudia Roden – became a famous cookery writer. In 1946, in the United States, Bernard Baruch drafted the first official American proposal for the international control of atomic energy, while Hungarian-born Edward Teller, a pre-war refugee from Nazism, emerged as the leading scientific

Sit. Com. *Gertrude Berg, Barbara Rush and Eli Mintz in the television show 'The Goldbergs'.*

Laughter at large. *Sergeant Bilko's fast-talking con-man act brought smiles to millions of television viewers. Phil Silvers, the actor playing Bilko, began his show business career as a boy singer in vaudeville before the Second World War, and appeared in his first film in 1940. From 1955 to 1959 he hosted 'The Phil Silvers Show' on television.*

advocate of the development of the hydrogen bomb. The Jewish contribution to television in the United States was seen in its earliest days, on 10 January 1949, when Gertrude Berg appeared as the host of a television show *The Goldbergs*. It was the first successful, long-term television situation comedy, running six years and appealing to Jews and non-Jews alike. Later, playing a Jewish widow in the *Gertrude Berg Show*, she carried on a lively dialogue in her Yiddish accent with a British actor who took the role of her English teacher. In 1950 the American comedian Jack Benny had his first television show. In 1953 Arthur Miller's play *The Crucible* challenged the Macarthyite anti-communist hysteria of the time with its powerful plea for tolerance, taking as a parallel the witchcraft trials of the early years of America.

Individual Jews continued to enrich American artistic life. On 29 October 1955 a young opera singer, Beverly Sills (born Belle Miriam Silverman) made her debut at the New York City Opera. She was to become one of the great American sopranos. She later left the operatic stage for almost a decade to look after two severely handicapped children, but eventually returned in tri-

umph. Leonard Bernstein's *West Side Story* was first performed in 1957, when it was directed by a fellow-Jew, Jerome Robbins (born Rabinowitz). American medicine benefited from research by Jews. Gertrude B. Elion – whose father, from a distinguished line of rabbis, had immigrated to the United States from Lithuania before the First World War – carried out research that was to revolutionize cancer treatment. She was thirty-two years old when she discovered the drug that was to have a dramatic effect on the survival of children with leukemia. The drug, thioguanine, was then developed by Elion to facilitate kidney transplants, as well as to treat severe arthritis, and gout. Tenacious in her researches, a decade later she discovered a drug that could combat shingles, genital herpes, chicken pox and encephalitis. In 1988 she was awarded the Nobel Prize, the first for thirty-one years to be awarded for drug research. Her methodological approach later enabled her former research unit to develop AZT, the drug authorized in the United States to treat AIDS.

Abstract Expressionist *painter Marc Rothko (above). He was a pioneer of Colour Field painting, using large areas of strong, unmodulated colour. Born in Russia, he emigrated to the United States with his parents when he was seven.* PHOTO: HENRY ELKAN]

A helping hand. *The American composer and conductor, Leonard Bernstein, at the piano. Twice when Israel was at war he travelled from the United States without hesitation to play to soldiers and civilians alike, enormously boosting morale.*
[PHOTO: LISL STEINER]

In 1953 two American Jews, Julius and Ethel Rosenberg, husband and wife, were convicted of spying for the Soviet Union and passing on atomic secrets. They were the first civilians to be executed for espionage in United States history. A year later, in contrast to the Rosenbergs' divided loyalties, Admiral Hyman George Rickover, who had come to the United States with his parents at the age of six from Russian Poland in 1906 – his father was a tailor – made a leading contribution to the construction of the world's first nuclear submarine, *Nautilus*, giving the United States a dominant deterrent.

In a turning point in popular journalism, on 16 October 1955 Ann Landers – born Esther Pauline Friedman, in Sioux City, Iowa, the daughter of Jewish immigrants from Russia – wrote her first daily advice column in the *Chicago Sun Times*. Within a decade she was receiving a thousand letters a day. By the end of the twentieth century she had become the most widely syndicated newspaper columnist in the world. Asked what influence Judaism had on her work – giving advice to people in personal distress – she replied: 'I am inclined to support the underdog.'

Being the underdog had never inhibited Jewish creativity, or the Jewish contribution to universal thought and reflection; indeed, it may have enhanced it. In 1960 the Hungarian-born Elie Wiesel, a survivor of Auschwitz and Buchenwald, and a future Nobel Prize winner, published an account based on his personal experiences in the Holocaust, *Night*, which was to become a beacon for those who sought to grasp the enormity of what had happened. The primacy of individual actions for good was also a basic Jewish belief – much debated in the post-Holocaust years. To the question 'Where was God at Auschwitz?', Hugo Gryn, a former inmate, answered with the question: 'Where was man?'

CHAPTER SEVEN

SUCCESSES, THREATS AND DILEMMAS

1961-1980

IN THE SOVIET UNION, MANY INDIVIDUAL JEWS, WORKING within the Communist system, did well during the 1960s. The economist Yevsey Liberman, who was at the centre of the post-Stalin era debate about economic reform, published an article in *Pravda* in 1962 in which he suggested moving away from central planning and giving factory managers more responsibility. He also argued that profit rather than output should be the measurement of successful management. 'Libermanism' became the beacon of economic change in the Soviet Union: Liberman himself received thousands of letters of support from Soviet citizens anxious to see a relaxation of the economic straightjackets imposed upon them. Another Soviet Jewish achievement in 1962 was the award of the Nobel Prize for Physics to Lev Landau. Twenty-five years earlier, not long after becoming head of the leading physics institute in Moscow, Landau had been imprisoned on charges of spying for Germany. He was quickly released because of his scientific eminence – the absurdity of the charges being irrelevant to Stalin.

The success of individual Jews inside the Soviet Union did not, however, diminish anti-Jewish Soviet policy or attitudes. On the 'nationality' line of their identity cards, many of the country's two million Jews inscribed themselves as 'Jew' – one of the dozens of so-called 'nationalities' that made up the peoples of the Soviet Union. Yet they were given no national identity or region – beyond the token and farcical Autonomous Jewish Region of Birobidjan in eastern Siberia – they were often singled out for taunts and abuse, found themselves up against unwritten quota systems for university entrance, and were unable to emigrate to Israel, the Jewish 'national' home. Between July 1961 and March 1963 a series of 'economic' trials found just over a hundred defendants guilty of what was described in court as 'speculation' in clothing, footwear or furs. All were shot; at least sixty-eight of them were Jews. In an upsurge of anti-Semitic comment in the Soviet newspapers,

New immigrants from Russia
*at the housing project built specially for them at Neve Sharett,
just outside Tel Aviv, 1968.* [PHOTO: MICHA BAR-AM]

many of the accused were said to have had a Zionist, a Jewish Social-Democrat or a 'bourgeois-nationalist' past, or to have helped American and British spies to 'penetrate Soviet factories'. In 1964, in Kishinev, the scene of the notorious pogrom of 1903 and the massacres of 1941, a booklet on *Contemporary Judaism and Zionism* stated: 'Judaism is the worst of all religions; pessimistic, nationalistic, anti-feminine and anti-popular.'

On 12 October 1963 a conference on the status of Soviet Jews was held in New York, sponsored by Martin Luther King among others. It led to the establishment of an American Jewish Conference on Soviet Jewry, to co-ordinate public concern throughout the United States. Six months later, on 27 April 1964, a group of young American Jewish students met at Columbia University, New York, to protest against the treatment of Jews in the Soviet Union. Four days later they organised a silent march to the Soviet Mission to the United Nations. Thus began the Student Struggle for Soviet Jewry, one of whose leading spirits, Glenn Richter, was to devote the next two decades and more to its cause. The campaign was partly successful. In 1966 just over 2,000 Jews were allowed to leave for Israel. If the numbers wanting to leave were to grow substantially, it was unclear whether they would be allowed out. Strict Soviet rules, enforced by the KGB, forbade the private teaching of Jewish history to young people, and small Hebrew-language classes, eagerly attended by Jews hoping to emigrate to Israel, were often broken up by the authorities.

In Israel, the building up of the Jewish State continued, with farming still the main livelihood. Mounds of oranges being picked for export were a favourite visual advertisement. At the same time, industry was expanding. Exports included polished diamonds, with Israel becoming a hub of a largely Jewish profession along with the two other diamond trade centres, Antwerp and New York.

At Yad Vashem, in Jerusalem, exhibitions, ceremonies and archival collections stressed not only the mass murder of Jews and Jewish resistance, but drew the attention of the Israeli public to the thousands of non-Jews who saved Jewish lives during the Holocaust, at the risk of their own. In 1960 a dramatic event propelled the Holocaust forward into the public consciousness of Israel and the world. On the afternoon of May 23 word spread throughout the Knesset building in Jerusalem that Ben Gurion was about to make an extraordinary statement. The Knesset Chamber and the public galleries rapidly filled to capacity, but no one knew what they were about to hear. As Cabinet Ministers, to whom Ben Gurion had just confided the secret, entered the Chamber, it was clear that something unique in Israel's history was about to be revealed. Called to the rostrum by the Speaker, Ben Gurion then told an astonished gathering that the man responsible 'for what they call the final solution of the Jewish question, that is the extermination of six million Jews of Europe' – Adolf Eichmann – was at that very moment in Israel, under arrest, and would be brought to trial.

Searching for Nazis. *Simon Wiesenthal (above), who survived five years in concentration and slave labour camps, and whose mother was murdered at Belzec, founded the Jewish Historical Documentation Centre in Austria after the war, with thirty other survivors. It assembled evidence to help track down former Nazi war criminals. Weisenthal's motto was: 'Hope lives when people remember.'*

For more than ten years Eichmann had been living in Argentina under a false identity. Israeli agents had found him, kidnapped him and flown him to Israel. His trial began in Jerusalem on 11 April 1961. Although courts of law do not allow foreign advocates to appear before them to plead on behalf of a defendant, Israel allowed Eichmann to be defended by Dr Robert Servatius, a German counsel who had appeared for the defence in the Nuremberg Trials of the leading Nazis fourteen years earlier. Eichmann was found guilty and hanged. Neither before, nor since, has the death penalty been carried out in Israel. Even in the case of the worst terrorist actions against Israeli civilians, the death sentence has always been commuted.

Adolf Eichmann *(right), chief organiser of the Nazi mass murder operation, in a courtroom in Jerusalem during his trial. He is being questioned by the chief Israeli prosecutor, Gideon Hausner (back to camera). On the left, with earphones, is Eichmann's German defence counsel, Dr Servatius.* [PHOTO: MICHA BAR-AM]

The Israeli census of 1961 gave Israel's population as 1,932,400 Jews — just over 88 per cent of the total population. There were also 250,000 non-Jews — Muslim and Christian Arabs, and Muslim Druse. The Druse, some 24,000 in all, are a Muslim group that for centuries had been fierce warriors in the region. While Israeli Arabs did not have to serve in the army, many Druse volunteered to do so, and served with distinction. The Government of Israel tried not to neglect the rights of its Arab minority, but its relationship with the Israeli Arabs was strained because of the long conflict with the Arab States across Israel's borders. A Military Administration had been established over the Arab-inhabited areas of Israel in the first days of statehood, to prevent hostile activities against the State from within. Its five main regulations permitted the arrest of a person for being in a prohibited area, allowed police supervision over a person for up to one year, provided the legal basis for administrative detention by military commanders, allowed for house arrest, and permitted military commanders to declare certain areas closed areas, with

Discovery in a cave. *In March 1961, archaeologists and volunteers excavating in a cave near the Dead Sea discovered a cache of letters written by Jews who had fled from Roman vengeance after the crushing of the Bar Kochba revolt in 135 AD. The letters included one from Bar Kochba himself to one of his military commanders, reminding him of the religious duty to provide Sabbath accommodation for visitors.*

[PHOTO: DAVID HARRIS]

special permits needed for Arabs to enter or leave them. Gradually the regions to which these regulations applied were reduced. In 1962 the Druse were exempted from the restrictive legislation. Even when the Military Administration was lifted in its entirety in 1966, the Emergency Regulations which it embodied could still be implemented by the heads of the regional military commands.

The Arab population had the right to vote in Israeli elections, and had several Arab parties to vote for. But whether the Arab minority in Israel, feeling disadvantaged as Muslims in a predominantly Jewish State, would ever be attracted to some wider, even militant form of Arab nationalism was a question thoughtful Israelis often asked. For its part, Jewish nationalism received a boost as Israel's links with its Biblical roots were strengthened by the continuing excavations of Yigael Yadin. Assisted by thousands of volunteers, many of them from abroad, Yadin worked between 1963 and 1965 on Masada, the mountain fortress built by King Herod in the Judaean desert

Archaeologists at work *during the exploration of the Judaean desert caves. In the centre, with woolly hat, is Yigael Yadin, former Chief of Staff of the Israel Defence Forces, and later Professor of Archaeology at the Hebrew University. Known affectionately by his English friends as 'Yig the Dig', he was also to excavate at Masada, Hazor and Megiddo (Armageddon).* [PHOTO: MICHA BAR-AM]

overlooking the Dead Sea. It was at Masada that the last of the Jewish rebels against Rome, the Zealots, had held out under siege until imminent defeat led them to draw lots for the taking of their own lives. Yadin's team discovered the stones on which those lots were cast, as described by the Romano-Jewish historian Flavius Josephus. The excitement at Yadin's discoveries was nation-wide, giving Israelis a sense of their long-time attachment to the land, and

Sun and fun. *At En Gedi, Israelis enjoy the buoyant salt waters of the Dead Sea and the perennial fresh water stream falling 656 feet down through the gorge in the dry bare mountains. They could drive from the centre of the country in four or five hours to this popular picnic and recreation area, which has changed little since Biblical times, when David sought refuge there from Saul.*

[PHOTO: DAVID HARRIS]

confirming the stories of heroes from a distant age. Each year, Israeli army officers hold their graduation ceremony on Masada, the symbol of Jewish defiance against an overwhelming enemy. After Masada, Yadin turned his archaeological energies to the hill fortress of Megiddo – the Biblical Armageddon – where evidence of a flourishing city was found.

In 1963 the Israeli Foreign Minister, Golda Meir, was in Florida when President John F. Kennedy, who was on holiday there, asked to see her. She told him that the Government of Israel was in many ways 'no different from any other decent government. It cares for the welfare of the people, for the development of the State, and so on'. But there was, she continued, 'one other great responsibility, and that is for the future. If we should lose our sovereignty again, those of us who would remain alive – and there wouldn't be very many – would be dispersed once more. But we no longer have the great reservoir we once had of our religion, our culture, and our faith. We lost much of that when six million Jews perished in the Holocaust.' Kennedy's answer was:: 'Mrs Meir. Don't worry. Nothing will happen to Israel.'

Despite the refusal of Israel's Arab neighbours to make peace, even the border areas began to be developed. At En Gedi, on the Dead Sea, a mere five miles from the barbed wire and concrete barriers of the border with Jordan, a resort village provided much-needed leisure for Israeli adults and children alike. But defence remained a priority for the government of Israel, as the bordering Arab nations increasingly aligned themselves with the Soviet Union. Soviet arms were forming the basis of new military strength for both Syria and Egypt. In January 1964, at an Arab summit meeting in Damascus, the Syrian Government proposed making use of the 75,000 Palestinian Arab refugees who had been living in refugee camps in Syria since 1948, and the far larger number living in other Arab lands, in a way which could destabilise Israel. The Syrian proposal was accepted, the Arab summit authorising the Palestinians, wherever they might be living, to 'carry out their role in liberating their homeland and determining their destiny'. Later that year the Jordanian government allowed an 'Assembly' of Palestinian Arabs to meet in East Jerusalem. As a result of the Assembly's discussions, a new organisation was created, the Palestine Liberation Organisation (the PLO), whose aim, in the words of its founding manifesto, was to 'attain the objective of liquidating Israel'. To this end, a Palestine Liberation Army was established. The PLO received substantial financial backing from the Arab governments. President Nasser, hoping to win patronage of the Palestinians from Syria, placed both Sinai and the Gaza Strip at the PLO's disposal for military training, and as a base for raids across the border into southern Israel.

On 1 January 1965, while the Christian world – including Israel's Christian Arab population – celebrated New Year's Day, yet another new Arab organization was born, with Syrian encouragement. It called itself the Movement for the National Liberation of Palestine, soon known by its Arabic acronym 'Fatah' – Victory – and was led by a Palestinian Arab, Yasser Arafat.

Fatah commandos, usually working in small teams of three or four, crossed into Israel and planted bombs. Syria, as a precaution against retaliation, would not allow them to cross from Syria but only from Lebanon. Their first action, of which they boasted to the world in a 'victory' communiqué that New Year's Day, was in fact an unsuccessful one, the Fatah commandos being stopped by a Lebanese policeman on the border and turned back. On 28 February 1965 another Fatah team crossed into Israel from Jordan, penetrated three miles into Israel, and damaged a grain silo.

Raid and counter-raid between Fatah and Israeli forces became the order of the day. But it was the Syrian dimension that gave Israel greatest cause for alarm. On 19 May 1965 the Syrian authorities hanged Eli Cohen in front of a vast crowd in Damascus. Cohen was a Jew who had been born in Egypt. Recruited by Israeli military intelligence, he pretended to be a Chilean citizen of Arab descent. Living in Syria he became a popular figure in the Syrian military establishment, whose most secret decisions he sent back to Israel. He also sent back photographs which he himself had taken of the Syrian defences on the Golan Heights. Syrian television covered his execution. His body was left hanging for six hours as crowds filed past.

On May 25 a small Fatah commando unit penetrated across the River Jordan to the town of Afula. There it blew up a house, badly injuring a woman and her two children. Two days later, in response, a paratroop attack organised by the Chief of Staff, Yitzhak Rabin, destroyed two Fatah bases on Jordanian territory.

Amid these strains and struggles, Israel's normal life continued. Her artists, orchestras and theatre groups toured the United States. American Jews in particular, but also Jews from throughout the Diaspora, contributed to the building up of theatres, music academies, concert halls and cultural centres, educational institutions and museums, throughout the country, and to the Israel Museum, situated on a hillside in Jerusalem. Also in Jerusalem, the Israeli parliament – the Knesset – was provided with a new building thanks to the British Rothschilds, who three decades later also made possible a magnificent new Supreme Court building. For the Knesset, Marc Chagall painted a vast mural. In 1965, Viennese-born Teddy Kollek became mayor of Jerusalem, a divided city, where he had to stand on a rooftop on the Jewish side if he wished to glimpse the Wailing Wall, Judaism's holiest site, then under Jordanian rule, and barred to Israelis. Kollek could also see, from a vantage point in West Jerusalem, the Hebrew University buildings on Mount

Mayor of Jerusalem. *Teddy Kollek (left), was elected Mayor of West Jerusalem in 1966, and presided over the united city from 1967 for more than two decades, improving the quality of urban life for Jews and Arabs alike.* [PHOTO: TIM GIDAL]

Scopus, to which the Jordanians had effectively denied access since 1948. Books had to be smuggled out of the campus to a new one that had been built in West Jerusalem.

In 1966 an Israeli citizen, S.J. Agnon, won the Nobel Prize for literature, the first time that the prize was given to a Hebrew writer. He had been born in the Austro-Hungarian town of Buczacz, first emigrating to Palestine in

Learning redeemed. *Books from the Hebrew University library on Mount Scopus, to which the Jordanians denied the Jews free access between 1948 and 1967, brought to the new campus (below) in West Jerusalem.* [PHOTO: DAVID HARRIS]

293

SHMUEL YOSEF AGNON – NOBEL-PRIZEWINNER. *Born in Austria-Hungary from a Hassidic background, he lived in Palestine from 1908 to 1912, then went to Germany, where he joined a circle of Hebrew writers in Hamburg. Salmann Schocken, a German-Jewish businessman, supported him and published his books. He lived in Jerusalem under the Mandate, when many of his books and manuscripts were destroyed in the riots of 1929.*

[PHOTO: DAVID RUBINGER]

ISAAC BASHEVIS SINGER – NOBEL-PRIZEWINNER. *Born in Russian Poland, of a rabbinical family, it is the vibrant inter-war life and history of Polish Jewry which fills the pages of his Yiddish novels and short stories. After 1935 he worked in New York, where he wrote for the leading Yiddish newspaper, the* Jewish Daily Forward.

[PHOTO: MICHA BAR-AM]

MARTIN BUBER – THEOLOGIAN AND EDUCATOR. *Born in Vienna, he edited at Theodor Herzl's request the official Zionist journal, and in 1916 he founded* Der Jude *(The Jew) a journal for German-speaking Jewry. He brought the tales of the Hassidic masters to the attention of the western world, and in Palestine he advocated both Jewish-Christian and Jewish-Arab rapprochement. He became the first President of the Israel Academy of Sciences and Art.*

[PHOTO: DAVID RUBINGER]

1908. A second Nobel Prize for literature was awarded in 1966, also to a Jew – the poet Nelly Sachs, who wrote in German. Born in Berlin seventy-five years earlier, she had found refuge in Sweden in the early months of the Second World War. In her acceptance speech she said: 'Agnon represents the State of Israel; I represent the tragedy of the Jewish people.' That tragedy had destroyed a vast reservoir of Jewish talent which would have enriched Israeli life. The contribution that the pre-war refugees from Nazism had made emphasised the scale of the loss. The philosopher Martin Buber, who had left Germany for Palestine in 1938, was one of the founders of the College for

Teachers of Adult Education, aimed at making new immigrants, especially those from Islamic countries, an integral part of Israeli society, and doing so by training teachers from among the new immigrants themselves.

Israel's social, cultural and intellectual life was cruelly interrupted in May 1967, when the Egyptian President, Gamal Abdul Nasser, closed the vital Straits of Tiran to Israeli merchant ships bound for Eilat. He had already closed the Suez Canal to Israeli ships, so this forced all Israel's Far Eastern trade to go the long way round the Cape of Good Hope and through the Atlantic. In hostile mood, Nasser massed his troops along Israel's Negev border. On 24 May 1967, as a gesture of support for Egypt, an armoured brigade from Kuwait was landed at Cairo International Airport. A few hours later the Secretary-General of the United Nations, U Thant, flew from New York to the same airport to persuade Nasser not to commit his forces to war. Nasser would make no such commitment, and U Thant flew back to New York.

A national unity government was formed, the first in Israel's short history. Menachem Begin, head of the Herut opposition, and hitherto a pariah in the eyes of the Labour leadership, was brought into the government. Israel's military position was, on paper, precarious. Egypt, Syria and Jordan had 200,000 men and 1,600 tanks ready for action. A further 150 Iraqi tanks were moving into Jordan to join what was being called in the Arab world 'the final battle'. West of the Suez Canal, Egypt had a further 140,000 troops and 300 tanks ready to be transferred eastward. Against this substantial Arab force, deployed on three fronts, Israel had, with the full mobilisation of the civilian reserves, 264,000 soldiers and 800 tanks. An estimated 700 Arab combat aircraft were also ready for action. Israel had only 300.

At a meeting of Israel's national unity government on June 4, reports were read out of the determination of the Egyptian generals to take action. Moshe Dayan, then Minister of Defence – and himself a former Chief of Staff – proposed that Israel take the initiative before she was attacked. On the morning of June 5, Israeli warplanes, many of them French-made Mystère fighters, carried out a three-hour-long attack – five hundred sorties in all – against air bases throughout Egypt. In a dramatic example of the success of the element of surprise in warfare, one third of Egypt's Soviet-made Tupolev, Ilyushin and Sukhoi war-planes were destroyed on the ground, and almost all Egyptian airbase runways rendered unusable. Syrian, Iraqi and Jordanian warplanes then launched a series of attacks on targets in Israel, but Israeli radar and signals intelligence knew that they were on their way, and within two hours the attackers were shot down or driven back. All of Jordan's twenty-two British-made Hurricane fighters were destroyed. Ironically, the Commander of Israel's air force, General Mordechai Hod, had trained at a Royal Air Force flying school in Britain, where he had been the outstanding pilot of his class.

Masters of the skies, Israeli warplanes then proceeded to destroy the Syrian and Jordanian air forces both in the air and on the ground. Iraq's main desert air base was also destroyed. Israel was no longer vulnerable from the air.

Battle for East Jerusalem. *Israeli soldiers getting ready to attack the Old City from Mount Scopus. Behind them is the Hadassah hospital, which had been cut off from Israel since 1949.*

[PHOTO: DON MCCULLIN]

In the assessment of Yitzhak Rabin, Israel's Chief of Staff, the elimination of Arab air power undermined the fighting spirit of the Arab military force, while 'precisely the opposite happened within Israel's political and military leadership and its combat units'. Still, however, Rabin added, 'we were not over-confident and were certainly not itching for a fight merely to demonstrate our prowess'.

The main victim of Israel's air superiority was King Hussein, but he need not have been. Using both an American and an Israeli intermediary, Israel had offered him its strict neutrality, provided he took no action against Israel. But the Commander-in-Chief of the Egyptian Army, Field Marshal Amer, had informed the Jordanians during the first morning of battle that 70 per cent of the Israeli air force had been destroyed, and Hussein believed him. He also accepted a report from Nasser that Egyptian forces had broken through the Israeli border in the south and were advancing across the Negev towards the Hebron hills. The Iraqis added to the Jordanian King's sense of urgency in committing his troops when they told him that Iraqi aircraft had bombed Tel Aviv, causing considerable destruction. All three claims were false, but on the basis of them, Hussein ordered his forces to attack, and began shelling West Jerusalem. The Knesset was among the buildings hit: its members continued their deliberations in the shelter. As a gesture of support for Israel, Leonard Bernstein flew in to conduct the Philharmonic Orchestra, even as Jordanian shells fell.

A Jordanian Brigade, sent up from the Jordan Valley during the first night of the war, was spotted by the Israeli air force which, using flares to illuminate the desert, attacked it from the air, so disrupting its advance that it arrived only after the Israelis had effectively secured East Jerusalem, and was unable to take effective action.

Late on the afternoon of June 7, King Hussein appeared on Jordanian television, calling on his people 'to fight to the last breath and the last drop of blood'; hours after he had in fact agreed to accept a ceasefire, which was formally accepted at seven that evening. Jordan had lost East Jerusalem and the whole of the West Bank.

In the Sinai desert, General Ariel 'Arik' Sharon – who had fought in the Battle of Latrun during the War of Independence as a lieutenant – parachuted with his division more than sixty miles behind Egyptian lines, then drove westward to the Suez Canal. The Egyptian fortified positions at El Arish, on the northern route to the canal, were captured by tank forces commanded by Colonel Shmuel 'Gorodish' Gonen, who had been trained at the United States School of Armour at Fort Knox. By the sixth day of battle Egypt had lost the Gaza Strip and the vast expanse of the Sinai desert, up to the eastern bank of the Suez Canal. In all, 650 Israeli soldiers were killed on the Egyptian and Jordanian fronts.

In the heart of the city. *Watched by a young Orthodox Jew, Israeli soldiers celebrate the liberation of the Western (or Wailing) Wall on 12 June 1967, immediately after the Six-Day War.*
[PHOTO: WERNER BRAUN]

JOYOUS ORTHODOXY. *Young Orthodox Jews sing and dance their way from the Western (Wailing) Wall to their Jerusalem homes, after their first visit there following the reunification of the city in June 1967.* [PHOTO: LEONARD FREED]

A LIFE CYCLE. *Georgian Jews (above), emigrants to Israel from the mountains of the Caucasus, celebrate a wedding, 1973. Mothers and their babies (top, right), at Kibbutz Givat Hayyim, 1973. The* *kibbutz, in the coastal plain, was founded by Jews from Austria and Czechoslovakia. An elderly couple in Tel Aviv, 1967 (right).*

[PHOTO ABOVE AND TOP RIGHT: MICHA BAR-AM]

[PHOTO BELOW RIGHT: ERICH HARTMANN]

Golan Heights fortification. *Israeli civilians stand in front of a trench at a former Syrian military outpost six hundred feet above the Sea of Galilee. Syria had used the heights to shell Israeli villages, one of which, Ha'on, with its fish ponds, can be seen at the sea shore.* [PHOTO: MICHA BAR-AM]

On the Golan Heights, the Israeli tanks were preceded by bulldozers to enable them to move up the steep and stony terrain. All the bulldozers were hit, and some lost several crews during the advance; but still they came on, the tanks following close behind. When tanks were knocked out, their surviving crewmen followed the remaining tanks on foot, fighting as infantry. Following the Jordanian surrender on the West Bank, two Israeli armoured brigades, with one victory already raising their morale, moved rapidly to the

SOVIET JEWS

Golan battlefield, helping to push the Syrians back to Kuneitra, less than thirty miles south-west of the Syrian capital, Damascus. One of the peaks of Mount Hermon was seized by Israeli parachute troops, a major intelligence vantage point facing Damascus. In the fighting for the Golan, 1,000 Syrian and 115 Israeli soldiers were killed.

In the course of a single week, from appearing the imminent victim in danger of total destruction, Israel had became the victor, and an occupying power. Her occupation of Sinai was to continue for a decade; of the Golan Heights, and of the West Bank and Gaza Strip, for four decades. The West Bank and Gaza occupations, involving a considerable Israeli military presence, including that of thousands of army reservists brought back each year from their civilian life, stimulated Palestinian nationalism and violence.

With the Israeli victory, Soviet Jews felt a sense of pride in the country which, on the first day of the war, Radio Moscow had described as doomed. They also gained the courage to ask to emigrate. Beginning on a tiny scale in September 1967, and rising rapidly in the following four months, exit visas were granted by the Communist authorities to 379 Soviet citizens who had received the required formal 'invitation' from Israel, authenticated as it had to be by an Israeli notary, and sent openly in the post from Israel to the Soviet Union. Thousands of Soviet Jews now began to ask for these invitations, the first step in a long and complicated procedure for an exit visa. This included the requirement that adult applicants obtain their parents' permission to leave. By giving permission, parents could risk their jobs. Seeking an exit visa also involved the applicant revealing to his or her employer and local Party organisation the intention to leave, thereby risking, the loss of all official work. Hundreds of refuseniks – as those denied exit visas were called – were to be found working in boiler houses, or cleaning streets.

On 22 March 1968 Soviet Jews were surprised to read in *Pravda* the full text of a speech by the Polish Communist leader Wladyslaw Gomulka, according to whom there were many 'Jewish Polish citizens' who were not 'tied to Poland by feeling and reason, but to the State of Israel'. Of these citizens Gomulka went on to say: 'They are certainly Jewish nationalists. Can one have a grudge against them for this? Only the same kind of a grudge as Communists have against all nationalists, no matter what their nationality is. I suppose that this category of Jew is going to leave our country sooner or later.' To those who considered Israel their 'homeland', Gomulka added, 'we are ready to give emigration passports.' Poland, in the grip of a sudden upsurge of anti-Semitism, allowed any Jew who wanted to, to leave for Israel – getting rid of the historic 'outsider' whose people had enriched Polish life for centuries. Tens of thousands emigrated. To Jews in the Soviet Union, the fact that the Communist Party newspaper *Pravda* should reproduce Gomulka's remarks in full, and without hostile comment, seemed a hopeful sign. For many months, Soviet Jews spoke excitedly of 'the Gomulka variant'. However, the number of Jews actually allowed to leave the Soviet Union in

1968 – only 230 – was lower than for any year during the previous six, almost the lowest since 1955.

This did not deter the awakening of Jewish national consciousness. In September 1968, several hundred Jews gathered at Babi Yar, the ravine in Kiev where more than 30,000 Jews were massacred by the Nazis in September 1941. During the ceremony the official Soviet speakers, while honouring the dead, also abused the State of Israel. Among the Jews present was a twenty-two-year-old student, Boris Kochubievsky. 'What's going on here?' he heard a man ask, to which a woman replied, 'Here the Germans killed a hundred thousand Jews.' 'That', commented the man, 'was not enough.' Kochubievsky protested to the authorities. For his pains, he was sentenced to three years in a labour camp.

Manifestations of Jewishness continued. In October 1969 several thousand Jews gathered in Archipova Street in Moscow, outside the Moscow synagogue. It was the eve of Simhat Torah, the Jewish festival of the Rejoicing of the Law. In a quarter-mile section of the narrow street, these Jews, most of them aged between eighteen and twenty-four, sang and danced in the cold drizzle until late into the night. Some sang Yiddish songs, others took up the refrains in Hebrew, the language of the Jewish State of which they wished to be part. Some had pieces of paper on which they had written out such words as they knew in modern Hebrew; these words were avidly swapped and spoken. One of the songs heard that night was a jingle mocking Soviet anti-Semitism. But when 1969 came to an end it was clear that no substantial emigration was to be allowed. Three thou-

Prayer shawls in Moscow *at the Archipova Street synagogue. Jewish meetings in Moscow were illegal except in this synagogue and in the street outside it.*

[PHOTO: JESSE ZEL LURIE]

Campaign medals from the Second World War *displayed by a Georgian Jew in the immigration hall at Ben Gurion airport. When he saw the photographer he proudly opened his overcoat to reveal his decorations.*

[PHOTO: DAVID HARRIS]

sand Jews received their exit visas, the largest number in any year since the 1917 Revolution; but that number was in sharp contrast to the 34,000 who had asked to leave in the sixteen months since September 1968.

World Jewry began to take up the cause of Soviet Jewry. In December 1970, when two Jews were sentenced to death for their part in trying to seize a twelve-seater airplane and fly it from Leningrad to Sweden, an international outcry led to the death sentences being commuted to fifteen years in prison and labour camp. The campaign for Soviet Jewish emigration grew, both inside and outside the Soviet Union, and was successful; during the course of almost a decade more than 100,000 Jews were allowed to leave the Soviet Union for Israel; 50,000 more emigrated to the United States. But more than a thousand others continued to be refused permission to leave, lost their jobs, had to do menial work to survive, and faced imprisonment if they became too active in fighting for the right of all Jews to leave. By 1980 more than a hundred Soviet Jews had been imprisoned for their part in the emigration struggle. Persistent and prolonged campaigns by world Jewry eventually secured the release of most of these 'Prisoners of Zion', but after each release, others were arrested and imprisoned, among them Anatoly Shcharansky, who was sentenced to thirteen years 'deprivation of liberty', to be served in prison and labour camp, on the false charge of spying for the United States. For long periods Shcharansky, a free and defiant spirit who never relinquished his small book of Psalms, was kept in solitary confinement. The campaign for his release, vigorously conducted by Jewish groups worldwide, lasted almost a decade, and was unremitting in its energetic ingenuity, until he was finally allowed to live in Israel.

Within the Communist world, Jews were still able to flourish. In 1964, a Jewish woman athlete, Irena Kirszenstein, a Polish citizen, won a gold medal for Poland at the Tokyo Olympics. A year later she was named Poland's 'Athlete of the Year'. She went on to win two more Olympic gold medals. In 1965 the 'Queen of Yiddish Theatre', Ida Kaminska, who had been performing on the stage in Yiddish in Poland since the age of five, starred in a film, *The Shop on Main Street*, which was made in another Communist country, Czechoslovakia. Kaminska, then sixty-six years old, played a Jewish widow of eighty whose senility and deafness prevented her from understanding what was happening to her and her fellow Jews during the German invasion of Czechoslovakia. The film won an Academy Award in 1966 for the best foreign film.

With the upsurge in anti-Semitism in Poland in 1968, Ida Kaminska found refuge first in Vienna, and then in the United States. There she made an energetic attempt to establish a permanent Yiddish repertoire. But the language spoken by so many millions when she was in her prime had been turned virtually into a dead language as a result of the Holocaust. What had once been the language of Jewish daily life, the vehicle of so much Jewish humour, has passed into history.

In Israel, in the immediate aftermath of the Six-Day War, a music unit of the Israel Defence Forces produced 'A Song for Peace', which expressed the longings of many Israelis, including those who had fought in the war. Several senior Israeli generals told the Chief of Staff, Yitzhak Rabin, that they regarded 'A Song for Peace' as too pacifist, and that it should not be part of the army repertoire. Rabin overruled them; the song became an antidote to the triumphalism of victory that can overcome any army (see page 343).

Stopping for a drink in an Arab café. *In the aftermath of the Six-Day War, Orthodox Jews could make their way to the Western (Wailing) Wall for the first time since 1948, and did so along an Arab street*

*leading to the Old City's Damascus Gate.
Arabic and Hebrew advertisements, as well
as the customers, show the owner ready to
serve both Jews and Arabs.*

[PHOTO: DAVID HARRIS]

In March 1969 Golda Meir became Prime Minister of Israel. Her first public announcement was: 'We are prepared to discuss peace with our neighbours, all day and on all matters.' Within three days President Nasser replied: 'There is no voice transcending the sounds of war, no call holier than the call to war'. Egyptian artillery opened fire on the Israeli forces stationed on the east bank of the Suez Canal. Israel returned the fire. What became known as the War of Attrition had begun. On 5 January 1970 a nine-man Egyptian unit crossed the Suez Canal and, supported by artillery fire from the western bank, attacked an Israeli army post. All nine Egyptians were killed. Two days later the Israelis began bombing Egyptian military camps near Cairo. Other Israeli warplanes flew more than eighty miles into Egypt. At the same time there were Israeli air strikes on terrorist bases in Lebanon and Jordan that were being used for attacks inside Israel.

Champion of fair play,
*the South African novelist
Nadine Gordimer was an
outspoken opponent of
apartheid.*

The War of Attrition ended in August 1970. In just over a year, 593 Israeli soldiers and 127 Israeli civilians had been killed by Egyptian bombardments, almost as many Israeli deaths as during the Six-Day War. It was not only external enemies with whom Israel was confronted. The inhabitants of the occupied territories – the West Bank and Gaza – had entered the national and international arena as a force to be reckoned with, despite the fact that Golda Meir had gone so far as to say that there was 'no such thing as a Palestinian'. Even among Israeli Jews, groups were formed to champion the rights of the Palestinians under Israeli occupation, and to protest when they had their fields confiscated, their homes bulldozed, or were subjected to harsh treatment, even torture.

Not only in Israel, but in many regions of the world, Jews fought for civil and human rights. In South Africa, Helen Suzman, the daughter of Lithuanian Jewish immigrants to South Africa, became in 1961 the only Progressive Party Member of the South African Parliament. As non-Whites had no representation there, she alone spoke up for them in the legislature, and did so fearlessly. When criticised by supporters of apartheid, she replied: 'If we are serious about wanting to restore our position as a respected member of the Western community of nations, we have simply got to realise that our old prejudices and practice of discrimination must go.'

The South African novelist Nadine Gordimer, the daughter of a Jewish watchmaker from Lithuania, was also a fearless opponent of the apartheid regime, which banned three of her novels from publication in South Africa. Unhappy at the close relationship between South Africa and Israel, which was selling arms to South Africa, she later wrote: 'I think for all Jews it was a sorrow, really, and a shame'. In 1991 she was awarded the Nobel Prize for Literature, the first woman to receive one for twenty-five years.

During the South African Treason Trial which ended in 1961, of the twenty-three Whites accused, two-thirds were Jews. All five Whites arrested at the start of the Rivonia Trial – which led to Nelson Mandela being sentenced to life imprisonment – were Jews. The State Prosecutor in the Rivonia Trial was also a Jew, Percy Yutar. In the words of David Saks, a senior researcher at the South African Jewish Board of Deputies: 'Percy Yutar gained lasting ignominy for the manner in which he conducted the trial, showing a vindictiveness many felt went beyond the call of duty.' Yutar was undoubtedly motivated by a desire to demonstrate Jewish loyalty to South Africa, and thereby combat widespread official anti-Semitism.

American Jewry had reached a high point of participation in all walks of life. Numbering more than five million, there were twice as many of them as in the Soviet Union and three times as many as in Israel. The strongly-held Zionist belief that a Jew could only be finally secure in his own land, ruled by fellow-Jews, had been disproved there for the foreseeable future – although as Churchill once reflected, 'The future, though imminent, is obscure'. All citizens of the United States, except Native Americans are members of some immigrant group which has arrived within historic memory, even the Founding Fathers of the seventeenth century.

Lower East Side to the Senate. *Jacob Javits began his career helping his mother to sell kitchenware from door to door in New York. Becoming a distinguished trial lawyer, and Attorney-General for New York State, he was elected to Congress in 1946, as a liberal Republican, going on to the Senate eight years later, where he served for twenty-four years. Civil rights and urban redevelopment were among his priorities. He helped create the Prison Reform Act and the National Endowment for the Arts, as well as helping draft, in the aftermath of the Vietnam War, the War Powers Resolution, restricting the ability of future Presidents to make war without full Congressional approval.*

Civil rights march leaders at the Lincoln Memorial, *Washington, August 1963. Philip Randolph (second left), veteran labor leader who helped to found the Brotherhood of Sleeping Car Porters and organiser of the demonstration, turns to talk to Rabbi Joachim Prinz, President of the American Jewish Congress.*

The exclusion of Jews from clubs or certain suburbs, and the quotas on Jewish admission to universities, was rapidly becoming a thing of the past. More and more Jews were in positions of power, their hands on the levers of power; they could give orders as well as receive them, acting as enablers, not suppliants. They had entered the heart of the American establishment, forming an important segment of the nation's elite in the law courts. colleges and universities, hospitals, Hollywood and Wall Street. There were frequent articles in the newspapers about the decline of the White Anglo-Saxon Protestants (the Wasps), but no such worries about the Jewish professional classes.

Jewish writers celebrated their Jewishness while making mainstream contributions to American literature. Cynthia Ozick, drawing on anti-Semitic experiences in her childhood, and Jewish family traditions, was influential across the whole spectrum of the American novel. Chaim Potok, the son of a Hassidic rabbi, was a master craftsman of the novel, plays and children's books. Philip Roth characterized and caricatured Jewish life, but also satirised President Reagan, and won America's coveted Pulitzer Prize for fiction. Studs Terkel was another earlier Pulitzer prizewinner, for pioneering the art of oral history.

LITERARY TALENT. *Philip Roth (far left), novelist. Roth's fellow-novelist Norman Mailer (opposite above) speaks into the microphone in the Garment District, New York, during his unsuccessful campaign to be Mayor. Next to him is the journalist Jimmy Breslin. The novelist and playwright Joseph Heller (far left, below), in front of a poster advertising his play* We Bombed in New Haven. *The Canadian-born novelist Saul Bellow (immediate left), at* a pro-Israel rally in New York's Central Park. The cartoonist Saul Steinberg in whimsical artistic mode (above) acts out his laconic, witty drawings. In the Nevada desert, the playwright Arthur Miller (above right) takes a brief rest while on location during the film shoot of his play* The Misfits. *The chair next to him is designated for his wife, Marilyn Monroe.*

[PHOTO OPPOSITE TOP LEFT: EVE ARNOLD]
[PHOTO ABOVE LEFT: INGE MORATH]

The rapid rise of Jews in American public life could be seen in all sectors. When New York went bankrupt, it was a Jewish financier Felix Rohatyn, who rallied Wall Street and reorganised the city's finances. As well as commerce, banking and business expansion, social change was also an area where Jewish involvment was prominent. In 1963, an American Jewish feminist, Betty Friedan, born Betty Noami Goldstein, published *The Feminine Mystique*, in which she argued that women must strive, despite male dominance in society, to obtain 'the fulfilment of their own femininity'. Her inspiration came as a reaction to the traditional part taken by women in Jewish life. 'For me,' she explained, 'as for other Jewish feminists, religion perpetuated the patriarchal tradition that denied women access to Judaism's most sacred rituals and enshrined them within the strict confines of their biological role.' The artist Judy Chicago born Judy Cohen, was among those who raised the – in her case colourful – banner of women's rights, whatever their social background, race or creed. Her monumental *The Dinner Party* was a landmark in recognising women's achievements throughout history, and worldwide. Like many of American Jewry's most impressive contributions it had a universal aspect.

Feminist leader Betty Friedan. *In her youth it was said that she thanked young men opening doors for her by kicking them in the shin. In 1979 she and Bella Abzug (opposite) were among the founders of the National Women's Political Caucus, aimed at encouraging women to seek political office.* [PHOTO: JOAN ROTH]

Jewish students and rabbis were active in the Civil Rights movement. The attorney William Kunstler, a Bronze Star veteran of the Second World War, was at the centre of the defence of those in the American Civil Liberties Union who challenged the racial laws in the American South, serving as Special Counsel for Martin Luther King – just as, in South Africa, Jews were leaders in the African National Congress struggle for equality. In 1969 Kunstler secured the acquittal of the Chicago Seven who had been charged with conspiracy to incite violence at the previous year's Democratic National Convention. Another American Jew, Luis Kutner, co-founded Amnesty International in 1961, and was also the originator of the concept of the 'living will', whereby an individual could instruct next of kin against using life support methods 'in the event the signer was unable to tend to his own affairs'. Among those who helped to draft the Civil Rights Act of 1964, and the Voting Rights Act of 1965 – landmarks in the emancipation of the American Blacks – was Bella Abzug, the first Jewish woman to be elected to the United States Congress. On her first day in Congress, in 1970, she asked for the withdrawal of American troops from Vietnam. She also formed a mass movement, Women Strike for Peace, to bring a halt to nuclear testing by both

Congresswoman extraordinaire Bella Abzug, *known as 'Battling Bella'. A lawyer before being elected to Congress, she had acted for many of those named by Senator McCarthy as suspected Communists. In 1979, when she accused President Carter of paying only lip service to women's rights, he dismissed her as an adviser.*

313

the United States and the Soviet Union. Parallel with Jewish radicalism, Jewish religious Orthodoxy was also on the rise. The ultra-Orthodox Hassidic sects, which had been such a prominent feature of eastern European life until virtually wiped out during the Holocaust, found a renewed vigour in the United States. As a result, Jewish traditional worship and self-expression was revived, and continues to thrive in the new century. There is a new confidence in and willingness to be seen as Orthodox, and a new zeal in finding, among lapsed Jews, receptive adherents to the stricter tenets of the Jewish faith.

Aaron Copland, *America's best-known classical composer, at the Brooklyn Academy of Music in 1976. He had begun writing music, often using jazz rhythms, in the 1920s. His ballet score* Appalachian Spring *won the Pulitzer Prize for composition in 1944. He died in 1990 at the age of ninety.*
[PHOTO: BRUCE DAVIDSON]

In entertainment, Jews continued to make noted contributions. On 22 March 1962 the musical *I Can Get It for You Wholesale* opened on Broadway. The star was a nineteen-year-old actress, Barbra Streisand. When she was a young girl, her grandmother had called her *farbrent* – the Yiddish for 'on fire'. Her energy as a singer was extraordinary, and in the film *Yentl* she rejected suggestions that she tone down her Jewishness.

Aaron Copland, the American composer, the son of immigrants from Russia, spent 1965 at the Music Centre at Tanglewood which he had founded twenty-five years earlier: it was his last composing year there. That year, twenty-two year old James Levine, a 'child prodigy' at the piano at the age of ten, became assistant director of the Cleveland Orchestra: it was the start of a conducting career that would see him spend three decades at the Metropolitan Opera in New York. Also in 1965, Woody Allen (born Allen Stewart Konigsberg) wrote and starred in the film *What's New Pussycat?* So far he has won four Oscars.

At Dropsie College, William Chomsky, who had reached the United States from Russia in 1913, at the age of seventeen, was continuing to argue, as he had done in books and articles for many years, that without a

Two much-loved musicians, *Vladimir Horowitz, playing the piano, watched by the violinist Isaac Stern. Horowitz, noted for the flawless tone of his playing, was thirty-one when he moved from Russia to America. Stern won an Oscar for his television documentary* From Mao to Mozart *and it was his violin millions heard in the film* Fiddler on the Roof. [PHOTO: INGE MORATH]

familiarity with the Hebrew language and classical writings there could be neither vigorous creativity nor intelligent participation in Jewish life, given that in most important Jewish writing more than half the vocabulary was Biblical Hebrew. In 1969 his son Noam, professor of linguistics at the Massachusetts Institute of Technology and pioneer of a revolutionary theory of language, published *American Power and the New Mandarins*, part of his strong criticism of American involvement overseas, especially in Vietnam, and of what he saw as the flagrant abuse of power by multinational corporations. He was also a strong critic of the policies of the State of Israel.

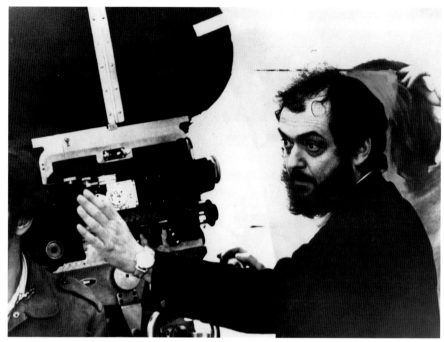

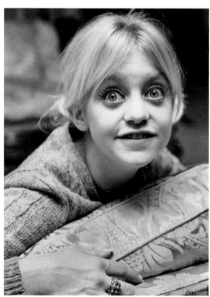

SATIRE AND MOVIES. *Lenny Bruce, born Leonard Schneider (top left) a comedian who flayed the world around him. A veteran of the Anzio and Salerno landings in Italy, he fell from public grace after facing obscenity and narcotics charges, and was banned from the stage. The film director Stanley Kubrick (top right). Among his cinema classics were* Lolita, Dr Strangelove,

A Clockwork Orange *and* 2001. *Goldie Hawn in teasing mood (below left), about the time she first made her name on the satirical NBC Television* Laugh-In *shows. Her mother was Jewish, her father a Protestant musician. She excels as an actress, producer and businesswoman. Barbra Streisand, singer, actress, director and producer (below centre).*

Walter Matthau (below right), dressed as a woman between takes on the film House Calls. *His father, who left the family soon after Walter was born, was a Catholic priest from Russia, his mother, who brought him up in New York, was a Jewish Lithuanian. Woody Allen, comedian, writer, director, actor, in Paris (opposite).*

[PHOTO TOP LEFT: DENNIS STOCK]

Rabbi Marc Tanenbaum was one of the first Jewish leaders in the United States to take part in dialogues with Catholic scholars, in search of improvement in Jewish-Catholic relations. Seeking a way to change the anti-Semitic elements in the Church's teaching, he was welcomed in Rome by Pope John XXIII, and was the only Jew to take part in the Second Vatican Council. His

Bob Dylan, *at the centre of the revival of folk song in the 1960s, writing 'Blowing in the Wind' 1962) and 'The Times They Are a-Changing' (1964).* [PHOTO: VAL WILMER]

Steely Dan. *Donald Fagen, American-born singer and keyboard player, in this pop group renowned for its jazz-influenced music in the 1970s and 80s. He and his chief collaborator, Walter Becker, split in 1990, but toured again as a duo in 1996 throughout Europe. In 2001 they won a Grammy award for their album* Two Against Nature. [PHOTO: DAVE ELLIS]

Simon and Garfunkel. *Singers and song-writers Paul Simon and Art Garfunkel met in a sixth-grade production of* Alice in Wonderland. *They recorded their first top-fifty disc in 1957. Their album* The Sound of Silence *reached Number One in the charts in 1966. Four years later they had their third Number One album,* Bridge Over Troubled Water, *after which they went their separate ways. Only once did they perform together again, in Central Park, New York, in 1982.*

[PHOTO: MICHAEL OCHS]

was a major influence in the document *Nostra Aetate*, which repudiated anti-Semitism and rejected altogether the popular Christian belief that all Jews were responsible for the death of Christ.

In 1970, at Princeton, Saul Kripke, an observant Jew, gave three lectures – published two years later as *Naming and Necessity* – which marked him out in the minds of his colleagues as 'the greatest living philosopher'. In 1971, Eric Segal, a classicist at Harvard, and the tutor of a future Presidential candidate, Al Gore, made publishing history when his novel *Love Story* became the fastest selling best-seller of its time. In 1973 a Jewish journalist, Carl Bernstein, won a Pulitzer Prize with his non-Jewish colleague Bob Woodward for unmasking a White House cover-up by President Nixon. For the film of their book, *All The President's Men*, two Jews won Academy Awards: William Goldman for Best Writer and Jason Robards for Best Supporting Actor.

Jewish songsters also had a noted part on the American musical scene. In 1962 the singer and songwriter Neil Sedaka had his first number-one hit, 'Breaking Up is Hard To Do' and the same year, Bob Dylan (born Robert Zimmerman) composed 'Blowing in the Wind', followed two years later by 'The Times They Are a-Changing'. In 1969, Burt Bacharach wrote the much-loved, much-hummed 'Raindrops Keep Falling on My Head'.

WORK AND PRAYER IN THE UNITED STATES.

A Jewish registered nurse, Hennie Cherrick (left), identified as orthodox by her head covering, attends her tiny patient at the Neo-natal Intensive Care Unit, Chicago. A young boy lights the candle (above) during the third night of the festival of Chanukkah, celebrating the victory of the Maccabees over the Seleucid Greeks in 164 BC. A Bar Mitzvah boy (right), chants his portion as he takes on the responsibilities of manhood in Wisconsin, watched by his family, friends and his local synagogue congregation.

[PHOTO OPPOSITE: YVES MOZELSIO]

[PHOTO ABOVE: JOAN ROTH]

JUREK BECKER *(above), German novelist, a survivor of the Lodz ghetto and several concentration camps, his novel* Jakob the Liar *told the story of ghetto life.* TOM STOPPARD *(right), an English playwright of Czech Jewish origins, brought to Britain just before the outbreak of war, and active in helping the campaign for Soviet Jewry.* CLAUDE LEVI-STRAUSS *(above, right, on the right), Belgian-born anthropologist who questioned the assumed superiority of Western logic and rationalism.* MURIEL SPARK *(opposite above), born Muriel Camberg in Scotland, wrote her best-known novel,* The Prime of Miss Jean Brodie, *in 1961.* ELIAS CANETTI *(opposite, top, right) born in Bulgaria, and brought up as a Ladino speaker. After spending some years in Germany and Austria, and publishing his novel* Auto-da-fé *in 1935, in which a scholar figure representing civilisation is tricked and robbed by brutal mass-man, he emigrated to England in 1938. His analysis of*

mass behaviour, Crowds and Power, *was published in 1960. In 1981 he was awarded the Nobel Prize for Literature.* EUGENE IONESCO *(above), Romanian-born French playwright whose mother was Jewish. He created the 'Theatre of the Absurd', depicting the idiocy of daily life in bourgeois society. His play* Rhinoceros *showed fascism as a disease that turned humans into rhinoceroses.* PRIMO LEVI *(far left), the Italian chemist and writer, who survived Auschwitz as a slave labourer and who afterwards made it his task to record his experiences for posterity in books, among them* If this is a Man. *He committed suicide in 1987.* LORD WEIDENFELD *(left), Viennese born, emigrating to Britain after the Anschluss, a publisher of distinction and leading advocate of a tolerant, cultured and humanistic European tradition.*

Acts of terror continued to mar life in Israel. In May 1972 three Japanese gunmen, working for Arab terrorists, opened fire in the arrival hall of Lod airport, killing twenty-seven passengers. Unknown to the killers, most of their victims were Christian pilgrims from Puerto Rico. Four months later, at the Munich Olympics, a PLO hit-squad murdered eleven Israeli athletes. But Israeli life maintained its vigour, and in May 1973 the country celebrated its twenty-fifth anniversary. Walter Eytan, a diplomat who had worked at the centre of state-building in the founding days, reflected in an anniversary article that on the West Bank and Gaza Strip the Arab population 'is more prosperous, and probably freer, than at any time before, bound by increasingly close economic and personal ties with Israelis. Something like 40,000 of these Palestinians work each day in Israel.' The situation of Gaza had been transformed. 'Where formerly unemployment was endemic and terrorism rife, today every able-bodied person can find work either in Israel or in the Gaza Strip itself, while terrorist action for the most part belongs to a nightmare of the past.'

Beneath the surface, however, Arabs resented occupation and fostered their own national ambitions, while the future of the West Bank had become a contentious issue among Israelis. The National Religious Party, which since the foundation of the State had always put its Knesset seats behind the Labour-led coalitions of the day, voted at a Party convention to resign from any government that agreed to give up any part of the West Bank. It called the West Bank the 'inheritance of the Patriarchs', the heartland of the biblical Jewish kingdoms of Judaea and Samaria. Moshe Dayan told a BBC television interviewer: 'I do think that Israel should stay for ever and ever and ever and ever in the West Bank, because this is Judaea and Samaria. This is our homeland.' Dayan wanted the Labour Party platform to incorporate his ideas. He advocated a substantial Jewish urban and industrial expansion around Jerusalem, and he wanted individual Jews to be allowed to buy land and to build homes and settlements anywhere on the West Bank. Hitherto only the Israeli government had acquired land in the Occupied Territories, especially in East Jerusalem. Dayan also wanted to construct a port city in the Rafa Salient, on the northern coast of Sinai, which had been captured from Egypt in 1967, cutting Gaza off from Egypt, eclipsing it economically, and establishing Israel permanently in Sinai.

Dayan was opposed by the Finance Minister, Pinhas Sapir, who feared that if Israel incorporated the occupied territories, adding more than a million West Bank and Gaza Arabs to the existing 400,000 Israeli Arabs, she would cease to be a predominantly Jewish State. No Israeli spoke of a Palestinian State in the West Bank and Gaza, but many saw occupation as draining the moral resources of the occupier, and denying the rights of self-government, however defined, to hundreds of thousands of people. Hebron and Nablus, Bethlehem and Jenin, Jericho and Ramallah, were Palestinian towns, yet they were under Israeli rule. On 23 August 1973 the Israeli government authorised

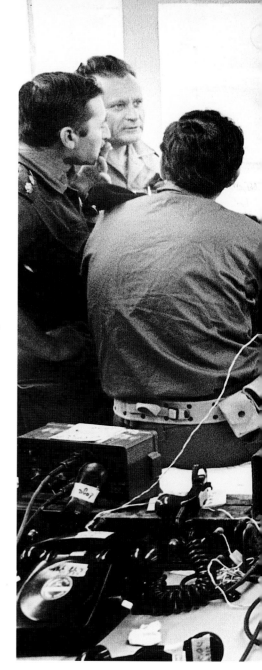

Inside the war room. *Stunned by the rapid Egyptian advance in the south and Syrian advance in the north in the early stages of the 1973 war, Chief of Staff David Elazar and his senior advisers stare at the situation map in the war room. Israel was caught unprepared but managed to turn the tide within a few days.*

[PHOTO: DAVID RUBINGER]

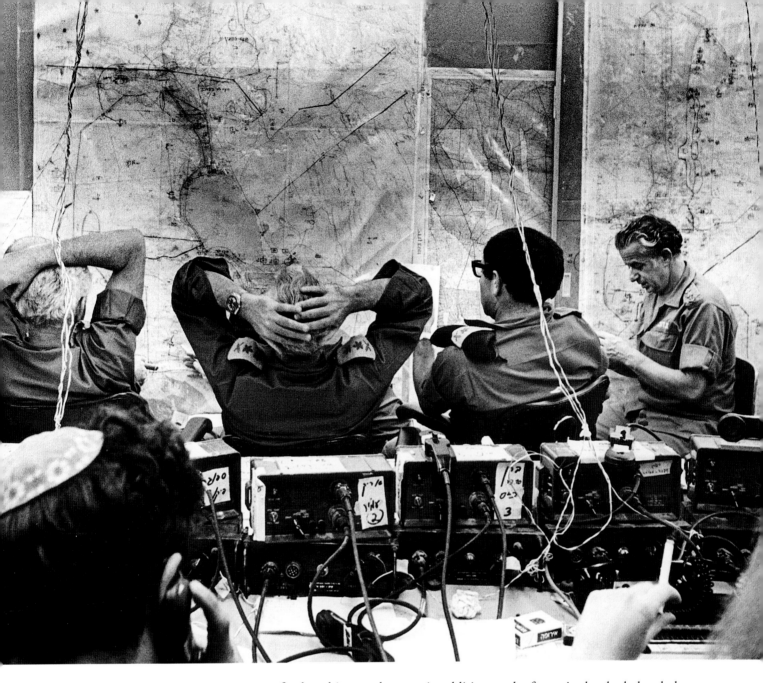

a further thirty settlements in addition to the forty-six that had already been built on the West Bank. All these settlements, Dayan insisted, would be 'inside Israel's final borders'.

On the morning of 6 October 1973, the Day of Atonement, a day of fasting and prayer, Egyptian and Syrian forces attacked Israel simultaneously. Israeli civilians suddenly felt endangered, as much if not more so than in 1967, their only contact with the unfolding events being radio and television. At 5 p.m., fifteen minutes after a radio announcer had reported the Egyptians had 'crossed the canal at several points' and that there was 'fighting on land and in the air', a news flash stated: 'Syrian planes are in action in the Upper Galilee. A fierce air battle is in progress.' Syrian shells had fallen in the Huleh

Valley. Israeli outposts on the Golan had been attacked. At 5.10 p.m. a further radio announcement told all citizens to black out their windows. Three-quarters of an hour later another message advised people to stick tape over all windows, mirrors and pictures – advice that raised the spectre of Syrian bombing raids on Israel's main cities.

Five minutes after this announcement Golda Meir spoke over the radio, only to have her words interrupted by a high-pitched wail, followed by a mobilisation message in code, ordering members of particular units to their bases. At 6.05 p.m. it was announced that three Egyptian bridgeheads had been established over the Suez Canal. The radio announcer added that eleven Egyptian helicopters carrying troops had been shot down. An 8 p.m. news flash reported that all women and children had been evacuated from the Golan Heights. At 8.50 p.m. there was another news flash: everyone was asked not to use the telephone 'unless it is absolutely necessary'.

Among the many Jews who flocked to Israel to show their solidarity with the Jewish State in danger was Danny Kaye, who immediately set about entertaining the troops. Slowly, by means of a harsh daily confrontation in Sinai, Israel pushed back the attackers, crossing over the Suez Canal to the Egyptian side. After four days and and three nights the few surviving Israeli tanks defending the Golan Heights were down to their last shells and their crews could hardly stay awake. Then Lieutenant Colonel Yossi, recalled from his honeymoon in the Himalayas, arrived with thirteen tanks which had been recovered from the battlefield and repaired, to supplement the seven left to the 7th Brigade. Thirty Syrian tanks were immediately knocked out, and this was enough to turn the tide. The Syrians were pushed back beyond the 1967 ceasefire line to within sight of Damascus.

When the war ended Israel's land, its towns and settlements, were intact, but the shock of the surprise attack, the initial Arab successes, the harsh fighting needed to regain the initiative, and the 2,800 Israeli war dead, were a blow to confidence and self-esteem. So too was the revelation, by an official committee of enquiry, of a serious Intelligence failure on the eve of the war. The Chief of Staff, General Elazar, was criticised for failing to appreciate the full implication of Intelligence reports. He was sacked, as were the Chief of Army Intelligence and the general commanding Southern Command.

Once the war was over, yet more settlements were built on the West Bank, stimulating Palestinian resentment. Terror and reaction reached new depths: on

'The only man in her Cabinet', *Golda Meir just outside the Knesset. As smoking was forbidden in the chamber she would stand at the open door and listen to the debate while having a cigarette. Prime Minister of Israel since 1969, her failure to agree to a pre-emptive strike when she learned of the impending Egyptian attack in 1973 was held against her, and she resigned after the war. She believed it would have put Israel in the wrong in the eyes of the world to have struck the first blow, as in 1967.* [PHOTO: DAVID RUBINGER]

Victorious warriors. *General Ariel Sharon (his head bandaged), commander of an armoured division in the 1973 war, and the Israeli Minister of Defence Moshe Dayan, jubilant that Sharon's troops, on the tenth day of the war, had crossed the Suez Canal into Egypt.* [PHOTO: MICHA BAR-AM]

the night of 14 May 1974 – the twenty-sixth anniversary of Israel's independence – a PLO squad penetrated across the northern border and murdered twenty-two Israeli pupils while they were asleep in a school house in the town of Ma'alot. Politically, Israel was under international scrutiny. On 22 November 1974, six months after the Ma'alot massacre, the United Nations General Assembly voted to accept the Palestine Liberation Organisation as an observer at all United Nations meetings, as the 'representative' of the Palestinian Arabs, whose right to 'national independence and sovereignty' and 'to return to their homes and property' the Assembly asserted by a substantial majority.

To nearly all Israelis, Arafat's emergence as an accepted figure in the international forum was deeply distressing. His commitment to Israel's destruction seemed one of the few certainties of the Fatah and PLO cause. Only eleven days before Arafat made a first appearance at the United Nations, gun in holster, he had declared: 'We shall never stop until we can go back home and Israel is destroyed. The goal of our struggle is the end of Israel, and there can be no compromise or mediations. We don't want peace, we want victory. Peace for us means Israel's destruction, and nothing else.'

Inside Israel, a fanatical extremist religious group calling itself Gush Emunim (Bloc of the Faithful), headed by Rabbi Moshe Levinger, demanded the widest possible Jewish settlement of the West Bank. It described the Palestinian Arab presence in the West Bank – which predated modern Zionist settlement there by several centuries – as 'foreign rule'. The Israeli government already encouraged Jewish settlement in the largely unpopulated Jordan Valley, in order to form a defensive line of settlements between Israel and Jordan. Gush Emunim rejected this geographic limitation, regarding every square mile of the unpopulated parts of the West Bank and Gaza Strip as areas of predestined settlement, however close they might be to Arab villages or centres of Arab population.

Gush Emunim organised a series of marches and protest demonstrations in favour of unrestricted settlement. At several sites its members organized sit-ins until they were pushed away by the Israeli army. In December 1975, Gush Emunim held talks with the Minister of Defence, Shimon Peres, and with Prime Minister Rabin's Intelligence Adviser, Ariel Sharon – himself a former Likud member of the Knesset, who favoured substantial Israeli settlement on the West Bank and the annexation of most of it too. Gush Emunim was given permission to move 'temporarily' into a former Israeli army camp in the Samarian hills. Soon afterwards it moved to a nearby site east of Nablus. It was never forced to withdraw. The impetus given to Gush Emunim by the government's compromise was enormous. Within ten years there were 40,000 Jewish settlers in several dozen such settlements throughout the West Bank and within twenty years, the number had risen to 140,000.

At the end of June 1976 an Air France passenger airliner on its way from Tel Aviv to Paris was hijacked by Arab terrorists shortly after take off from Athens. It was then diverted to Libya, where the Israeli and Jewish passengers were separated by the hijackers, and the non-Jews released. The Jews - ninety-eight of them - were flown on to Entebbe in Uganda, 2,500 miles

Rabbi Moshe Levinger, *who organised the return of Jews to Hebron after the Six-Day War. A founder of the Gush Emunim movement for Jewish settlements throughout the West Bank and Gaza. After shooting dead an Arab bystander near a Hebron store, allegedly in self-defence, he was imprisoned for manslaughter. When he ran for the Knesset in 1990 he and his Party received less than the minimum threshold of votes to win a single seat.*

[PHOTO: MICHA BAR-AM]

A vigorous trio. *Three young Orthodox Jewish students in France sing out in class.*

[PHOTO: WERNER BRAUN]

from Israel, where they were held hostage at the airport. Their captors were joined by other Palestinian terrorists, and by units of the Ugandan army which guarded the airport building, some of them on its roof. As a young soldier, the Ugandan President, Idi Amin, had won his parachute wings in Israel.

The highjackers demanded the release of fifty convicted terrorists who were being held in prison in Israel, West Germany, Kenya, Switzerland and France. The balance of public opinion in Israel was that the freedom of the hostages must be assured by accepting the hijackers' demands, including the release of Fatah terrorists being held in Israeli prisons. Menachem Begin, leader of the Likud opposition, accepted this. But on July 3, the Israeli Cabinet, meeting with military leaders and intelligence experts, decided on an airborne commando raid against Entebbe airport to bring the hostages back to Israel. The raid would be carried out by a force composed entirely of volunteers, two hundred men in all.

The raid was daring in the extreme. The airborne troops, together with jeeps, armoured cars, a medical team and a Black Mercedes car of the type Idi Amin was known to use, together with two Land Rovers of the sort that always accompanied him – a brilliant deception – were flown in four Hercules

Safe and free. *The Entebbe hostages back in Israel from Uganda after their ordeal. In the left foreground is the French captain of the hijacked Air France aircraft.*

[PHOTO: DAVID RUBINGER]

aircraft from Sharm el-Sheikh, at the southern tip of the Sinai peninsula, to Entebbe. The flight, which took seven hours, was timed to come in immediately behind a British cargo plane, so as not to be noticed. The noise of the British plane landing and taxi-ing masked the noise of the Hercules.

As soon as the first Hercules landed, a unit commanded by Lieutenant-Colonel Jonathan ('Yoni') Netanyahu set off with the Mercedes and the two Land Rovers for the terminal building, posing as Idi Amin. The unit reached the terminal building and, after a short shoot-out, rescued the hostages, who were then taken from the terminal to the Hercules and – only fifty-seven minutes after the first plane had landed – flown back to Israel.

All thirteen terrorists and thirty-five of the Ugandan troops were killed. There were two Israeli deaths: one of the hostages, Dora Bloch, an elderly woman who had to go to hospital while being held hostage and was murdered after the raid, while still in hospital, and Yoni Netanyahu, who was mortally wounded by a shot fired from the airport control tower: he was safely evacuated with the hostages, but died later.

Elections were held in Israel in May 1977, bringing victory for Menachem Begin and his Likud Party, the parliamentary opposition since statehood had been declared twenty-nine years earlier. Settlement building was intensified on the West Bank and in Gaza, but at the same time, Begin began secret negotiations with the Egyptian President, Anwar Sadat, which culminated in one of the most dramatic events in Israel's history, the arrival on 19 November 1977 at Ben Gurion airport of Sadat himself, followed by his address to the Knesset and the start of a process aimed at a permanent peace with Egypt. This did not mean peace with the Palestinians, however. On 11 March 1978 a PLO unit from Lebanon landed by boat on the Israeli coast. Its first victim was Gail Rubin, an American-Jewish photographer who was working, by chance, at the point where they landed. She was killed without hesitation. The unit then hijacked a bus on the Haifa to Tel Aviv highway, forcing the driver to continue southward. The bus was stopped just before it reached Tel Aviv, and in the ensuing struggle thirty-nine of its passengers were killed.

Israel retaliated four days later by invading southern Lebanon – known in Israel as 'Fatahland'. Several dozen PLO soldiers were killed or captured, and a ten-kilometre strip of territory along the border was occupied by Israeli troops. All PLO installations there were systematically destroyed. Three months later, on June 13, the Israeli forces withdrew and United Nations troops, the United Nations Interim Force in Lebanon (UNIFIL), took over the policing of the region.

Peacemaking with Egypt had continued without interruption, and on 17 September 1978, after thirteen days of intense negotiations at Camp David – the American Presidential retreat in Maryland – an agreement was signed whereby Begin was to restore Sinai to Egypt, and Sadat to end the state of war with Israel. The Israeli settlements in Sinai, including the new town of Yamit, would be dismantled. The Camp David agreement also called for the implementation of an autonomy plan for the Palestinians of the West Bank and Gaza, to be followed after five years by a 'permanent settlement' there. Negotiations regarding that permanent status 'must also recognise', the agreement stated, 'the legitimate rights of the Palestinian people and their just requirements'.

The acceptance of a Palestinian identity, and of the 'legitimate rights' of the 'Palestinian people', was a revolutionary step for the Israeli public, and one which the Palestinians were in due course to use to the fullest advantage, pushing first for autonomy and then for statehood. A new era, of unexpected hope and latent conflict, had begun.

Enemies into friends. *Menachem Begin and Anwar Sadat during negotiations in Egypt in 1979, following the peace agreement between their two countries. It was less than two years since Sadat's visit to Jerusalem, and two years before his assassination.* [PHOTO: DAVID RUBINGER]

CHAPTER EIGHT

TOWARDS THE TWENTY-FIRST CENTURY

1981-2000

THROUGHOUT THE 1980S THE STRUGGLE BY SOVIET JEWS for exit visas continued, as did the demand by world Jewry that these should not be refused, and that those seeking them should not be punished. Pressure by American Jews led to the passing by Congress of the Jackson-Vanick amendment, linking American trade with the Soviet Union to Soviet performance on human rights. The Soviet response was to arrest many Jewish activists, but clandestine Hebrew classes, theatre performances, historical tours and history lessons went on.

On 11 February 1986 a vast crowd gathered at Ben Gurion airport to welcome Anatoly Shcharansky, who had been released that morning from the Soviet Union. But Shcharansky's release, though it provided an upsurge of hope and determination, did not end the Soviet policy of imprisoning Jews who were active in demanding the right to live in Israel, or open the gates to Soviet Jewish emigration, which that year stood at 914, almost the lowest for two decades. Shcharansky himself, taking the Hebrew first name Natan, was the driving force a year and a half later in organising the largest ever Soviet Jewry solidarity rally – 400,000 people in all – held in Washington. Within a decade, Russian Jews were allowed to leave without restrictions, and quickly became the largest single group of immigrants in Israel.

The Jews of the Soviet Union followed events in Israel closely. Since 1979, it had continued to fulfil its obligations under the peace treaty with Egypt, withdrawing not only from the whole of Sinai, but also from the Rafa Salient on the north coast of Sinai, a region which Moshe Dayan, among others, had been so determined to keep. The abandonment of the salient was a specific feature of the Israeli-Egyptian accords. Many of the settlers refused to go, and had to be taken away by force. The buildings of Yamit, its greenhouses and its orchards, were then systematically destroyed by the authorities, ostensibly to prevent the Arab population from establishing itself so close to the border.

Hebrew renaissance. *Three Polish women at a Hebrew language class at the Nozyk synagogue community centre in Warsaw in 1998. Klara Tuchanowska (centre), brought up a Catholic, had only found out five years earlier, at the age of sixteen, that her mother had been adopted by a Catholic family in the war.* [PHOTO: GARY GELB]

Forced exit. *Two women soldiers, themselves disturbed by their task, lead away a woman settler – who is clutching her Bible – from one of the settlements near Yamit that was being demolished by the Israeli army, to prevent it being used by the Egyptians when they reoccupied the area under the Begin-Sadat peace treaty, 1982.*

But one of the settlers, Motti Ben-Yannai, asked bitterly: 'Why was it necessary to uproot orchards? Why was a green and fertile area turned back into desert?'

The divisions inside society were deep. Begin was accused of 'betrayal' by those who did not want to give up land that had been conquered, cultivated and built on. Others resented the harsh nature of Israeli rule in the occupied territories, especially during General Ariel Sharon's tenure of the Defence Ministry. On 10 May 1982, six senior reserve officers, who had been carrying out his policies on the West Bank, spoke out. One of them, Benny Barabash, told the press conference: 'We are gradually losing our humanity. The local population are gradually becoming objects in our eyes – at best mere objects, at worst something to be degraded and humiliated.' The officers told of an Israeli soldier who wrote the identity numbers of detainees on their forearms. This had happened, one of the officers pointed out, on Holocaust Remembrance Day, 'and the soldier was not even aware of the implications of what he was doing'. Another of the six officers, Yuval Neriah, said 'The soldiers are pelted with rocks and bottles and the army does not provide us with adequate means to react. In the end all that we

Amos Oz *in his study in Kibbutz Hulda. Israel's leading novelist, born in Jerusalem, he fought in three of his country's wars (1956, 1967 and 1973). A forceful voice for Arab-Jewish reconciliation, he repeatedly urged greater tolerance towards the Palestinians.* [PHOTOS OPPOSITE AND RIGHT: MICHA BAR-AM]

Determined to stay in Yamit, *a group of settlers are hosed down with foam by the Israeli army, and eventually removed from their rooftop. They had been encouraged to build Yamit by the Israeli government, whose Ministerial Committee on Settlement was headed by Ariel Sharon, who ultimately advised Begin to give up the area in return for peace with Egypt.* [PHOTO: MARLOW]

have are our rifles.' In Tel Aviv, more than 80,000 demonstrators marched in protest to denounce Sharon's 'iron fist' policy.

On Israel's Independence Day, 28 May 1982, Sharon gave his approval to the establishment of more new settlements on the West Bank. Israeli Peace Now demonstrators were dispersed with tear gas, and Palestinians who had often experienced such treatment gave them pieces of peeled onion and drinks to alleviate the effects of the gas.

On 3 June 1982, a Palestinian gunman shot the Israeli Ambassador, Shlomo Argov, in London, paralysing him. The attack coincided with yet more PLO shelling, rockets and raids from bases in southern Lebanon on Israeli towns and villages in Galilee. On June 6 Israeli troops crossed the Lebanese border and drove northward. This was the beginning of the Lebanon War, the fifth war in Israel's thirty-four year history. The name given by the Begin government to the attack was 'Operation Peace for Galilee'. The Israeli writer Amos Oz commented: 'Whenever war is called peace, where oppression and persecution are referred to as security ... the defilement of language precedes and prepares for the defilement of life and dignity.'

In an act of apparently deliberate deception, Sharon had assured the Cabinet that the troops would not advance more than twenty-five miles into Lebanon, and that the operation would be completed within two to three days. On this basis the Cabinet approved it, as did the opposition leaders Yitzhak Rabin and Shimon Peres, whom Begin consulted. Sharon was determined, however, that a much larger military operation was needed, not only to drive the PLO out of its bases but, if Israeli troops continued to Beirut, to destroy the PLO headquarters there and drive out Yasser Arafat.

Begin failed to halt Sharon's plan, and on the afternoon of June 13, Israeli troops reached the eastern entrance to Beirut. For the next two months Israeli tanks and artillery bombarded West Beirut, while warplanes struck at PLO strongholds there. By the end of June more than 500 buildings were in ruins. The daily television pictures caused immense harm to Israel's international image, and much anguished discussion within Israel itself. Then, on August 11 the Israeli Air Force began a forty-eight-hour attack on the PLO-held areas and on August 12 the PLO agreed to leave Beirut.

A multi-national force, including 1,800 American Marines, was assembled to protect the PLO as it prepared to leave for Tunis by sea. All was set for Israel's Lebanese-Christian ally, the Phalange, to take control, but on September 14 the President-elect, Bashir Jemayel, was assassinated. His Christian Maronite followers were incensed against the Palestinian Muslims, who claimed responsibility for the assassination.

On September 15 the Israeli army occupied West Beirut. This was done, Begin explained, 'to protect the Muslims from the vengeance of the Phalangists'. The vengeance he had in mind was the killing by the Phalangists of the PLO fighters who had found refuge in the Sabra and Shatilla refugee camps. Israeli forces sealed off the two camps from the outside world: 'hermetically sealed' was how a senior general, Rafael Eitan, later described it. Israeli military searchlights also illuminated the camps at night as an added precaution. But on September 17, Phalangist forces entered the two camps and massacred the inhabitants, fighters and civilians alike. When newspaper reporters from around the world entered Sabra and Shatilla, the bodies – many of them mutilated – of 2,300 Palestinian men, women and children were found.

Many Israelis were outraged that the Sabra and Shatilla massacres had been allowed to happen, and 400,000 took to the streets. It was Israel's largest-ever demonstration. Sharon, censured by a commission of enquiry for his 'disregarding the danger of acts of revenge and bloodshed by the Phalange against the population in the refugee camps', was forced to resign as Defence Minister, but remained in the Cabinet. Protests continued and between

Sombre thoughts. *Prime Minister Shimon Peres (centre) and Defence Minister Yitzhak Rabin return from a visit to Israeli troops in southern Lebanon, 1984, shortly after a suicide bomber had killed thirty-six Israelis there. In late 1984 and early 1985 both men supervised a step-by-step withdrawal to the border with Israel, but continued to give military support to Lebanese Christian militia forces in a narrow zone just north of it.*
[PHOTO: MICHA BAR-AM]

Bombardment. *A moment during the Israeli air and artillery attack on PLO positions in West Beirut, 1982.*
[PHOTO: DAVID RUBINGER]

September 1982 and June 1983 sixty Israeli soldiers refused to do reserve duty in Lebanon and were imprisoned. It was not until 1985 that Israel withdrew from all but a five-mile deep Security Zone inside Lebanon, and only in 2000 did her soldiers leave Lebanese soil.

On 5 January 1985 a remarkable and hitherto secret episode in Jewish history came to an abrupt end, with the revelation of a secret airlift which had brought 10,000 Jews from Ethiopia to Israel. Operation Moses, as it was called, would have continued, had it not been leaked to the newspapers. Before 1984 no more than two hundred Ethiopian Jews had been able to make their way to Israel, given the hostility of the Ethiopian government to their emigration. The airlift was organised by the government of Israel to rescue as many as possible from a region wracked by famine and civil war. The Black Jews of Ethiopia had been living in the country for two thousand years,

A Palestinian stone thrower *watches Israeli soldiers in Gaza, December 1987. Just in front of him are some of the burning tyres used by Palestinians to block roads.*

[PHOTO: MICHA BAR-AM]

and were known locally as 'Falashas' (Strangers). In 1905 a Polish Jew, Jacques Faitlovitch, visited Ethiopia and then began a campaign to have them recognised as Jews. He argued that the Falashas were 'the descendants of genuine Jews and an integral part of the Jewish people.'

In October 1986 one of the leading figures in Israel's labour movement, Shimon Peres, who had reached Palestine from Poland as a boy before the Second World War, became Prime Minister. He was determined to find some means of ending the continuing state of war with Syria, Lebanon and Jordan, and of assuaging Palestinian anger at Israeli occupation. Underlying his approach was the conviction that Israel's Arab neighbours, and the Palestinians, were equal participants in the problems and opportunities of the region. On 11 April 1987, following secret talks in London, Peres and King Hussein of Jordan reached an agreement on how a peace treaty could be negotiated between Israel and Jordan, and a wider settlement reached based on Israel's withdrawal from territories occupied in 1967, as called for by the United Nations. But this agreement was rejected by the Israeli Cabinet, intensifying Arab frustration. On 9 December 1987, after four Arab workers from the Gaza Strip were accidentally run over and killed by an Israeli truck, Israeli soldiers were attacked throughout the occupied areas – first with stones, then with Molotov cocktails and finally, in some instances, with guns. It was a popular uprising which took even the PLO in Tunis by surprise.

Many Arab villages sought to block the entry of Israeli soldiers. Strikes were declared, trade between Israel and the West Bank brought to a halt, and pamphlets circulated calling for a continuous struggle. Arab demonstrators raised the Palestinian flag on pylons and rooftops. This was declared illegal under Israeli military law and the flags were pulled down. Sometimes those trying to raise them were shot and killed. This was the 'Intifada' – the Uprising. It drew much of its numerical strength from the twenty-seven Palestinian refugee camps in the West Bank and Gaza.

In an attempt to suppress the Intifada the Israeli army used tear gas, rubber bullets, plastic bullets and – increasingly, when under extreme provocation – live ammunition. There were many examples, one of them filmed, of prolonged and savage beatings. Several Israeli soldiers were found guilty by Israeli courts of abuse of their powers, as were four Israeli border policemen who had seized and tortured four Arab hotel workers in Tel Aviv. In finding the four policemen guilty, and sentencing one of them to a year and the others to eight months in prison, Judge Moshe Talgam told the court: 'These acts cause me to shudder by the associations they raise precisely because I am a Jew.' Young Israelis were sent, as part of their three-year compulsory military service, to the West Bank and Gaza Strip. Instead of defending the borders of the State against external attack they were policing cities, villages and roads inside it, acting at times, as occupying powers inevitably do, with harshness. On 22 December 1987 the Security Council debated a resolution denouncing Israeli violence in the occupied territories. Earlier such attempts to censure Israel had been blocked, but the

United States, under President Reagan, now refused to exercise its veto, and Israel stood condemned by the United Nations.

In August 1988 a new organisation, Hamas, which drew its support from Islamic fundamentalists, and was largely funded by Iran, published its covenant, rejecting the 'legitimacy' of the PLO as the sole leader of the Palestinian people. It also rejected any permanent compromise that might be reached with Israel. The whole of Mandate Palestine, 'from the sea to the river', was declared a Muslim endowment (Waqf). Holy war (Jihad) was to be conducted not only against Israel but also against 'corrupt and degenerate' elements in Palestinian society.

External danger also threatened Israel when, at the beginning of the Gulf War in 1991, Scud missiles were fired against her from Iraq. The whole country took shelter during the attacks in the sealed rooms that had been hurriedly set up in every home. The gas masks they wore were a terrible reminder of the Holocaust. There were televised scenes of Palestinian youth cheering the Scud attacks, but the support of the United States under President George Bush, who sent protective Patriot missiles to Israel to defend it against the Scuds, was a lifeline of hope, reducing the widespread sense of isolation and danger. To man the Patriot missiles, Bush sent American service personnel to Israeli soil for the first time.

A new Likud government, the second to be led by Yitzhak Shamir, was determined not to recognize the PLO. When Ezer Weizman – the architect of the Likud electoral victory in 1977, and a Minister in Shamir's government – met Arafat in Vienna, he was sacked on the grounds that it was illegal to consort with the enemy. A formula was eventually found, largely as a result of United States efforts led by the Secretary of State, James Baker, whereby the Palestinians would be represented in negotiations between the Arabs and Israel – to take place in Spain – not by the PLO, but by individual Palestinians from the occupied territories who would be part of a joint Jordanian-Palestinian delegation.

The Madrid Conference, opening on 30 October 1991, did not come a day too soon. The leaders of the two Super Powers, President Bush and President Gorbachev, were the sponsors and opening speakers. Israel was represented by Shamir, the Arab States by their Foreign Ministers. Despite protests from Israel, the leading Palestinian delegate, Haider Abd al-Shafi, was given equal time with the other delegations to deliver his opening and closing speeches. Further talks also took place in Washington, facilitated by the State Department under James Baker.

As the negotiations continued, it became clear that Israel was not prepared to respond to questions of 'territorial concessions' to the Palestinians, but wished instead to limit the discussion to some form of limited Palestinian autonomy. The Likud formula was of autonomy for people, not for land. For the Palestinian Arabs this was a deceptive, disingenuous offer. Talks were still going on when Israel was plunged into another election. The result was a

Handshake for peace. *Yitzhak Rabin and Yasser Arafat shake hands on the White House lawn, 13 September 1993. Encouraging them to do so is President Clinton, the main facilitator of the agreement. Also watching are the Israeli Foreign Minister Shimon Peres (far left) and Warren Christopher, the American Secretary of State (to the right of Arafat).*
[PHOTO: RICHARD T. NOWITZ]

victory for Labour. Yitzhak Rabin, who had been Chief of Staff in the 1967 war, became Prime Minister. There was an immediate change in Israel's attitude to the peace process. In his first speech as Prime Minister, Rabin told the Knesset that his government would embark on the pursuit of peace with a 'fresh momentum', determined to turn 'a new page in the annals of the State of Israel'. By way of response, on 7 December 1991, the fifth anniversary of the start of the Intifada, three Israeli soldiers were murdered in Gaza City, and six days later Hamas militants kidnapped and killed an Israeli army sergeant. As the terror continued, a Palestinian from Gaza stabbed to death four people in Tel Aviv.

In the midst of this tragic violence, the first-ever talks had begun, in strictest secrecy, between Israel and the PLO on January 20, at a villa outside the Norwegian capital, Oslo. Rabin knew that Arafat and the PLO were the only viable element of secular Palestinian nationalism with which Israel could deal. On the West Bank and in Gaza, Hamas and Islamic Jihad wanted more radical, fundamentalist and violent solutions. On February 13 a draft Declaration of Principles was produced, and the talks continued, still in secret. The urgent need to find a new way forward was underlined on March 18 when it was learned that, let alone the deaths in earlier years, during 1992 eleven Israeli soldiers and eleven Israeli civilians had been killed by Palestinians, and a hundred Palestinians killed by Israeli troops. In addition, members of Hamas and Islamic Jihad had killed 220 fellow-Palestinians for opposing the Intifada and being willing to compromise with Israel.

On 20 August 1992 the Oslo Accords were initialled. The Palestine Liberation Organisation, hitherto a pariah for most Israelis, became a partner. But before the Accords could be signed, Israel insisted that Arafat renounce all further terror. He agreed to do so, signing a letter calling on the Palestinian people in the West Bank and Gaza Strip to reject 'violence and terrorism'. On 13 September 1993 Rabin and Arafat were in Washington, where they signed a Declaration of Principles, whereby Israel recognised the PLO and the PLO recognised Israel. The active support of the United States was crucial to this breakthrough, and to the subsequent continuation of negotiations towards what was hoped to be a final and comprehensive peace agreement. President Clinton devoted many hours of intense effort and consultation with both sides to keep the peace process on track, as did his Secretary of State Madeleine Albright and his special emissary to the Middle East, Dennis Ross.

As talks between Israel and the PLO continued, with Clinton maintaining his close watching brief, it was clear that peace had enemies on both sides. In February 1994 an Israeli gunman opened fire inside the main mosque in Hebron – the site of the Tomb of the Patriarchs venerated by Jews and Muslims alike – and killed twenty-nine Arab worshippers. In April a member of Hamas, a suicide bomber, killed eight Israelis in the northern town of Afula. Seven days later another suicide bomber killed six people on a bus in Hadera.

The peace talks went on. When Rabin and Arafat met in Cairo on May 3, it was to set up a Palestinian Authority, to be headed by Arafat, with 'legislative, executive, and judicial powers and responsibilities', including its own armed police force and full control over internal security, education, health and welfare, and the power to negotiate agreements with foreign governments on economic matters, regional development, and cultural, educational and scientific matters. Israel would retain control of foreign affairs and defence.

Nine days after the signing of the Cairo Agreement, all Israeli troops and administrative personnel withdrew from Jericho. Four days later they withdrew from the Gaza Strip and the Palestinian flag was raised over Jericho and over Gaza City. In Gaza, Palestinian self-rule extended to all the 800,000 Arab inhabitants, though the sixteen Israeli settlements there, with a total a population of 5,000, were excluded. These settlers had special access roads to reach them across the Gaza Strip, and were defended by Israeli troops.

An Israel-Jordan peace treaty was signed on 26 October 1994. President Clinton, on what he called 'a mission inspired by a dream of peace', flew specially to the signing ceremony on the Israeli-Jordanian border. But peace with moderate Jordan could not guarantee peace with extremist Palestinians. On 22 January 1995 nineteen Israeli soldiers and a civilian were killed in a snack bar. On April 2, seven Israelis and an American student were killed in two suicide bomb attacks. Rabin and Peres were determined, however, not to let terror halt the peace process. On August 20, with Clinton's special envoy Dennis Ross at the centre of the negotiations, Israel agreed to the immediate transfer of all fuel, petrol, agricultural, insurance and postal services to the Palestinian Authority. Then, on 28 September 1995, following Clinton's own intense behind-the-scenes help, Rabin and Arafat returned to Washington to sign Oslo II, which allowed for a phased withdrawal of Israeli troops from the

Following Yitzhak Rabin's funeral, *thousands of candles were lit, many of them by young people, on the ground near Rabin's grave in Jerusalem, and also in the square, in Tel Aviv – Kings of Israel Square – near which he was assassinated, and which was renamed Rabin Square. For many months an informal memorial service was held there each Friday, and candles lit again. The wall poster declaims: 'Something is rotten'.*

[PHOTO: KAREN BENZIAN]

A SONG FOR PEACE

Let the sun rise, and give the morning light
The purest prayer will not bring back
He whose candle was snuffed out and was
*   buried in the dust*
A bitter cry won't wake him, won't bring
*   him back*
Nobody will return us from the dead dark
*   pit*
Here, neither the victory cheers nor songs of
*   prayer will help*

So sing only a song for peace
Do not whisper a prayer
Better a song for peace
With a great shout.

main cities, from most of Hebron – the only West Bank city with a small Jewish presence – then from the Palestinian villages, and finally from the countryside. Israel would remain responsible for the Jewish settlements on the West Bank, and there would be a small Israeli military enclave for security purposes. But almost all the West Bank would be ruled and policed by the Palestinians, whose national flag, stamps, symbols and authority would be put in place for the first time in their history.

Inside Israel, the opposition parties reviled Rabin for Oslo II. Outside his apartment block in Tel Aviv, opponents of the peace process called out 'Traitor' and 'Murderer' whenever Rabin arrived, and once, when his wife Leah pulled into the driveway, someone in the crowd shouted out: 'After the next election, you and your husband will hang from your heels in the town square like Mussolini and his mistress.'

Oslo II was passed in the Knesset by the narrowest of margins, 61 to 59. At a rally in Jerusalem three weeks later, Rabin was denounced by several speakers as a traitor who was abandoning the Land of Israel. During the rally leaflets were distributed showing him dressed as a Nazi officer. To counter such hostility, on November 4 a mass rally was held in Tel Aviv in support of the government and the peace process. Rabin and Peres were both on the platform, Rabin speaking about the need for peace with the Palestinians, and also about the divisions within Israeli society which had become so harsh: 'In a democracy there can be differences, but the final decision will be taken in democratic elections, as in the 1992 elections which gave us the mandate to do what we are doing.'

As the rally came to an end, Rabin, normally a shy man, joined in the singing of 'A Song for Peace' which had been composed immediately after the October War. He then left the platform and, as he went to his car, was shot dead by an assassin. His murderer was a Jew, Yigal Amir, a religious student at Bar-Ilan University who considered the peace process a betrayal of Jewish values.

Within hours of Rabin's assassination A Song for Peace became an anthem to a lost hero, warrior, and peacemaker, sung softly and with infinite sadness in a thousand streets and at a thousand gatherings throughout Israel and in the Diaspora. In London it was sung the next day at a gathering of Mahalniks – the 1948 overseas volunteers – many of whom had served under Rabin on the Jerusalem Front. The shock of the murder created a stunned numbness throughout Israel. When President Clinton was told the news of Rabin's death, he came out on to the White House lawn, visibly shaken, and spoke a few words stressing how much Rabin had done to advance the peace process. Then, before returning inside, he said in a quiet voice the two words *Shalom haver* (Peace, friend). At Rabin's funeral Clinton spoke of how 'if people cannot let go of the hatred of their enemies, they risk sowing the seeds of hatred among themselves', and he added, in a powerful appeal: 'I ask you, the people of Israel, on behalf of my own nation, that knows its

MUSIC IN ISRAEL. *Yona (above), a drummer with her own band, who plays to women's audiences only. An enthusiastic audience at the Arad Festival (above right), an annual musical experience for young* *Israelis held in the desert town. It has become a symbol of youthful exuberance.*
[PHOTO ABOVE LEFT: JOAN ROTH]
[PHOTO ABOVE: MICHA BAR-AM]

long litany of loss from Abraham Lincoln to President Kennedy, do not let that happen to you.'

The divisions inside Israel reached a pitch of intensity never seen before. Palestinian fundamentalist violence continued, as did stern Israeli counter-measures. On 5 January 1996 one of the instigators of terrorist actions inside Israel, Yahiya Ayash, a West Bank university graduate known as 'the Engineer' because of his skills with explosives, was killed in Gaza City while talking on a portable telephone that exploded in his face. Israel did not deny responsi-bility. Hamas swore to be avenged and there were three suicide bombings killing fifty-six over the next three weeks.

The mood inside Israel was one of near despair. Rabin's successor as Prime Minister, Shimon Peres, warned Arafat that the future of the peace process hung in the balance unless the Palestinian Authority took immediate action against Hamas. These acts of terror by Hamas, Peres pointed out, 'occurred in spite of the fact that – even after the assassination of Rabin – we had rede-ployed our army from 450 villages and six cities in the West Bank, in the face of tremendous resentment.' He added, with understandable anger: 'Instead of thanks, we got bombs.'

The peace process continued amid growing scepticism during the pre-miership of Benjamin Netanyahu, the Likud leader. Once more President Clinton acted as host to try to bridge the gaps between Jews and Arabs. Then, in the year 2000, in the immediate aftermath of a major series of Israeli con-cessions offered by a new labour Prime Minister, Ehud Barak, which Clinton urged Arafat to accept, a second Palestinian uprising broke out. The insur-gents demanded full Palestinian sovereignty over East Jerusalem, and 100 per cent of the West Bank rather than the 95 per cent which had been offered by Israel. Whether negotiations ought to continue is a source of anguished uncertainty by most Israelis in the wake of killings and counter-killings that, within two months, left more than 250 Palestinians dead – most of them teenagers, some of them children. Thirty Israelis were also killed, including two soldiers who, having lost their way near the Palestinian-ruled town of Ramallah, were lynched and their bodies savagely abused.

Violence had proved a recurrent feature of the life of the Jewish State in its first fifty-five years. But there was much more to daily life than conflict. A nationwide health service provided free medical help for all citizens, Jews and Arabs alike. Film, music and the arts had many vibrant manifestations. The Israel Museum in Jerusalem displayed every aspect of Jewish history and cul-ture, and of Jewish roots in the Holy Land. The Diaspora Museum in Tel Aviv gave young Israelis a picture of Jewish life outside Israel from earliest times. University life flourished. Schools brought the children of new immigrants into the main stream of the world of Israeli youth. Each Sabbath, tens of thousands of Israelis went to the country's beaches, or picnicked in the forests. The new high-tech era saw a proliferation of computer-based enterprises. At the Tefen Industrial Park in Galilee, Israel's leading industrialist, Stef

Wertheimer, who had come to Palestine from Germany as a young man before the Second World War, encouraged young people, in particular soldiers who had completed their three-year compulsory military service – and women who had completed their two years – to enter productive industry. He also built a village nearby, called Kishorit, for the severely handicapped. In Tel Aviv, Shimon Peres established the Peres Peace Institute, dedicated to the economic as well as political well-being of the whole region.

Throughout the late 1980s and early 1990s, Russian immigrants reached Israel in huge numbers. To absorb them evenly across the country, every town

About to leave Baku, *capital of the Republic of Azerbaijan, Lileh and Isak Michalshvili, Georgian Jews, watch while a friend continues their packing.*

[PHOTO: ALIZA AUERBACH]

in Israel increased its population between five and ten per cent. The new immigrants began life in Israel with whatever skills they could muster, often as street sweepers or street musicians. Among the 300,000 who reached Israel between 1989 and 1991, 8,000 were doctors. In that same period, 120,000 Soviet Jews emigrated to the United States. More than 20,000 Ethiopian Jews also arrived in Israel in the 1990s. Incredibly, 14,194 of them arrived during an airlift that was completed within twenty-two hours. On one occasion I was present when several hundred Ethiopian and Russian Jews – among them Shcharansky's mother Ida Milgrom – reached Ben Gurion airport immigration hall at the same time, people from two different worlds

Numbered for easy identification, *an Ethiopian Jewish girl at the end of her long journey from famine and civil war to a new life in Israel.* [PHOTO: ALIZA AUERBACH]

who would have to make a life together despite their wide cultural divide. Two things would unite them: their common Jewish heritage – even if some of their respective practices were very different – and their desire to become Israeli patriots.

Despite the possibility of emigration, at least a million Jews remained in the former Soviet Union. For them, it was a time of hope. Synagogues and Jewish community centres opened in dozens of cities, and Jewish learning revived. More than fifty Jewish newspapers, many in Hebrew, and many libraries of Jewish books came back into existence, after almost seventy years of proscription. At the same time, amid the political uncertainty and economic hardships accompanying the collapse of Communism, there were spasmodic outbursts of anti-Semitic feeling which acted as a spur to continued emigration. By the end of the century, Russian Jews formed a substantial part of the Berlin Jewish community. In Lithuania, the remnant of a once flourishing Jewish community rebuilt its life in the 1990s, following four years of Nazi destruction and forty-five years of Communist suppression. A young Jewish member of parliament, Emanuelis Zingeris, was at the forefront of the Lithuanian independence movement. He was also active in helping to reestablish Jewish institutions, including a Jewish museum and library in Vilnius.

As the Holocaust receded in time it loomed large in memory. In the United States, the Museum of Tolerance in Los Angeles sought to warn young Americans of the dangers of prejudice and how race hatred could turn to mass murder. In Washington, the United States Holocaust Museum Memorial, supported at its inception by President Carter, brought the story of Jewish suffering and resistance to the very centre of the capital city, and became a focal point for visitors and students. A permanent Holocaust Exhibition was opened in London as an integral part of the Imperial War Museum. Berlin and Vienna also built Holocaust memorials and museums. Memorials had become a feature of Jewish community life. 'Contemplate that this happened', the words of the Italian author and survivor of Auschwitz, Primo Levi, were inscribed on a plaque at Rome's Tiburtina railway station from which 1,600 Jews were deported to their deaths on 16 October 1943. One Jewish imperative – encouraged by Yad Vashem in Jerusalem as an integral part of Israeli law – was the award of special medals and diplomas to non-Jews who had saved Jewish lives in the war, at the risk of their own lives. In 1993 Peter Aran, the Israeli ambassador in Vienna, accelerated the award to an eighty-three-year-old Armenian woman, Felicia Taschdjian, who together with her husband had hidden a Jew, Valentine Skidelsky, in the attic of their Viennese home for two and a half years.

Extremists who denied that the Holocaust had happened were challenged by Jewish historians and by survivors. In 1993 a Jewish historian in the United States, Deborah Lipstadt, published a book, *Denying the Holocaust,* in which she exposed the deniers for the falsifiers, neo-Nazis and racists that they

were. When brought to court in Britain by a British writer who was already banned from spreading his views in Austria, Germany and Canada, Lipstadt successfully staved off his challenge, and Holocaust denial was struck a severe blow.

To make the details of the Holocaust more widely known, more and more survivors – a dwindling band – published their memoirs in the last decade of the century. An estimated 50,000 survivors recorded their testimonies on video tape for Steven Spielberg's Survivors of the Shoah Visual History Foundation of Los Angeles, and for other oral history projects around the world. In Canada, a Belgian-born scholar, Alain Goldschläger – whose grandfather had been murdered by the Nazis – established a library of more than 2,000 printed memoirs.

For many Jewish organizations the need to compensate the survivors, an ever-dwindling band, and to obtain restitution for property seized and confiscated, remained a strong imperative. American Jews, some of them children of survivors, and who had reached the top of the establishment in law firms,

Remembering the Holocaust, *the entrance to the United States Holocaust Memorial Museum (left), just off the Mall, in Washington, DC. The memorial at the*

350

railway yard in Warsaw (above) from which more than 300,000 Jews were deported to Treblinka and murdered. There were too many names to inscribe on the memorial, so only first names were listed, in their Polish spellings: *Mosze, Dawid, Szoszana etc.* In the building on the right thousands of Jews were held before being deported.

[PHOTO TOP LEFT: TIMOTHY HURSLEY]

[PHOTO ABOVE: GARY GELB]

the media, universities and government, took a leading part in this, helping to instil shame and secure justice for the return of stolen money, lost insurance policies and art works from private collections. They also helped obtain compensation for individual suffering at the hands of industrial firms such as Volkswagen and Krupp, and institutions such as the Deutsche Bank, and German subsidaries of IBM, which had flourished after the war but never offered any form of amends. In a decisive move, President Clinton appointed Stuart Eizenstat, an observant Jew from the American South who had been President Carter's adviser on Jewish affairs, to conduct negotiations throughout Europe for compensation of the survivors. In October 2000, agreement was reached between the Austrian and United States governments for a $380 million compensation fund for slave labourers, men and women who had hitherto not been part of reparations agreements. In all, 150,000 former prisoners, non-Jews, as well as Jews, would benefit from the Austrian fund.

Individual Jews continued to make their mark in many different societies. David Marshall, a Singapore Jew – the son of immigrants from Baghdad – served after 1978 as Singapore's ambassador to France, Spain, Portugal and Switzerland. An activist in Singapore's earlier struggle for independence from Britain, after independence he became a strong critic of any abuse of human rights by his own government. In 1994, Richard Goldstone, who at different

Bernard-Henri Levy *(above), the French philosopher, at a mass demonstration in Vienna attended by 200,000 people, against the right-wing Austrian Freedom Party led by Jörg Haider, in 2000.*

[PHOTO: HERWIG PRAMMER]

Ruth Bader Ginsberg *wrote editorials in her New York school magazine on the meaning of the Magna Carta and the Bill of Rights. In 1993 she was sworn in as a Justice of the United States Supreme Court, where she emerged as a strong opponent of blurring the roles of Church and State. She voted against allowing Hassidic Jews to run their own public school on the grounds that it would constitute government-backed 'segregation'.*

Barbara Boxer *addressing the Democratic National Convention in 2000. Born Barbara Levy, she was active in the civil rights movement, and an opponent of the Vietnam War; she served five terms in the United States Congress. Her Boxer Amendment, which was vetoed by President Bush in 1989, was an attempt to make Medicaid funds available to pay for abortions for the victims of rape or incest. In 1992 she became a Senator for California, one of ten Jewish Senators out of a hundred.*

[PHOTO: DAVID J. PHILLIP]

times served on the South African Supreme Court, Appeal Court and Constitutional Court, was made chairman of the commission of enquiry into the political violence which had followed the lifting of the government ban on the African National Congress and the release of Nelson Mandela from prison. He was also appointed that year by the United Nations as the chief prosecutor of two international war crimes tribunals, one for Bosnia and the other for Rwanda, and in 1999 became chairman of the international enquiry on Kosovo. Above all, in the United States, Jews reached the highest levels of professional, public, artistic, academic and business life. In the Senate, Joseph Lieberman – later the first Jew to run for Vice-President – championed the Muslim victims of ethnic cleansing in Bosnia. In New York, Ed Koch was one of only three people in the whole century to be elected to three consecutive terms as Mayor. In the Supreme Court, Ruth Bader Ginsberg, the first Jewish woman to be appointed to the court, championed the liberal interpretation of the laws, and women's rights. Regarding her Jewishness as an integral part of her mental make-up, she commented: 'The demand for justice runs through the entirety of the Jewish tradition. I hope I will have the strength and the courage to remain constant to that tradition.'

STEVEN SPIELBERG –
A FORCE IN HOLLYWOOD.

Largely self-taught, he was only sixteen when he made his first film, the two-hour science fiction Firelight. *His first box office success was* Jaws *in 1975. Other triumphs were* ET *and* Jurassic Park. *With* Schindler's List *in 1995, he gave millions of people their first insight into the Holocaust, through the story of a non-Jew who saved more than a thousand Jews. He has recorded on video the recollections of more than 50,000 Holocaust survivors.*

[PHOTO: CHRIS PIZZELLO]

HENRY KISSINGER –
A FORCE IN INTERNATIONAL
DIPLOMACY, *left Germany in 1938 with his parents for the United States. In 1945 he returned to Germany as an American soldier. After teaching at Harvard he entered government, and in 1973 was appointed Secretary of State. A pioneer of 'shuttle diplomacy', he negotiated an end to the Vietnam War, initiated the first Strategic Arms Limitation Treaty (SALT I) with the Soviet Union, and arranged the disengagement of Israeli, Egyptian and Syrian forces after the 1973 war.*

[PHOTO: DAVID KARP]

BARBARA WALTERS –
A FORCE IN THE MEDIA.

In 1961 she was given her first on-air assignments, and soon began her career as an interviewer. In 1962 she covered Jacqueline Kennedy's trip to India, In 1977, having travelled with President Sadat on his historic journey to Israel, she set up a joint interview with Sadat and Begin. Her family lit the candles on Friday nights but they did not belong to a synagogue. 'The only way Judaism was important was socially,' she once explained. 'Our friends were Jewish.' [PHOTO: JOSHUA BUCKLAN]

GEORGE SOROS –
A FORCE IN INTERNATIONAL
FINANCE. *Born in Budapest in 1930,
he was educated at the London School of
Economics. He began work as an arbitrage
trader in New York, then as an economic
analyst, becoming one of the world's leading
financiers and wealthiest men. He served
from 1982 as a member of the Executive
Committee of the Helsinki Watch,
monitoring human rights abuse in the
Soviet Union. With the fall of Communism,
he put enormous financial resources and
personal energy behind the development of
liberal education in eastern Europe.*

[PHOTO: PATRICK AVIOLAT]

EDGAR BRONFMAN JNR –
A FORCE IN MULTI-NATIONAL
BUSINESS. *Canadian millionaire and
philanthropist, who sold his family's share
in the chemical giant Du Pont to buy
Universal Studios, in Hollywood. The
Bronfman family, originally from Tsarist
Russia, built up the Seagrams liquor
manufacturing company. Edgar senior, as
President of the World Jewish Congress, was
at the centre for two decades of the struggle
on behalf of Soviet Jewry, and of the quest
for reparations for Nazi-era slave labourers.
His brother Charles brought professional
baseball to Canada, and founded both the
Canadian Heritage Project to strengthen
Canadian unity, and the Jewish Peoplehood
Project for Jewish education worldwide.*

[PHOTO: MITCHELL GERBER]

RONALD LAUDER –
A FORCE IN PHILANTHROPY,
*son of cosmetics queen Estée Lauder,
describes himself as having grown up an
assimilated 'three-day-a-year' Jew. In 1986
he became United States Ambassador to
Vienna, where for the first time in his life
he was criticised as a Jew – for failing to
attend the inauguration of President
Waldheim, a former Wehrmacht officer. His
Ronald S. Lauder Foundation set up schools,
youth centres and summer camps throughout
eastern Europe to encourage the revival of
Jewish life, and has established a centre
in Cracow for Jewish communal life. At
the beginning of the Twenty-first Century
he was chairman of the Conference of
Presidents of major American Organisations.*

[PHOTO: BERNHARD HOLZNER]

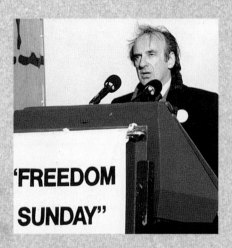

'FREEDOM SUNDAY"

The links between Jewish communities worldwide – links which at the beginning of the century had enabled protests against the Tsarist pogroms to take place all over Europe and the Americas – continued even stronger at the century's end. Hundreds of Jewish philanthropists put social welfare at the centre of their agenda. The Wolfson Foundation made enormous contributions to medical research in Israel. The Soros Foundation promoted democracy in the former Communist countries of Central Europe. The Abraham and Maimonides Foundations both put considerable resources into Arab-Jewish understanding. Jewish communities in Britain, Canada and the United States forged links with many of the eighty-two Jewish communities in the former Soviet Union which, with almost no resources of their own, were desperate for material and moral support. Jews in the former Yugoslavia were also

American protests. *Nobel-Prizewinner Elie Wiesel (left), whose 1963 book* The Jews of Silence *brought the Soviet Jewry struggle to a wide public, at Freedom Sunday, 6 December 1987, in Washington, calling for the right of Soviet Jews to emigrate. A moment at the demonstration (below). Two scenes (right) from a Peace Now rally in New York, 24 April 1988, calling on Israel to end its occupation of the West Bank and Gaza Strip. The person calling out (far right) is a counter protester wanting Israel to stay there.*

[ALL PHOTOS: SUSAN HARRIS]

PATTERNS OF JUDAISM. *The Bobover Rebbe, Shlomo Halberstam (above), dances with his granddaughter at her wedding in Brooklyn. The Bobovers are a Hassidic sect originating in Eastern Europe. The Rebbe, who escaped from the Nazis on false papers, restored his dynasty in New York in 1946. He died in 2000 and was succeeded by his son Rabbi Naftali. Of the 80,000 Hassidim in New York, 20,000 are Bobovers. A Sephardi family (above, right) examining an elaborate Torah scroll cover in their synagogue at New Rochelle, New York. Rabbi Shira Milgrom (right) leads a service – what she calls 'Shabbat morning spiritual lift' – in the reform synagogue in White Plains, New York.* [PHOTO ABOVE: JOAN ROTH]

[PHOTOS OPPOSITE: SUSAN HARRIS]

Hassidic leader, *Russian-born Menachem Mendel Schneerson, the Lubavicher Rebbe, head one of the many Hassidic sects that originated in eastern Europe and are now centred mostly in Israel and the United States. He is seen here at a funeral in New York accompanied by some of his followers, who believed him to be the precursor of the Messiah, and even the Messiah himself, and continued with this belief after his death in 1994, at the age of ninety-two. His movement, known as Habad, has established synagogues and houses of prayer wherever Jews live, including Alaska and Hong Kong. A tiny fraction of Diaspora Jewry, Habad is active in trying to bring Jews back to Orthodoxy.* [PHOTO: SUSAN HARRIS]

The ecstasy of revelation. *A Hassidic Rabbi, Reuven Flamer, a follower of the Lubavicher Rebbe, caught by the camera at a moment of intense prayer, during a Sabbath discussion in a private home near New York, while relaying the words of the departed Rebbe.* [PHOTO: SUSAN HARRIS]

helped. In 1999 the Beth Israel synagogue in Phoenix, Arizona, raised the money needed to build a new synagogue for the two hundred Jews of Skopje, the capital of Macedonia. In Poland, the former main synagogue in Oswiecim, situated less than a mile from the Auschwitz concentration camp, was restored as a study centre, for use by the many Jewish visitors to the camp.

As the twenty-first century began there were fifteen million Jews in the world, two million less than in 1939. Thus the Holocaust cast its grim shadow over Jewish life. Had not six million then been murdered, there might well have been more than twenty-five million Jews in the world in 1999, a far larger community, and one with particular strength in eastern Europe. The numerical loss can be calculated, ten million unborn Jews. The human loss is incalculable.

The largest Jewish population at the end of the century was that of the United States, with a total of nearly six million Jews. Israel had the second largest, nearly five million Jews, among a total citizenry of just over six million. No other country's Jewish population came near to these two, which between them constituted two-thirds of world Jewry. The former Soviet Union, which as Tsarist Russia had a Jewish population in 1900 of more than a million Jews, had fewer than one and a half million Jews when the century ended. Almost a million had emigrated to Israel in the final decades of the century, and the pattern continued as the new century began, at the rate of tens of thousands a year. The five next largest Jewish communities were in France, with 600,000 Jews, many of them originally from French North Africa; Canada with 360,000, Britain with 285,000, and Brazil and Argentina with a quarter of a million each. In Australia the Jewish community was 106,000 strong, including many survivors of the Holocaust and their

descendants. A mere 6,000 lived in Poland – as compared with more than three million in 1939; 11,000 in Lithuania, which had almost 150,000 in 1939; and 67,000 in Germany, one tenth of the pre-war numbers. A third of the German Jews at the end of the century were recent emigrants from Russia, Russian Jews who had decided that Germany, not Israel or the United States, was the place for them. Only Hungary had maintained a large Jewish community, 100,000, though even this was a third of its pre-war size. There were still 90,000 Jews of South Africa, and 25,000 Jews in Iran who had survived as a community in the midst of an Islamic regime. A similar number of Jews lived in Turkey, despite large-scale emigration to Israel. In Morocco, the Muslim rulers showed great tolerance towards their 7,000 Jews. At the start of the twenty-first century there were Jewish communities in a hundred countries. Some of these were extremely small, scarcely a dozen families, as in Albania and Zambia. Others had several hundred families, as in Croatia and Costa Rica. Jewish communities survived which could trace their origins back two thousand years and more, such as the 34,000 in Italy and the 4,800 Jews of Greece – which before the Holocaust had a Jewish population of 77,000.

In the most industrialised and modern nations, both in Europe and the Americas, Jewishness has been massively diluted. Jews, like Christians, were swept up by the almost universal secularism of the late twentieth century. Family life, which when the century began was a marked feature of Jewish existence, has faced the same strains and disintegrations that beset the

At home in Tunisia. *A Sephardi family from the community there which goes back to Roman times. Once 100,000 Jews lived here, but three-quarters emigrated to Israel in 1950. Today scarcely a thousand families remain.*

[BOTH PHOTOS: JOAN ROTH]

non-Jewish world amid the secularism and agnosticism of affluence and modernity. Synagogue attendance has fallen almost everywhere. Yiddish has almost gone, but Hebrew, except in Israel, has not replaced it as the language of millions of Jews on two continents. The lessening of persecution, and in many countries an end to virtually any discrimination, has weakened the bonds of Jewish communal solidarity. Intermarriage with non-Jews has

At home in Bucharest. *Two Romanian Jewish girls under the flag of the State of Israel. In a country where once a quarter of a million Jews lived – in a community which also dated back to Roman times – there are now only 14,000, a third of them in Bucharest.*

363

reached as much as fifty per cent in some communities, especially in the United States. In Western countries, the Jewish birthrate has fallen in tandem with the non-Jewish rate, except among ultra-Orthodox Jews, who are everywhere a minority Jewish group. Even in Jerusalem, Orthodox Jews make up less than a third of the city's Jewish population.

The political power of the Orthodox minority in Israel to make and break coalition governments has given them a feeling of strength which often leads to attempts to put pressure on the more secular minority, including attacks on Reform Jewish worship, even at the Wailing Wall, where women wearing skull caps and prayer shawls – against Orthodox practice – have been attacked. But such religious extremism has also led to a backlash among those Israelis who resent the power of the religious parties. At those times when the Arab threat diminishes, there are many Israelis who see the Jewish fundamentalist threat as a greater one. However, Israel remains an essentially secular society, with a parliamentary system and an independent judiciary, sensitive to religious feelings – as in the suspension of flights by El Al the national airline, on Sabbath – but not dominated by them. In defence of the Orthodox, many, including Israelis who dislike their politics, agree they are among the guardians of Jewish faith and traditions.

At the end of the twentieth century Jews had much to celebrate. Jewish life had survived the Holocaust. Anti-Jewish aspects of Roman Catholicism had been overturned by two successive Popes. Anti-Semitism, virulent in the first half of the century, had declined almost everywhere. Jewish sovereignty had been restored after two thousand years, the Jewish State making peace before the century's end with two of its neighbours, Egypt and Jordan. However, to the distress of many Jews in Israel and the Diaspora, a lasting accommodation with the Palestinians - the great desire - had so far eluded all efforts. Moses told the Children of Israel in their early days in the wilderness: 'Choose Life'. That wilderness is now a part of distant folk memory; today there is much more to Jewish existence than survival, but without a determination to survive, the creativity for which Jews strive, and in which they rejoice, would be at risk. The twentieth century saw dangers threaten to engulf Jewish existence. Those dangers were overcome. 'Choose Life', with all the struggle and hardship it can entail, remains the challenge for Jews all over the world, and their opportunity.

Bridging the divide. *At a wedding in Jerusalem, the Ethiopian-born mother-in law (left), and the European Ashkenazi mother (right), sit on either side of the bride.*
[PHOTO: JOAN ROTH]

ACKNOWLEDGEMENTS

There are many people to whom thanks are due for their help in the creation of this book. Our greatest debt is to the photographers, archivists and curators in Israel, the United States of America and the United Kingdom for their generosity with their time and with their work. In addition we wish to acknowledge a debt of gratitude and thanks to the following private collections, photographers and institutions for their generous and invaluable support for this book:

Ajex Archive London: Martin Sugarman. A.S.A.P., Tel Aviv. Austrian Archives, Vienna: Dr. Christian Brandstätter. Micha & Orna Bar-Am, Ramat Gan. Karen Benzian, Jerusalem. Bildarchiv Preussischer Kulturbesitz Berlin: Heidrun Klein. Werner & Anat Braun, Jerusalem. Bristol University, Theatre Collection. Bundesarchiv Koblenz: Martina Caspers. Cailingold Family, Jerusalem. Central Zionist Archive, Jerusalem. David Dangoor, London. Gary Gelb, New York. Pia Gidal, Jerusalem. Government Press Office, Jerusalem. David Harris, Jerusalem. Susan Harris, New York. Beth Hatefutsoth Photo Archives, Museum of the Jewish Diaspora, Tel Aviv: Ruth Porter, Zippi Rosenne. Keren Hayesod – United Israel Appeal: Yehoshua Amishav. United States Holocaust Memorial Museum Washington: Genya Markon, Judith Cohen, Christopher W. Sims. Hulton Archive: Leon Meyer, Peter Rohaston, Tom Worsley. Imperial War Museum, London. Institute for Labour Research in Memory of Pinchas Lavon, Tel Aviv: Yael Tadmor-Mastbaum. Israel Museum Jerusalem: Amalyah Keshet. Lady Immalie Jakobovits, London. Jerusalem Post: Eliot Jager. Rolf M. Kneller, Jerusalem. Jenny Kolsky, Long Beach California. Miki Krazman, Jerusalem. Alex Levac, Jerusalem. Irene Levitt, Jerusalem. Magnum Photos, London. Museum of the History of Tel Aviv/Jaffa: Batiya Carmel. Ilan Roth Collection, Herzliya: Ilan and Evelyn Roth and Hila Zahavi. Joan Roth, New York. Edmund de Rothschild, London. The Rothschild Archive, London: Victor Gray and Melanie Aspey. David Rubinger, Jerusalem. Rona Sela, Jerusalem. Moshe Shai, Tel Aviv. Marli Shamir, Jerusalem. SilverPrint Gallery Collection, Ein Hod: Vivienne Silver-Brody. Tel Aviv Museum of Art: Jaffa Goldfinger. Maurice Tiefenbrunner, Jerusalem. William Wake, London. YIVO Institute for Jewish Research, New York: Marak Web, Leo Greenbaum, Krysia Fisher.

PICTURE CREDITS
The following have kindly granted us permission to use the photographs on the pages listed below:

AJEX, Association of Jewish Ex-Service Men and Women, London, 219bl
Aperture Foundation, New York, 208
Archiv S. Fischer Verlag, Frankfurt am Main, 144
Associated Press AP, 308, 353b, 354l, 354m, 354r, 355l, 355r
Aliza Auerbach, Jerusalem, 347, 348
Austrian Archives, Wien /Christian Brandstätter, 23, 60t, 61, 152br, 206 /Franz Hubmann, 4, 36, 46, 47, 59, 68 /Lothar Rübelt, 143
Karen Benzian, Jerusalem, 342-343
Bildarchiv Preussischer Kulturbesitz, Berlin, 48, 58t, 128, 152tl, 177, 178, 179, 182, 200-201tm, 202t, 213 (Yad Vashem), 224, 323tr
Black Star, New York, 354r
Phil Blake, http://users.aol.com/hagdud/hagdud, 70, 89
Werner Braun, Jerusalem, 266, 275b, 282, 297, 329
Jack Brauns Family Archive, 242
Kevin Brownlow, Photoplay Productions, London, 83
Bundesarchiv Koblenz, 197, 198, 199, 204-5, 207, 225, 'An Unlikely Heroine' by Asher Cailingold, Jerusalem, 259
Cassell & Co, London, 323br (Behram Kapadia)
Central Zionist Archive, Jerusalem, 20, 21, 22, 24, 25, 54-5, 56, 84, 98, 132, 133, 136, 269
Collection of the Tel Aviv Museum of Art, 14, 17t, 17bl, 17br
Colorific, London, 296
Corbis Sygma, 41, 102, 341, 355m /Bettman, 6-7, 97t, 140, 321b /Reuters New Media, 353t
Dangoor Family Archive, 16t, 124t
Deutsche Presse-Agentur, Frankfurt am Main, 145, 322tl
Mary Evans Picture Library, London, 34
www.garygelb.com, from his book 'Who will say Kaddish? – A Search for for Jewish Identity in Contemporary Poland' 332, 351
Government Press Office, Jerusalem, 165t, 190-1, 253
Pia Gidal, Jerusalem, 149, 154, 163, 292
David Harris, Jerusalem, 267b, 274, 288, 290, 293, 305, 306
Susan Harris, White Plains, New York, 356-7, 359t, 359b, 360, 361
Beth Hatefusoth Photo Archives, Tel Aviv, 26, 243 /courtesy of: Diaspora Research Centre, Zanziper Collection, 85 /Dr. Elkan, 244 /Jewish Agency, Jerusalem, 91 /Johannesburg 'The Star', 57 /Uri Lilienfeld, 71l /Lasislav Lipscher, 233 /Polska Akademia Nauk, Warsaw, 85b, 72 /Salonika Collection, 16bl, 125 /Yad Vashem Photo Archive, Jerusalem, 241 /Zuskin Collection, 114
Hulton Archive, 10, 16br, 32,33t, b, 52, 58b, 63, 66-7, 74, 75, 78, 79l, 79m, 79r, 80, 81, 82, 96, 97b, 101, 105, 106, 107, 108, 126, 139, 141, 142, 151, 152tm, 152tr, 152bm, 153, 155, 156, 162t, 166, 167, 168, 172b, 173, 174t, 174bl, 174bm, 174br, 175tl, 175r, 184, 185, 192, 195, 215, 237, 240, 245, 246t, 246b, 247, 248, 249, 250-1, 254, 263, 270, 278, 281, 286, 304, 307, 310tr, 310bl, 310br, 311r, 313, 316tr, 316bl, 316bm, 316br,

317, 322tr, 322b (Roy Jones), 323tl, 323mr, 323bl (Bernard Gotfryd), 352
Timothy Hursley, Little Rock, Arkansas, 350
Imperial War Museum, London, 76, 90, 93, 94, 95b, 219tl
Jakobovits Family Archive, 275t
Jerusalem Central Archive of History of Jewish People /Hebrew University, 73
Jerusalem Post Archive, 258
Rolf M. Kneller, Jerusalem, 188, 255, 261
The Kobal Collection, London, 279
Labour Archives and Library, Tel Aviv, 71r
London Museum of Jewish Life /768 /41, 77
Magnum Photos, 2, 5, 262, 268, 272, 276-7, 285, 289, 294m, 298, 300, 301t, 301b, 302, 310tl, 311l, 314, 315, 316tl, 327, 328, 334t, 334b, 335, 337, 338, 345/courtesy of Government Press Office Jerusalem, 287
Marks & Spencer Ltd Company Archive, London, 44
Yves Mozelsio, Chicago, 320
Museum of Jewish Heritage /Centre for Holocaust Studies, New York, 202b
Museum of the City of New York, 50b
National Archives /Library of Congress, Washington, 18, 51, 88, 309
Österreichische Nationalbibliothek, Wien, 152bl
Redferns Music Picture Library, London, 318, 319t, 319b
Ilan Roth Collection, Herzliya, 38, 86-7, 95t, 124b, 130, 162b, 164-5, 180-1
www.joanroth.com, 312, 321t, 344, 358, 362, 363, 364-5
1988 Kate Rothko Prizel and Christopher Rothko, 280
The Rothschild Archive, London, 42, 43t, 43b
David Rubinger, Jerusalem, 238, 252, 256-7, 260, 267t, 271, 273, 294l, 294r, 326, 330, 336 /ASAP Jerusalem, 325, 331
Helena Rubinstein Archives, New York, 50t
Rona Sela Collection, Jerusalem, 158-9, 228
Marli Shamir, Jerusalem, 1
SilverPrint Gallery Collection, Ein Hod, 53, 92, 123, 127, 129, 134t, 134b, 135, 137, 157, 160, 161t, 161b, 193, 229, 265
Theatre Collection Bristol University, 45
Maurice Tiefenbrunner, Jerusalem, 219tr
Ullstein Bild, Berlin, 15, 19, 27, 60b, 110-11
courtesy of USHMM Photo Archives, Washington: American Joint Distribution Committee, 104, 187 /Archiwum Dokumentacji Mechanizny, 171 /Beit Lohamei Haghettaot, 221 /Bibliothèque Historique de la Ville de Paris, 172r, 200tl, 203 / Central Zionist Archive, 146 /Jabotinsky Institute, 131 /Jewish Historical Museum of Yugoslavia, 209 / KZ Gedenkstätte Dachau, 236 /David Laor, 231t, 231bl, 231br /Annette Linzer, 201b /Stefan Lorant, 176 /Museum of the Great Patriotic War, Minsk, Belorus, 210 /National Archives Washington, 222-3 /Nederlands Instituut voor Oorlogsdocumentatie, 200b /Hubert Pfoch, Dokumentationsarchiv des Österreichischen Widerstandes, 216 /Julia Pirotte, 232 /Rabbi Jacob Edermann, 226-7 /State Museum of Auschwitz-Birkenau, 150 /Helmut Stern, 194 /Yad Vashem, 201tr, 220, 234, 235 /Felix Zylbersztajn, 212
Yad Vashem, 217
YIVO Institute for Jewish Research, New York, 28, 29, 31, 35, 37, 40, 49, 64, 65t, 69, 71m, 99, 109, 112, 113, 115, 116t, 116b, 117, 118, 119, 120, 170, 211

INDEX